D1260168

THE THIRD WORLD IN SOVIET MILITARY THOUGHT

The Third World in Soviet Military Thought

Mark N. Katz

THE JOHNS HOPKINS UNIVERSITY PRESS
BALTIMORE, MARYLAND

© 1982 Mark N. Katz
All rights reserved

Published in the United States of America, 1982,
by The Johns Hopkins University Press,
Baltimore, Maryland 21218

ISBN 0-8018-2875-9
LC Number: 82-47502

Printed and bound in Great Britain

CONTENTS

TO NANCY

ACKNOWLEDGEMENTS

In undertaking this study, I have received the advice of many individuals to whom I would like to express my gratitude. I would particularly like to thank William E. Griffith and Donald L.M. Blackmer of the Massachusetts Institute of Technology and Raymond L. Garthoff of the Brookings Institution for their comments and criticism. I have also received much helpful advice from Herbert Dinerstein, Paul Henze and Michael MccGwire, as well as others. In addition, I would like to thank all those who participated in seminars I gave at M.I.T. and Brookings for their comments and suggestions. Special thanks are also due to Christine Helms. Finally, I would like to thank my wife, Nancy Yinger, for her help and encouragement throughout all phases of this study. All errors, of course, are completely my responsibility.

I received generous fellowship support from the Brookings Institution, the Earhart Foundation, and the Institute for the Study of World Politics. Tremendous assistance was given to me by the librarians of the Library of Congress, the Brookings Institution and the Harvard University Russian Research Center. I would also like to thank the Brookings Institution for the use of an office, and the Library of Congress for the use of a study desk.

INTRODUCTION

While many studies have already been written about Soviet military thinking on nuclear war and war in Europe,[1] and about Soviet actions in individual Third World conflicts,[2] little research has been done on Soviet military thinking about conflict in the Third World. However, during the Brezhnev years, the level of Soviet military involvement in the Third World has greatly increased. While wars of national liberation have always been of interest to the Soviet Union, they held a definitely subsidiary place in Soviet foreign policy through the mid-1960s. During the Brezhnev era, though, Soviet interest and involvement in Third World conflicts has evolved into one of the most central and active aspects of Soviet foreign and military policy. Along with this increased Soviet involvement, Soviet military thought about conflict in the Third World has evolved from a subsidiary position into a much more important element of military thinking in the Soviet Union.

Not only has Soviet military thinking about conflict in the Third World evolved in importance, but also in substance. Soviet military pronouncements on and judgements of Third World conflicts have become more complex as Soviet military writers have attempted to come to grips with this highly complex phenomenon. In addition, Soviet military thought has changed in many respects to reflect increasingly active Soviet military involvement in the Third World. It is the purpose of this study to examine what Soviet military thinking about conflict in the Third World has been and how it has changed over time, as well as to assess its importance for the conduct of Soviet foreign policy.

The methodology employed in this study is what William E. Griffith has referred to as the 'deciphering of Soviet esoteric communications'.[3] Soviet military literature was examined to determine how Soviet formulations about conflict in the Third World have changed over time. In addition, military writings were compared with Party/civilian writings to determine what policy differences have occurred between the military and other groups in the Soviet Union. Finally, Soviet military thinking about the Third World was compared to Soviet foreign policy actions in the Third World in order to examine the relationship between military thinking and foreign policy in the USSR.

This study focuses primarily on the Brezhnev era, as this is the period during which conflict in the Third World became a subject of major

9

importance to Soviet military thought. Chapter 1, though, discusses the pre-Brezhnev years, especially the Khrushchev era when the Soviets first began to think about the Third World in some depth. Chapters 2, 3 and 4 treat the early (1964-68), middle (1969-75) and late (1976-81) Brezhnev years, respectively. This division of the Brezhnev era into these three periods is somewhat arbitrary, though the periods do correspond with important phases of Soviet military thinking about and foreign policy toward the Third World. After discussing each of these periods, the conclusions of the study are presented in Chapter 5 and the Epilogue.

Soviet military thinking about conflict in the Third World was found to consist of six different aspects: (1) the relationship of local war to world war; (2) the nature and types of war in the Third World; (3) the relationship of peaceful coexistence to local wars; (4) the Soviet view of indigenous forces in the Third World; (5) the Soviet view of American ideas about and actions in local wars; and (6) the role of the Soviet Union in Third World conflicts.

Briefly, Soviet military thinking about each of these aspects has changed in the following manner during the Brezhnev era: (1) The Soviet military at first stressed that local wars could lead to world war, but later emphasised the ability of the Soviet Union to keep local war localised through its growing military strength. (2) While at first rejecting Khrushchev's attempts to combine ideological factors with non-ideological ones in classifying the nature and types of wars, the Soviet military gradually moved from a purely ideological classification system to a more complex one that included non-ideological factors as well. (3) Although the Soviet military was not enthusiastic about peaceful coexistence with the United States during the 1960s, peaceful coexistence came to be regarded in the 1970s as a means of avoiding world war while at the same time providing greater opportunity for the Soviet Union to assist revolutionary forces in the Third World. (4) The Soviet military was at first optimistic about the ability of indigenous forces in the Third World (such as radical leaders or armies) to bring about socialism and become Soviet allies, but recently they have adopted a more pessimistic assessment in this regard. (5) While at first criticising American involvement in Third World conflicts from an ideological perspective, after the Vietnam war criticism was made from a military perspective; very recently, the Soviet military has evaluated favourably the success of certain American military actions in Vietnam. (6) Soviet military writers have advocated progressively greater Soviet involvement in Third World conflicts during the Brezhnev era; all of these recommendations, however, have always appeared after their introduction in practice and not before.

Regarding civil-military relations, it will be seen that although the Party dominates the military in the Soviet Union, during the Brezhnev era the Party has allowed the military a strong role in formulating Soviet ideas about conflict in the Third World. On occasion, military writers have differed with Party/civilian writers on certain issues. When the Soviet military had reservations about positions adopted by high Party leaders, though, it expressed them with great circumspection. However, when the military differed with lower level civilian academics, the military expressed its position much more strongly. Basically, though, the Party and the military share the same goals in relation to Soviet foreign policy toward the Third World.

Soviet military thinking sheds light on the changing expectations that the Soviets have of the Third World which shape Soviet foreign policy toward conflict there. The early years of the Brezhnev era (1964-68) were a period in which the Soviet military did not envision a large role for the Soviet Union in Third World conflicts. As the US encountered increasing difficulties and eventually withdrew from the war in Vietnam, the middle Brezhnev years (1969-75) saw the Soviet military become more optimistic about the ability of the Soviet Union to achieve foreign policy gains through low-level, low-cost Soviet involvement in these conflicts. However, in the late Brezhnev years (1976 to the present), there has been growing Soviet pessimism about the ability of the USSR to achieve and maintain foreign policy gains in Third World conflicts with anything less than a relatively large-scale, long-term and costly commitment to them.

In examining each of the six aspects of Soviet military thinking about conflict in the Third World, it will be shown that Soviet military thought is not a rigid set of ideas that seeks to explain all past events and predict all future ones in terms of unchanging Marxist-Leninist principles. While many rigid and doctrinaire elements do exist in Soviet military thinking, it is also an adaptable instrument that seeks to change with changing conditions. Its pronouncements at any given time are not to be regarded as binding for all time. A Soviet general described the role of Soviet military doctrine in the following manner:

In doctrine past experience finds its incorporation in an indirect form. It exists for the present and near future, within the framework of determined needs and potential of military organizational development. It indicates the assignments to be met by the organizational development for a comparatively limited period — only until new conditions and factors, which radically change the situation — come into full effect.

Doctrine must and can to a certain degree ignore new phenomena in military affairs, until they come into force.[4]

Not only, then, is Soviet military thought of a tentative and temporary nature rather than definitive and permanent, but large elements of it are reactive to change as new phenomena are not incorporated into it until they 'come into force'. Indeed, much of the change in Soviet military thinking about conflict in the Third World has been reactive to events and actions, including Soviet ones, rather than predictive of them, as will be shown here.

Notes

1. See Herbert S. Dinerstein, *War and the Soviet Union* (Praeger, New York, 1959); Raymond L. Garthoff, *Soviet Strategy in the Nuclear Age* (Praeger, New York, 1958); Raymond L. Garthoff, *Soviet Military Policy: A Historical Analysis* (Praeger, New York, 1966); Thomas W. Wolfe, *Soviet Strategy at the Crossroads* (Harvard University Press, Cambridge, Mass., 1964); and Thomas W. Wolfe, *Soviet Power and Europe, 1945-1970* (Johns Hopkins Press, Baltimore, 1970).

2. Recent works that examine several case studies each of Soviet military involvement in Third World conflicts include Robert H. Donaldson (ed.), *The Soviet Union in the Third World: Successes and Failures* (Westview Press, Boulder, Colo., 1981); Stephen S. Kaplan *et al.*, *Diplomacy of Power: Soviet Armed Forces as a Political Instrument* (Brookings Institution, Washington, 1981); and Bruce D. Porter, *Soviet Military Intervention: Russian Arms and Diplomacy in Third World Conflicts, 1958-78*, PhD dissertation, Harvard University, September 1979.

3. William E. Griffith, 'Communist Esoteric Communications', in Ithiel de Sola Pool, *Handbook of Communication* (Rand McNally, Chicago, 1973), p. 514.

4. Major General S. Kozlov, 'Voyennaya doktrina i voyennaya nauka', *Kommunist Vooruzhennykh Sil*, no. 5, March 1964, pp. 13-14.

1   PRELUDE TO THE BREZHNEV ERA

Certain of the changes in Soviet military thinking about conflict in the Third World that occurred at the beginning of the Brezhnev era were made in reaction to ideas that had been predominant during the Khrushchev era. In order to more fully understand these changes, this chapter will focus on military thinking during the Khrushchev years. Since the ideas expressed during that period were also a reaction to contemporary events in international affairs and to Soviet military thinking that had predominated earlier, Soviet ideas about conflict in the Third World during the Lenin and Stalin years will first be examined briefly.

The Lenin and Stalin Years

The first major Soviet statement about conflict in the Third World was made by Lenin at the Second Comintern Congress held in 1920. At this Congress, Lenin stated that the colonial and semi-colonial nations would experience a two-stage revolution. The first stage would be a national revolution to establish independence and would be led by the national bourgeoisie who would institute bourgeois democracy. The second stage would be a socialist revolution led by the proletariat to establish the dictatorship of the proletariat. Before the second stage could occur, though, Lenin believed that the first stage bourgeois-democratic revolution must have been completed.[1]

At the Congress, Lenin was strongly challenged on this idea by the Indian communist N.M. Roy. Roy believed that the national bourgeoisie in the Third World was so weak and so dependent on the colonial powers that it could not lead the first stage of the revolution to establish national independence. The proletariat would have to lead the first stage of the revolution as well. Although this revolution would also establish bourgeois-democracy, the proletariat would be in a better position to carry out the second stage of the revolution, thus allowing socialism to triumph sooner than Lenin expected.[2] Lenin's reaction to Roy was that revolution in the colonial nations was so far away that the differences in their formulations did not matter, and so the Comintern Congress passed resolutions approving both Lenin's and Roy's contradictory theses.[3]

The differences in Lenin's and Roy's formulations, however, did indeed matter very much, since revolution in the Third World began to occur much sooner than Lenin had anticipated. As early as the mid-1920s, the Soviet Union was faced with the choice in China of supporting a bourgeois-nationalist party (the Kuomintang) or a communist party. The Soviet leadership was divided on this issue, with Trotsky advocating Soviet support of the Chinese Communist Party and Stalin advocating Soviet support of the KMT since he considered the CCP too weak to lead the revolution by itself.[4] Stalin prevailed against Trotsky and the CCP was ordered to join forces with the KMT. In 1927, though, the KMT under Chiang Kai-shek turned against the communists, and destroyed most of the forces they had at that time, thus setting the stage for the emergence of the bitterness the Chinese communists held toward the Soviet Union.

Returning to Soviet military thinking, the Third World did not figure to a great extent in Soviet ideas about war during the Stalin era. During this period, one of the major themes of Soviet military thought was that war between imperialism and socialism was inevitable — the two antagonistic social systems were destined to clash. In this conflict, socialism would achieve a decisive victory over imperialism. This conflict between socialism and imperialism was seen to take place on a worldwide scale.[5]

During the Stalin era, all wars were classified into four different types or categories: (1) war in defence of the socialist homeland; (2) civil wars between the proletariat and the bourgeoisie; (3) national liberation wars; and (4) wars between imperialist states. The second category, civil wars, was seen as occurring only in the developed capitalist states and would lead to the dictatorship of the proletariat; these were not seen as occurring in the colonial and semi-colonial world until after the third category, national liberation war, had taken place. While wars between imperialist states might be waged to divide colonies, the only type of war in the Third World that involved indigenous popular forces were wars of national liberation.[6] The Stalinist view of this type of war did not differ from that expressed by Lenin: wars of national liberation would be led by the national bourgeoisie to establish national independence and bourgeois democracy — not socialism.

During the Stalin era, peaceful coexistence was regarded as possible, but only in a tactical sense. In other words, as long as the Soviet Union was weak, it should do anything it could to prevent a war with the imperialists in order to use this time to build up its military strength. Since war between socialism and imperialism was inevitable, this was a necessary measure so that the USSR would be strong when the war finally came.

In comparing the ideas about wars of national liberation expressed during the Lenin and Stalin years to actual events, a dichotomy becomes apparent. In those areas where Soviet armed forces were able to defeat any opposition in a country, the first stage of national liberation was quickly dispensed with and the second stage of socialist rule was imposed. Following the Second World War, the pretence of the first stage of national liberation was maintained only for three years, at most, before all the nations under Soviet domination were declared to be pursuing socialist transformation. In addition, Mongolia in 1921 passed directly to the second stage of national liberation through the help of Soviet military intervention.

Where Soviet armed forces did not directly control events in a country, however, Stalin was extremely hesitant about supporting the local communists. As was mentioned earlier, Stalin ordered the CCP to work with the KMT in China during the 1920s. Even after the KMT turned against the communists, Stalin still supported it and as late as 1948 Stalin was urging Mao Tse-tung to join a coalition government with the KMT.[7] During the Second World War, Stalin gave support to the royalist forces in Yugoslavia; his inability to control Tito led to the Soviet-Yugoslav rift in 1948. This event alone must have reinforced Stalin's fears about independent communists coming to power as well as confirmed his resolve not to allow any others to do so.

Yet while Stalin may not have wanted independent communists to come to power, he did not believe that the colonial powers would voluntarily depart from the Third World either. When the British did just this in the Indian subcontinent, Stalin believed that it was a trick – the rulers left behind in these nominally independent nations were seen as merely puppets of the imperialists. Stalin believed that true independence, even if only for a bourgeois democracy, must be won in a national liberation war. With regard to Asia after the Second World War, however, Stalin implicitly abandoned for a time Lenin's formulation expressed at the Second Comintern Congress that the national bourgeoisie would lead the first stage of revolution (national liberation), and embraced N.M. Roy's formulation that the bourgeois-democratic revolution could be led by the proletariat. Thus, in the wave of communist led insurrections in Asia during the late 1940s, communist parties announced that they were fighting for national independence even in those countries such as India, Burma, the Philippines and South Korea that were already independent.[8]

Nevertheless, while Stalin may have greatly encouraged these insurrections, he did very little to support them, and almost all of them failed. In only one country did the local communists have a chance both of defeating the colonial power and of installing itself in power — Vietnam. Yet even here, Stalin gave the local communists almost no support at all.[9] Further, during the Korean War, in which a communist state established by the Soviet Army came close to being completely defeated, the USSR limited its assistance to arms transfers and Soviet-flown aircraft support; Soviet ground forces did not enter the fighting.[10]

Despite the creation of the Mongolian People's Republic on its border and a certain degree of involvement in the Chinese revolution, the Soviet Union did not envision a major role for itself or for communist parties in the Third World during the Lenin and Stalin years. Before and during the Second World War, the USSR was preoccupied with its own defence, while after the war Europe was the area of greatest concern to it. Socialist revolution was envisioned for the Third World at some point in the future, though in practice Stalin appeared more interested in retarding it than encouraging it.

Soviet military thought about the Third World did not differ from the ideas expressed by Lenin and Stalin — indeed, Soviet military thought did not really exist independently during much of the Stalin era, but merely repeated Party doctrine instead. Concerning wars of national liberation, Soviet military thinking had nothing to say about situations in which the Soviet Army found itself predominant, such as in Mongolia or Eastern Europe. Where the Soviet Army was not present, and especially after the communist rebellions of the late 1940s in Asia failed, Stalin used the notion of a two-stage revolution as a means of trying to restrain independent communists from coming to power. The Third World, however, played only a minor role in Soviet military thought and Soviet foreign policy by the time of Stalin's death in 1953.

The Khrushchev Years

During the Khrushchev era, the Third World grew in importance both to Soviet military thought and to Soviet foreign policy. This change was caused by events in the 1950s and early 1960s that both provided opportunities for Soviet foreign policy and at the same time caused problems for it. These events also led to a change in both military and Party thinking about conflict in the Third World during this period. There were three main events that contributed to this reassessment:

(1) changes within the Third World itself; (2) the development of large nuclear arsenals by both the United States and the Soviet Union; and (3) the Sino-Soviet rift.

Although Stalin had considered the leaders of Third World nations that were granted independence to be the puppets of the colonial powers, events proved that this was not true. During the Korean War, India played an independent neutral role seeking an end to the conflict while its former colonial ruler, Britain, fought on the American side. Independent leaders prepared to challenge the West and to seek Soviet friendship arose in Egypt, Iraq, Ghana, Guinea, Mali and Indonesia, among others. Most spectacular of all, the revolutionary leaders of Cuba declared their government to be a Marxist-Leninist one. Not only did armed insurgency occur in Cuba during this period, but also in Vietnam, Malaya, Algeria and Kenya as well. Because many of the new Third World nations were involved in political, economic, and sometimes military conflict with the West, the entire region appeared to offer the Soviet Union an opportunity both to find allies against the imperialists and to advance the spread of socialism.

With regard to nuclear weapons, so long as the United States alone possessed them, Stalin disparaged their importance and claimed that they would not be decisive in war. However, after the Soviet Union acquired nuclear weapons and both superpowers increased their nuclear capability, Soviet recognition of the destructive power of these weapons was swift.[11] Khrushchev especially felt that a nuclear war would be extremely harmful to the Soviet Union, and thus should be avoided. There remained, however, the Marxist-Leninist dictum that Stalin upheld which saw war between socialism and imperialism as being inevitable. Lenin had certainly not envisioned the power of nuclear weapons when predicting war between socialism and imperialism and could not have foreseen, as Khrushchev saw quite clearly, that a world war between opposing social systems involving nuclear weapons could lead to the destruction of mankind instead of the triumph of socialism. Thus, in addition to all the other dramatic announcements signalling de-Stalinisation, Khrushchev proclaimed at the 20th Party Congress in February 1956 that war between socialism and imperialism was no longer inevitable since socialism was now so strong.[12]

However, while de-Stalinisation was welcomed by many communists in the USSR, it was not welcomed by communists in China. Indeed, one of the causes of the Sino-Soviet rift was the de-Stalinisation that Khrushchev announced at the 20th Party Congress. The Chinese communists did not accept Khrushchev's revision of Marxist-Leninist orthodoxy that war between socialism and imperialism was no longer inevitable. The Chinese believed at that time that such a conflict was inevitable, and even if nuclear weapons were involved, socialism would still triumph. Being less fearful of a world war, the Chinese advocated a policy of active socialist involvement in national liberation wars in order to advance socialism. Khrushchev, on the other hand, was not at all in favour of active Soviet involvement in these wars. He had said only that war between opposing social systems was no longer inevitable, not that it was no longer possible. As a result, one of the issues about which the Chinese heatedly criticised the Soviet Union in the increasingly bitter polemics between Moscow and Peking was the lack of Soviet support to national liberation movements.[13]

Yet while change in the Third World, growth in the nuclear arsenals, and the Sino-Soviet rift were the three major events of the Khrushchev era which affected Soviet military thinking about conflict in the Third World, the consideration of such conflict still played only a minor role in Soviet military thought. Of much greater importance were discussions of how nuclear weapons would affect a world war and war in Europe. With this background in mind, the various aspects of Soviet military thinking about conflict in the Third World may be more clearly understood.

The Relationship of Local War to World War

When Khrushchev stated at the 20th Party Congress in 1956 that world war between socialism and imperialism was no longer inevitable, his revision of previous Marxist-Leninist doctrine was readily accepted by the Soviet military. The Chinese communists, however, argued that socialism must be brought about through violent revolutions supported by the existing socialist states, and that excessive Soviet fear of world war led the USSR to shrink from its duty in this regard. The Chinese believed that the United States was a paper tiger that feared defeat and that even if there was a world war, socialism would triumph in it.[14]

This issue, which had been debated by the Soviets and the Chinese since 1957, was also discussed at the Moscow Conference of Eighty-one Communist Parties held in 1960. Khrushchev argued that world war between socialism and imperialism would not lead to the victory of the former, but to the destruction of both and that local wars which involved the nuclear powers would lead to world war. As a result of this he concluded that local wars should be avoided.[15] Khrushchev believed that there existed an escalatory link between local war and world war.

This idea was taken up by the military as well. It was stated in the first edition of *Voyennaya strategiya,* written under the direction of the noted Soviet military theorist Marshal V.D. Sokolovskiy, that any armed conflict will 'develop, inevitably, into a general war if the nuclear powers are drawn into it'.[16] Another highly influential Soviet military thinker, Major General N. Talenskiy, also stated that it would be impossible to keep war limited in the nuclear era.[17]

Although Khrushchev regarded the link between local war and world war to be inevitable, Thomas Wolfe has noted that many Soviet military thinkers differed from this point of view by describing the link as being only possible (albeit highly so).[18] The most interesting example of this was a letter by four of the Sokolovskiy authors published in *Krasnaya Zvezda* on 2 November 1963, in which they complained that the American editors of their book misrepresented them through translating one sentence to read that local wars 'inevitably' led to world wars, whereas they believed only that this was possible, pointing out that over seventy local conflicts after 1945 had not led to world war. As Wolfe observed, though, this letter was an odd one since the American editors had accurately translated the sentence in question while the Sokolovskiy authors themselves deliberately misquoted it in this letter, leaving out the word 'inevitably' which had appeared in their book.[19]

Some Soviet military thinkers even suggested that a conventional local war could be fought.[20] Nevertheless, the predominant point of view expressed by Soviet military thinkers at this time was that local war could lead to world war. The difference between Khrushchev and the military writers indicated that some in the military were less pessimistic than Khrushchev was on the subject of local war. Yet while the military may not have seen all local wars as necessarily growing into world war, they never indicated how a local war was to be kept localised. Although less pessimistic than Khrushchev, the military still considered local wars to pose a grave danger for wider conflict.

During the Khrushchev era, most Soviet commentary on the relationship between local war and world war focused on the possibility of a war in Europe involving both superpowers (at this time, most American commentary on this subject focused on Europe too). Relatively little attention was paid to conflict in the Third World. In the few statements that were made regarding conflict in the Third World, however, the possibility of local war escalating into world war was also emphasised, as may be seen from the following statement by Colonel General N. Lomov in 1962:

In recent times in the imperialist camp, much has been said not only of local wars, but of the formation of special forces to be employed in such wars. A special theory of brushfire wars has been elaborated. In actuality, such wars cannot remain local for long: they contain a threat for all humanity. A small imperialist war, as N.S. Khrushchev has noted, regardless of which of the imperialists started it, can develop into a world nuclear conflict.[21]

A similar statement was made by Colonel V. Morozov in the July 1963 *Voyennaya Mysl'* (the restricted circulation journal of the Soviet General Staff not intended for the public in either the Soviet Union or any other country):

This question [of local wars], by the way, has great significance, since local wars are considered by many bourgeois ideologists as a means of preserving the remnants of the colonial system and strengthening the capitalistic structure. It would be proper to expose the danger of local wars for the cause of peace, the possibility of their developing into a world nuclear war. It is all the more necessary to do this, since certain political figures of the West openly declare that they will not hesitate to use nuclear weapons in local wars. Thus, local wars, unleashed by the imperialists, are a direct path to a world nuclear catastrophe.[22]

What is clear from both of these statements is that the authors regarded local wars as a means of conflict in the Third World launched exclusively by the imperialists, not as a means of conflict that the Soviet Union could also initiate and wage successfully. The identification of local wars as an instrument of force available only to the imperialists would account for the attribution of evil to local wars made by almost all Soviet Party and military commentators on this subject. From the Soviet perspective, the United States had used its great nuclear advantage in the 1950s to threaten the USSR with massive retaliation. When the Soviet Union finally acquired a credible second strike nuclear capability to counter this threat, the US shifted to a strategy of local wars. The peace-loving Soviet Union had only acquired nuclear weapons to prevent world war, but did not wish to see the US make strategic gains through local war either.

Soviet statements about the link between local war and world war not only signalled to the Chinese that the Soviet Union was unwilling to become directly involved in local wars, but also served as a warning to the United States that the USSR could raise the magnitude of a conflict to world war if American involvement in a local war seriously damaged Soviet interests. Thus, the possibility of local war escalating into world war was emphasised as a means of deterring American involvement in local wars. At the same time, these warnings of the danger of escalation were an admission that the Soviet Union did not have the capability to respond to American involvement in local wars in the Third World through conventional means on the local level. Indeed, local wars were not seen as a foreign policy instrument that the USSR could use to achieve its goals in the way that the US did. During the Khrushchev era, then, both Party and military could only hope that the threat of Soviet nuclear retaliation against the United States would deter American involvement in local wars. However, the Soviet desire to avoid an actual world war combined with Soviet inability to project conventional forces into Third World conflicts meant that there was little the USSR could do to stop the US if the US was not deterred by Soviet threats.

The Nature and Types of Conflict in the Third World

At the beginning of the Khrushchev era, Soviet military thinkers retained intact the classification of wars that had been established during the Stalin years: (1) war in defence of the socialist homeland; (2) civil wars between the proletariat and the bourgeoisie; (3) national liberation wars; and (4) wars between imperialist states.[23] A change in the first category was made in the second edition of *Marksizm-Leninizm o voine i armii* that appeared in 1961. Wars in defence of the socialist homeland became wars 'between imperialist and socialist states'.[24] This change was meant to show that the Soviet Union no longer faced the imperialist nations alone, but was a member of a larger group of socialist nations that would defend one another.

An explanation of this classification of types of wars, which will be referred to as the 'traditional' Soviet military view of types of wars, is required here in order to understand why changes were made in it later and what sort of ideological problems these changes caused. Soviet military thinkers classified wars not only by type (civil wars, national liberation wars, etc.), but also by nature: just or unjust. Designations of just and unjust were not assigned to wars themselves, but to the contending parties in wars. Whether a contender in a war was just or unjust, however, depended on what it was fighting for in any of the four given types of war. In wars between socialist and imperialist states, the socialist states were always just and the imperialist ones always unjust. Similarly, in civil wars the proletariat was always just and the bourgeoisie always unjust, while in national liberation wars the forces fighting for independence were always just and the colonial powers always unjust. In wars between imperialist states, both sides were always unjust.[25]

Thus, given the four types of war and the concept of justness, the just and unjust side in any given conflict could be quickly and unambiguously determined. Further, although it was possible for both sides in a war to be unjust (wars between imperialist states), no more than one side could ever be regarded as just in a war. It was considered impossible for two just sides to fight each other. Because two just sides could not fight each other, it was not considered possible for war between socialist states ever to take place.

The elaboration of the nature and types of wars, then, was made solely on the basis of their ideological or sociopolitical characteristics. Non-ideological factors, such as scale of warfare or type of weapons employed, did not affect how wars were classified. Ideological factors alone determined which side (if any) the Soviet Union would support in any given war.

Concerning the types of wars themselves, Soviet military writers considered wars between imperialism and socialism to be the most just type of war socialism could fight. Such a war was usually envisioned as taking place on a worldwide scale. Civil wars, as during the Stalin era, were seen as being fought between the proletariat and the bourgeoisie in the advanced capitalist countries; victory by the proletariat would result in the establishment of socialism. This type of war was not envisioned as taking place in the Third World where national liberation of colonies or semi-colonies had to occur first before the question of social liberation would arise. Although the proletariat and peasantry participated in national liberation wars, they were led by the national bourgeoisie who would establish capitalism. Even this, however, was considered progressive compared to the continuation of colonial domination, and thus deserved the support of the socialist community.

The question that arose during the Khrushchev era was how much support the socialist community should give to national liberation wars. As was mentioned earlier, the Chinese felt that the Soviets should give a large amount of assistance to national liberation movements; they considered the spread of socialism so worthwhile that it made the risk of causing war with the imperialists acceptable. In addition, Mao Tse-tung believed that the two stages of national liberation, which Lenin saw as first establishing capitalism and then socialism, could be converted into one step leading directly to socialism.[26] The Chinese, then, had greater expectations concerning the success of national liberation wars for the spread of socialism than did the Soviets.

Chinese criticism of the Soviet Union for its lack of aid to national liberation forces threatened to make the USSR appear distinctly unrevolutionary within the world communist movement. Khrushchev sought to defend Soviet actions by arguing that the Soviet Union did support national liberation wars but that it also sought to avoid a world war that could destroy all of mankind. The way Khrushchev made this argument was through revising the traditional Soviet military classification of the nature and types of war.

In his speech reporting on the 1960 Moscow World Conference of Eighty-one Communist Parties, Khrushchev abandoned the traditional Soviet military classification with four types of war and substituted his own classification which contained three categories: world wars, local wars and wars of national liberation. Applying the concept of justness to these three categories, Khrushchev declared that national liberation wars were just, and thus should be encouraged and supported. A world war, however, was an unjust war because it threatened to destroy everything, including socialism. In addition, local wars were also unjust because they led to world war. Thus, both world war and local war were to be avoided. In distinguishing national liberation wars from the types that were to be avoided, Khrushchev noted that national liberation wars 'must not be identified with wars between states, with local wars'.[27]

By declaring national liberation wars to be just, unlike the other two types, Khrushchev appeared to be signalling Soviet support for them. As both Raymond Garthoff and Thomas Wolfe have pointed out, however, this seeming support of national liberation wars involved a contradiction: while national liberation wars were to receive Soviet support, the Soviet Union was also to avoid potential clashes with the United States in local wars.[28] In other words, Soviet support would be forthcoming only up to the point when a national liberation war threatened to become a war 'between states'. The USSR would not become involved in local wars which the US entered.

In revising the traditional Soviet military classification of types of wars, Khrushchev for the first time combined ideological factors with non-ideological ones. For the categories of world war and local war, the scale of the conflict was more important to Khrushchev than the socio-political objectives of the belligerents in these types of wars. The category of national liberation wars appeared to be a more purely ideological one, but even here this would only be true if it could avoid becoming a local war. Thus for Khrushchev, the scale of a conflict was more important for determining what the Soviet attitude toward a war should be than the class basis and objectives of the contending parties.

This revision in the traditional military view of the nature and types of war, made by Khrushchev in the context of the Soviet desire to avoid nuclear war and to appear responsibly revolutionary in the growing Sino-Soviet polemics, did not at all please the Soviet military. What they especially did not like was the classification of wars according to scale and then the categorisation of both world wars and local wars as unjust types of conflict *per se*; Khrushchev implied that all participants in them would be unjust and did not distinguish between the forces of socialism and imperialism in this regard. Thus, in the 1962 edition of *Voyennaya strategiya,* the authors outwardly accepted Khrushchev's revision of the classification of types of wars, but transformed them to reflect the importance of the criterion of sociopolitical content:

> Soviet military strategy starts with the fact that in the present era, the following basic categories of war are theoretically possible:
>
> *World war* between the imperialist and socialist camps, which – if not prevented – would be, in political essence, a decisive armed clash of two opposing world systems. Such a war would be aggressive, rapacious, and unjust on the part of imperialism and a liberating, just, revolutionary war on the part of socialism.
>
> *Small imperialist wars* on a local, limited scale, started by the imperialists for the purpose of suppressing national liberation movements and for maintaining colonies. Small, local wars are also possible between imperialist countries. All these wars are aggressive and unjust on the part of imperialism.
>
> *National liberation, civil, and other popular wars,* for the repulse of the aggressive, predatory attacks of the imperialists and for freedom and independence. These wars are just, liberating and revolutionary.[29]

In addition, although Colonel General Lomov acknowledged Khrushchev's classification of types of wars, he then criticised this means of classification (but not Khrushchev himself) for ignoring ideological factors:

> local wars cannot be evaluated from the standpoint that they are waged within local territorial limits. If we do this, we should also

have to include national liberation and civil wars in this category — that is, just wars which are also waged within territorial limits. But this would be quite incorrect. There exists only one criterion for determining the character of wars; this criterion is their sociopolitical content.[30]

Finally, the two editions of the influential *Marksizm-Leninizm o voine i armii* published during the Khrushchev era after the First Secretary had revised the classification of types of wars expressed their disapproval by ignoring Khrushchev's categorisation altogether and by publishing the traditional Soviet military one instead.[31]

It is clear from these statements that the Soviet military did not accept the classification of wars based on non-ideological factors (such as scale), but sought to reassert ideological ones instead. In the Sokolovskiy volume, the authors did not apply the concept of justness to types of war *per se*, but to the contenders in them. In a world war, the socialists would be just and the imperialists unjust. Only the imperialists fought unjust local wars — for their opponents, these wars were just. Lomov also explicitly rejected scale as a factor in classifying wars, claiming that only ideological content could be used to do this.

This disagreement between the leader of the Communist Party and the Soviet military over an issue as important as the classification of types of wars was unprecedented. This issue was important, not simply because it revealed ideological differences between Khrushchev and the military, but because these ideological differences had differing foreign policy ramifications.

For Khrushchev, world war would be a catastrophic event that would destroy socialism, and thus had to be avoided. Further, if the US and the USSR became involved in a local war, Khrushchev felt there would be no way to restrain the conflict from escalating. In addition, given the growing discussion in the United States of the possibility of limited war, Khrushchev wished to deter the US from undertaking such a war by warning that it would not necessarily remain limited. The Soviet Union, for its part, would not become involved in dangerous local wars, nor should the United States.

The Soviet military did not wish the US to become involved in local wars either, but when the US did, what then should the Soviet Union do? Not to become at all involved because local war was unjust according to Khrushchev meant that the USSR could not do anything to help the just side in the conflict. But if the Soviets did nothing, the United States might be victorious. A certain amount of Soviet support, though at a low level, might prevent this.

This difference of opinion between Khrushchev and the Soviet military, then, was a large one. Nevertheless, the military did not explicitly criticise the First Secretary himself. The ideas he expressed were criticised circumspectly compared to how they would be treated after he was forced from office. Yet while the military did not criticise Khrushchev directly on this issue while he was in office, what is remarkable was that they dared to disagree with him at all. The military would not have presumed to have a different opinion from the Party leader during the Stalin era. What this dispute shows is that during the Khrushchev era, the Soviet military could develop independent positions on issues that were of particular importance to it.

Peaceful Coexistence

During the Stalin era, peaceful coexistence with the imperialists was considered a temporary policy to allow the USSR to grow stronger before the inevitable war between them took place. At the 20th CPSU Congress in 1956, though, Khrushchev transformed peaceful coexistence with the imperialists into a policy that was to be pursued permanently. He had declared at this Congress that world war was no longer inevitable. Through pursuing a policy of peaceful coexistence, the Soviet Union would make sure that world war did not occur.[32]

As part of the policy of peaceful coexistence, Khrushchev said that the Soviet Union would not 'export' revolution.[33] He was implying here what Soviet leaders would later state outright: that the export of revolution was something the Chinese advocated. It was this type of adventurousness on the part of the Chinese that Khrushchev feared would result in world war for the Soviet Union. Instead of spreading socialism through violence, Khrushchev believed that socialism could be spread through peaceful means as well. Thus, peaceful coexistence was compatible with the struggle for communism worldwide.[34] From Khrushchev's statements on peaceful coexistence, though, it was evident that he saw the spread of communism as only a secondary goal over which the primary goal of avoiding world war took precedence.[35]

The Soviet military favoured the revision Khrushchev made that world war was no longer inevitable. However, the military appeared to be much less enthusiastic than the Party about peaceful coexistence judging from the paucity of references Soviet military writers made to it at this time. Even when they did mention it, their comments were not particularly favourable. In 1962, for example, Marshal of the Soviet Union R. Ya. Malinovskiy described peaceful coexistence as something that the Communist Party offered to other nations but did not mention the Soviet military as sharing the same desire.[36]

The Soviet military instead emphasised the necessity to be prepared for conflict with the imperialists, should they force it upon the Soviet Union. This argument may have been made more in reaction to the question of allocating resources between the military and civilian sectors of the Soviet economy than to the question of supporting conflict in the Third World. Here again was an issue over which the Party and the military differed, though the military did not explicitly attack the policy of peaceful coexistence.

Indigenous Third World Forces

The optimism Khrushchev had expressed at the 20th Party Congress that peaceful coexistence was compatible with the spread of socialism appeared to be justified during the period of his rule by events in the Third World. Many of the leaders that came to power in the former colonies of Africa and Asia declared themselves against capitalism and many of them even espoused socialism. Among these were Sekou Touré of Guinea, Kwame Nkrumah of Ghana, Mobido Keita of Mali, Gamal Abdel Nasser of Egypt, Ben Bella of Algeria, Ne Win of Burma and Achmed Sukarno of Indonesia. Fidel Castro even went so far as to proclaim his government to be a Marxist-Leninist one. The prospects of socialism appeared to be growing strongly in the Third World with no more than diplomatic and some economic support required of the Soviet Union.

With the exception of Castro, the Soviet Union recognised that Third World leaders were not true communists. Even those who espoused socialism often brutally suppressed their country's communists. Further, the advocacy of 'African' or 'Asian' socialism drew criticism from the Soviet Union since these forms of socialism were not of the 'scientific' variety that the USSR pursued.[37] Despite these misgivings, though, the non-capitalist path of development that these nations were following greatly enhanced their prospects of achieving socialism. One important Soviet scholar on the Third World, G. Mirskiy, expressed the optimism of the Khrushchev era on this score: 'If the conditions for proletarian leadership have not yet matured, the historical mission of breaking with capitalism can be carried out by elements close to the working class.'[38]

To this end, local communists in Third World countries were directed not to oppose the ruling parties, but to co-operate with them by joining them and seeking to guide them to socialism from within.[39]

The Soviet view of guerrilla armies fighting for both national liberation and socialism was more ambivalent. On the one hand, these groups were obviously struggling for a progressive cause. On the other hand, the Soviet Union could not approve of the supremacy of the guerrilla army over the communist party. This was seen as the error Mao Tse-tung advocated which led to the incorrect path being followed by China. Further, the Maoists were advocating guerrilla warfare on the Chinese model as the only path to national liberation and socialism in the Third World. The question of guerrilla armies, then, was caught up in the Sino-Soviet dispute. Opposing China's position that it was the only way to revolution, the Soviets asserted that socialism could also be achieved by peaceful means. Finally, there was also the Soviet fear that once guerrilla armies espousing socialism came to power, they might not follow 'scientific' socialism, or in other words, they might not submit themselves completely to Soviet influence, as was the case in China and Yugoslavia.

When a guerrilla army, such as in Algeria, did not actually espouse Marxism-Leninism, the problems created for the Soviet Union were less severe. Such an ideology was obviously representative of petty bourgeois and peasant influences. National liberation was a progressive step by itself that made the establishment of socialism that much likelier in the future. In addition, the anti-capitalist stance of Algeria made it a suitable ally for the USSR, despite Algeria's treatment of its communists.

When a guerrilla army that did espouse Marxism-Leninism came to power, and its interpretation of Marxism-Leninism differed from that of the Soviet Union, a greater problem was created for the USSR, as in the case of Cuba. The Communist Party of Cuba played only a very minor role in the Cuban revolution, which was won by Castro's guerrilla forces. Castro chose later to adopt the Communist Party into his government. This experience was elevated by Castro and Che Guevara into a revolutionary theory which they saw as applicable to all of Latin America. In their view, the Latin American communist parties were not revolutionary organisations. They advocated, instead, the formation of guerrilla armies that would later take over the communist parties.[40] This Cuban ideology which Guevara was later to try unsuccessfully to convert into practice in Bolivia, was directly at variance with Soviet ideology. First, the Latin American communist parties were supported by the USSR, as were their efforts at achieving socialism peacefully. Secondly, the Soviets objected to a guerrilla army controlling a communist party, believing that the reverse was essential to the success of socialism. This difference led to polemics between Moscow and Havana that threatened friendly relations between them in the 1960s.[41] The Soviet Union was not willing to tolerate an interpretation of Marxist-Leninist ideology different from and competitive with its own.

Soviet discussion of indigenous forces within the Third World was undertaken primarily by the Party during the Khrushchev era. The Soviet military had very little to say about this subject then. What little was said, though, did not differ from the position expressed by the Party.[42] Differences on this issue, though, would soon emerge between Party/civilian and military writers during the Brezhnev era.

American Ideas and Actions in Local Wars

Soviet military thinkers have commented relatively frequently on both American ideas about and American actions in Third World conflicts. Their treatment of each of these aspects, however, has changed in emphasis over time. During the Khrushchev era, Soviet military thinkers focused almost exclusively upon American ideas about local wars and not upon American actions in them.

The American discussion about limited and local war in the late 1950s and early 1960s was considered by the Soviet military to be a victory for the Soviet Union in one sense. They characterised the imperialists as wanting to attack and destroy the Soviet Union in a world war. The development of nuclear weapons by the USSR, however, forced the imperialists to abandon a policy of launching world war and to resort to local wars instead to achieve their aggressive aims.[43]

However, the Soviet Union could not regard this as a complete victory because even though it could now deter world war, it could not deter local wars. As was seen earlier, one way in which the USSR attempted to restrain the US from involvement in local wars was through emphasising how such wars could be transformed into world war. One Soviet military writer, A.Y. Yefremov, sought to demonstrate how an imperialist power could never achieve its goals through launching local wars. First he noted that the First World War and the Second World War were the result of local wars escalating into world wars.[44] He then noted that both the Korean War and the first Indochina war had threatened to become wider than the imperialists had wanted and that the US had not succeeded in conquering North Korea while the French were actually defeated by the Vietnamese communists.[45] The conclusion to be made was that local war was a very dangerous policy and that local war 'theorists' in the West should not assume as they did that a local war could be kept localised.

The basis of Soviet military criticism of American ideas about local war was the belief that local war could escalate into world war, and that the Americans should thus realise that the notion that local war could be kept localised was incorrect. This was, in essence, the sole comment upon American ideas about local war made by the Soviet military. What this criticism rested on, of course, was the Soviet view of the relationship of local war to world war. If the Soviet position on this subject changed (which it later did), then their view of American ideas about local war would also, necessarily, have to change. This, however, did not happen during the Khrushchev era. During this time, the criticism of American local war theory on the basis that local war could grow into world war showed that local war was a policy that the Soviet Union wished to deter the US from following. The fact that the Soviets had nothing favourable to say about the concept of local war at this time indicates that they did not envision it as a policy that they themselves could pursue successfully. It was a policy that only the imperialists sought to pursue and which the Soviets sought only to prevent them from pursuing.

The Soviet Role in Third World Conflicts

While Khrushchev had proclaimed that national liberation wars were just wars that the Soviet Union supported, the Soviets were extremely reticent in discussing the nature of the support they would give. As Raymond Garthoff pointed out in 1966, the Soviets frequently announced their support of national liberation movements, but only in very general terms; little was ever said about what the USSR would do specifically to help them, especially militarily.[46]

Sometimes Soviet support of national liberation movements would only be described as economic and political support, with no mention being made of military support at all.[47] The most Soviet leaders, including Khrushchev himself,[48] would acknowledge in the military realm was arms transfers. Even this policy, however, was described in hesitant terms. In 1963, for example, a *Pravda* editorial stated, 'The CPSU and the Soviet people consider it their international duty to give all-round political and economic support, and if necessary, the help of arms too, to the national liberation struggle of the people.'[49] Only economic and political support were described as 'all-round' here, while the 'help of arms' was not. Since a national liberation struggle, almost by definition, would require arms, the qualification 'if necessary' seems strange unless it meant that the USSR would be the one to define when arms transfers were necessary. However, even on those occasions when Soviet arms transfers were acknowledged, no further details were revealed. The Soviets would never describe what kind of or how many weapons were transferred.

Soviet military writers were even more reticent about discussing what sort of military support the USSR was giving national liberation movements. Usually military writers would make vague statements that the USSR supported national liberation movements without specifying what this support consisted of,[50] or they would mention Soviet 'material support' to these struggles without saying whether material support included military support.[51] Late in the Khrushchev era, Soviet military writers would also acknowledge that Soviet arms had been sent to national liberation movements, in response to Chinese charges that the USSR was doing nothing at all to help them.[52]

Although the Soviet military began to discuss Soviet arms transfers only in 1963, the USSR had transferred arms to the Third World as early as 1955 when an arms agreement was made with Egypt through Czechoslovakia.[53] This was the beginning of a pattern that would continue throughout the Brezhnev era as well. Soviet military thinkers would never discuss a policy that involved the USSR in a Third World conflict (or potential conflict) until that policy had already been successfully undertaken by the Soviet Union.

Concerning the Khrushchev era, the vague and hesitant statements made about how the USSR would support national liberation movements indicated that relatively little military assistance was forthcoming from the USSR at that time. The most that would be given was arms. No more direct involvement on the part of the Soviet Union in Third World conflicts was then envisioned by either the Party or the military. More than any other aspect of Soviet military writing about Third World conflicts, these statements about the role of the Soviet Union revealed the gap between the verbal support and the limited extent to which the USSR was actually willing to become involved in national liberation wars.

Conclusion

The most notable change in Soviet military thinking about conflict in the Third World from the Stalin era to the Khrushchev era was that during the latter period, thinking about conflict in the Third World became much more developed. During the Stalin era, very little attention was paid to this subject, and certainly no role was envisioned for the Soviet Union in national liberation wars. During the Khrushchev era, the Third World became much more important to both the military and the Party, although the threat of world war and war in Europe absorbed more attention.

Also significant was the fact that during the Khrushchev era, the military possessed ideas about conflict in the Third World different from those held by the Party leader. This would not have been conceivable during the Stalin era. This independent military line signified that on issues in which the military had an interest, it was now willing to state its own opinion. In general, the differences between the military and the Party over conflict in the Third World indicated that the military was more willing than Khrushchev to support Third World groups that favoured Soviet interests, or at the minimum, opposed Western interests, to come to power through armed conflict.

Although the Soviet military had different opinions than the Party on conflict in the Third World, it was the ideas of the Party, particularly of Khrushchev, that were of primary importance during this period. It was Khrushchev who made major revisions in the Marxist-Leninist view of the relationship of local war to world war (which the Soviet military accepted), the nature and types of wars in the Third World, and peaceful coexistence (both of which the military did not accept). The military never criticised Khrushchev directly, and Khrushchev did not criticise or even acknowledge the traditional Soviet military view of the nature and types of wars that he revised. Further, where the military disagreed with Khrushchev, they did not develop new ideas, but merely reasserted old ones that had been dominant during the Stalin era. Thus it was Khrushchev and the Party that took the lead in formulating a new Soviet position on conflict in the Third World while the military merely reacted to these new ideas by reasserting old ones when they disagreed.

What was the relationship between the ideas expressed about conflict in the Third World and the concrete policies the USSR adopted toward them? At most, Soviet Party and military writers said that the USSR would ship arms to national liberation movements. Many statements did not even mention arms transfers, but only referred to aid generally. Soviet statements about this aid were relatively hesitant, yet during this period the USSR shipped arms to Egypt, Algeria, Indonesia,

Iraq, Yemen and Cuba. Nothing in Soviet military or Party writing suggested that the USSR would send nuclear weapons to Cuba in 1962 – an event which resulted in the Cuban missile crisis. Also, as mentioned earlier, the USSR began to ship conventional arms to the Third World well before discussing the policy of arms transfers in print. It would appear that the Soviet Union was much more active militarily in the Third World than Soviet statements would indicate.

However, in looking at all these cases except Yemen and Algeria, Soviet arms shipments were not made to national liberation movements, but rather to established governments which had requested them. During the 1956 Suez crisis, Soviet nuclear threats were not made to Britain and France until the crisis was practically over. Algeria and Yemen were ongoing conflicts, but Soviet arms reached the side they favoured primarily through Egypt. The most serious crisis of the Khrushchev era in the Third World was the Cuban missile crisis. This situation, though, was primarily the result of the Soviets misjudging American reactions to their foreign policy rather than anything else. Cuba had been accepted by the Soviets as a communist state; after the Bay of Pigs incident in 1961, it was apparent that the US would not make much effort to topple the Castro regime. Once the US adopted this position, Khrushchev undoubtedly saw it as natural to have Soviet nuclear weapons emplaced on a communist ally's territory as it was for the US to have nuclear weapons on the territory of its European allies. The crisis did not arise until the Kennedy Administration noticed the weapons and called it a crisis, after which the Soviets very quickly backed down to avoid a world war. As a communist country, Cuba was no longer an ordinary part of the Third World to the USSR, though the incident did indicate the degree to which the USSR was willing to become militarily involved with any Third World country that turned into a communist state (at least, before the Cuban missile crisis).

With the exception of the Cuban missile crisis, the USSR was extremely cautious about undertaking military actions in the Third World, including arms transfers. The role of the USSR in Third World conflicts, though, was only one aspect of Soviet military thought on this subject. The differences between military statements from the Stalin era to the Khrushchev era and the differences between military and Party statements during the Khrushchev era did indicate a greater Soviet military interest in Third World conflicts over time. The belief that world war was no longer inevitable and the disagreement with Khrushchev over the classification of wars (in which the military classified belligerents in wars on an ideological basis alone and objected to the classification of wars themselves as just or unjust depending on their scale) signalled changes in attitude about Third World conflicts that had foreign policy ramifications.

In military terms, Soviet foreign policy toward the Third World during the Khrushchev era was one of responding to the opportunity of gaining allies through limited arms shipments when this posed little risk for the USSR of conflict with the United States. Only limited risks with limited costs would be accepted. This was the attitude toward the Third World that both Party and military writing expressed. The Soviets were relatively optimistic during this period about their ability to make foreign policy gains in the form of acquiring allies with little effort expended on the part of the USSR. The Brezhnev era, though, would soon show that allies gained so easily could also be lost easily, and events in the Third World would force a reassessment of Soviet military thinking about conflict there.

Notes

1. *Second Congress of the Communist International* (New Park, London, 1977), pp. 110-11.

2. Ibid., pp. 117-18.

3. Richard Lowenthal, *Model or Ally? The Communist Powers and the Developing Countries* (Oxford University Press, New York, 1977), p. 179.

4. Ibid., p. 180.

5. Herbert S. Dinerstein, *War and the Soviet Union* (Praeger, New York, 1959), p. 66.

6. A. Geronimus, *Marksizm-Leninizm o voine i armii* (Partizdat, Moscow, 1932), pp. 72-3.

7. Adam B. Ulam, *Expansion and Coexistence: Soviet Foreign Policy 1917-73*, 2nd edn (Praeger, New York, 1974), pp. 486-9.

8. Lowenthal, *Model or Ally?* pp. 184-5.

9. Mark N. Katz, 'The Origins of the Vietnam War 1945-1948', *Review of Politics*, 42:2 (April 1980), pp. 141-2.

10. O.B. Borisov and B.T. Koloskov, *Sovetsko-kitayskiye otnosheniya 1945-1970* (Mysl', Moscow, 1971), pp. 54-5.

11. Dinerstein, *War and the Soviet Union*, Ch. 5.

12. N.S. Khrushchev, *Otchetnii doklad Ts.K. KPSS XX sy"exdu partii* (Politizdat, Moscow, 1956), pp. 39-41.

13. See Raymond L. Garthoff, *Soviet Military Policy: A Historical Analysis* (Praeger, New York, 1966), Ch. 10.

14. See Lu Chih-ch'ao, 'Examination of the Question of War Must Not Run Counter to the Marxist-Leninist Viewpoint of Class Struggle', *Red Flag*, 15 August 1963, and 'Statement of the Chinese Government: A Comment on the Soviet Government Statement of August 21', *Radio Peking*, September 1 1963, both quoted in Garthoff, *Soviet Military Policy*, pp. 196-7.

15. N.S. Khrushchev, 'Za noviye pobedi mirovogo kommunisticheskogo dvizheniya', *Kommunist*, no. 1, January 1961, p. 18.

16. Marshal of the Soviet Union V.D. Sokolovskiy (ed.), *Voyennaya strategiya*,

1st edn (Voyenizdat, Moscow, 1962), p. 222.

17. Major General N. Talenskiy, 'Sovremennaya voina: kharakter i sledstviya', *Mezhdunarodnaya Zhizn'*, no. 10, October 1960, p. 36.

18. Thomas W. Wolfe, *Soviet Strategy at the Crossroads* (Harvard University Press, Cambridge, Mass., 1964), pp. 118-24.

19. Ibid., pp. 123-4. For other statements in which military authors say that local wars 'can' lead to world war instead of that they 'will' do so, see Colonel General N. Lomov, 'O sovetskoy voyennoy doktrine', *Kommunist Vooruzhennykh Sil*, no. 10, May 1962, p. 16; Colonel V. Morozov, 'The Third Edition of "Marxism-Leninism on War and the Army"', *Voyennaya Mysl'*, no. 7, July 1963, CIA FDD Trans. no. 956, p. 81; and the note by RAND Corporation editors of V.D. Sokolovskii, *Military Strategy* (Prentice-Hall, Englewood Cliffs, NJ, 1963), pp. 289-93.

20. See, for example, Major D. Kazakov, 'Teoreticheskaya i metodologicheskaya osnova sovetskoy voyennoy nauki', *Kommunist Vooruzhennykh Sil*, no. 10, May 1963, pp. 11-12, and Colonel L. Belousov, 'Konferentsiya o sovetskoy voyennoy doktrine', *Voyenno-Istoricheskiy Zhurnal*, no. 10, October 1963, p. 123.

21. Lomov, 'O sovetskoy voyennoy doktrine', p. 16.

22. Morozov, 'The Third Edition of "Marxism-Leninism on War and the Army"', p. 81.

23. Colonel I.N. Lebanov, Colonel B.A. Beliy and Colonel A.P. Novoselov (eds.), *Marksizm-Leninizm o voine i armii*, 1st edn (Voyenizdat, Moscow, 1957), pp. 79, 111-12. Three previous editions of this book were published (1932, 1949 and 1956), but in 1957, this work was greatly expanded; all subsequent editions (1961, 1962, 1965 and 1968) are enumerated from this 1957 edition.

24. Colonel G.A. Fedorov, Colonel N. Ya. Sushko and Colonel B.A. Beliy (eds.), *Marksizm-Leninizm o voine i armii*, 2nd edn (Voyenizdat, Moscow, 1961), p. 87.

25. Lebanov *et al., Marksizm-Leninizm o voine i armii*, 1st edn, pp. 74-84.

26. Peter Van Ness, *Revolution and Chinese Foreign Policy* (University of California Press, Berkeley, 1970), pp. 70-2.

27. Khrushchev, 'Za noviye pobedi mirovogo kommunisticheskogo dvizheniya', p. 20.

28. Garthoff, *Soviet Military Policy*, p. 212, and Wolfe, *Soviet Strategy at the Crossroads*, pp. 124-5.

29. Sokolovskiy, *Voyennaya strategiya*, 1st Russian edn, pp. 208-9.

30. Lomov, 'O sovetskoy voyennoy doktrine', p. 16.

31. Fedorov *et al., Marksizm-Leninizm o voine i armii*, 2nd edn, p. 87, and Colonel G.A. Fedorov, Major General N. Ya. Sushko and Colonel B.A. Beliy (eds.) *Marksizm-Leninizm o voine i armii*, 3rd edn (Voyenizdat, Moscow, 1962), p. 85. What was referred to as wars 'between imperialist and socialist states' in the second edition was called 'wars for the defense of the socialist countries against aggressors' in the third edition. This change made clearer that the editors believed that even a world war would definitely be a just war on the part of socialism.

32. Khrushchev, *Otchetnii doklad Ts.K. KPSS XX sy''ezdu partii*, pp. 39-41.

33. Ibid., pp. 37-8.

34. Ibid., p. 38.

35. Ibid., pp. 36-44.

36. Marshal R. Ya. Malinovskiy, *Bditel'no stoyat'na strazhe mira* (Voyenizdat, Moscow, 1962), p. 19. In the same paragraph, Malinovskiy expressed the sincere desire of the Soviet Union for total disarmament; one wonders if his desire for peaceful coexistence was as sincere.

37. Lowenthal, *Model or Ally?*, p. 220.

38. G. Mirskiy, 'The Proletariat and National Liberation', *New Times*, no. 18,

May 1964, pp. 8-9.

39. Lowenthal, *Model or Ally?*, pp. 221-4.

40. For a highly sympathetic description of the Cuban theory of revolution, see Régis Debray, *Révolution dans la révolution?*(François Maspero, Paris, 1967).

41. Andrés Suarez, *Cuba: Castroism and Communism 1959-1966* (M.I.T. Press, Cambridge, Mass., 1967), pp. 186-91.

42. See Colonel Ye. Dolgopolov, *Natsional'no-osvoboditel'niye voini v sovremennuyu epokhu* (Voyenizdat, Moscow, 1960).

43. Lomov, 'O sovetskoy voyennoy doktrine', p. 16.

44. A.Y. Yefremov, *Za shirmoy 'organichennykh' voin* (Voyenizdat, Moscow, 1960), pp. 38-9.

45. Ibid., p. 55.

46. Garthoff, *Soviet Military Policy*, p. 213.

47. Boris Ponomaraev, 'Nekotoriye voprosi revolutsionnogo dvizheniya', *Problemi Mira i Sotsializma*, no. 12, December 1962, pp. 9-10.

48. N.S. Khrushchev, *Predotvrashcheniye voini – pervostepennaya zadacha* (Inyazdat, Moscow, 1963), pp. 81-2.

49. 'Za edinstvo i splochennost' mezhdunarodnogo kommunisticheskogo dvizheniya', *Pravda*, 6 December 1963.

50. Sokolovskiy, *Voyennaya strategiya*, 1st Russian edn, p. 209.

51. V.D. Sokolovskiy, *Voyennaya strategiya*, 2nd edn (Voyenizdat, Moscow, 1963), p. 229.

52. See D. Vol'skiy and V. Kudriantsev, 'Real'naya deistvitel'nost' i domisli raskol'nikov', *Krasnaya Zvezda*, 10 October 1963.

53. Jon D. Glassman, *Arms for the Arabs: The Soviet Union and War in the Middle East* (Johns Hopkins University Press, Baltimore, 1975), p. 7.

2 THE EARLY BREZHNEV YEARS: 1964-1968

The flamboyance of Khrushchev gave way to caution in international affairs on the part of Brezhnev and Kosygin in their early years in power. Gone were the blustering threats that Khrushchev often dramatically made as well as such risk prone policies as the attempt to emplace nuclear weapons in Cuba. Instead, the new Soviet leaders pursued a steady buildup in both nuclear and conventional forces. The arms race with the United States and the rift with China continued during this period. However, several changes did occur in the Third World which affected Soviet military thinking.

Certainly one of the most visible events was the American military involvement in Vietnam. These were the years during which American armed forces grew to their greatest extent in Southeast Asia. North Vietnam and other communists began to put pressure on the USSR (especially at the 23rd Party Congress in 1966) to help Hanoi repulse the United States.[1] The USSR was faced with the dilemma of either risking some form of military confrontation with the United States if it militarily helped North Vietnam or losing its leadership role in the world communist movement if it did not aid Hanoi while China did. (On a smaller scale, the US also intervened militarily in the Dominican Republic in 1965.)

In addition, the recently decolonised Third World countries were beginning to experience conflicts between themselves, such as the 1967 Middle East war and the 1965 Indo-Pakistani war, as well as regional conflicts within nations such as the Nigerian civil war. Although this type of conflict had occurred before — India and Pakistan fought their first war as early as 1948 — they were different now in that the Third World nations involved began to call upon the USSR to help them. As with the war in Vietnam, the problem facing the Soviets was the extent to which it should become involved without either provoking a wider conflict with the US or losing influence to the Chinese. Further, conflicts that had their origins solely in disputes between or within Third World countries posed another problem: should the Soviet Union attempt to extend its influence by acting primarily as a peacemaker to all sides involved (as it did for India and Pakistan in 1965), or should it militarily help certain Third World countries in their disputes against certain others?

The difficulties created by the first alternative were that first the USSR could not impose peace on contending parties, but could only help them arrive at it themselves, if they wanted to; and secondly once peace had been achieved, the parties involved would not necessarily have any further reason to look toward the USSR for foreign policy guidance. By becoming involved in conflicts on the side of one of the parties, the USSR could establish (what it hoped would be) a long-term security relationship with a Third World country which would be in a dependent position *vis-à-vis* the Soviet Union. However, this would also tend to create a long-term adversarial relationship with the opponent of the USSR's Third World ally. Further, the dependent ally might use its Soviet military support to pursue its conflict to a greater extent than the Soviets desired, risking a US response. Thus, while conflicts that had their source in disputes between and within Third World nations presented an opportunity to extend Soviet influence in this region, they also posed difficult policy problems for the USSR.

Finally, another change that occurred in the Third World during these years was a most unwelcome one to the Soviets. Many of the radical Third World leaders who advocated non-capitalist development and friendship with the Soviet Union were overthrown by right-wing military coups. This happened in Indonesia in 1965, Ghana in 1966, and Mali in 1968, among others. The optimism of the Khrushchev era about the ability of progressive Third World leaders to lead their countries toward socialism came to an end early in the Brezhnev era. The problem to be addressed was how best to ensure that Third World nations remained on the path to socialism once they had chosen that path.

During this period, Soviet military thinking was still primarily concerned with the prospect of nuclear war and war in Europe; war with China also became an increasing concern. Nevertheless, these developments in the Third World forced Soviet military thinkers to pay more attention to conflict in this region. While Soviet military thinking was to a certain extent a reaction to the innovations made by Khrushchev, it began also to change from its own traditional view in order to better understand both the opportunities and the problems that conflict in the Third World presented for the USSR.

The Relationship of Local War to World War

No change occurred in the Soviet military view of the relationship of local war to world war from the Khrushchev era to the early years of the Brezhnev era. Military writers emphasised the possibility, though not the inevitability, of local war growing into world war. The most succinct statement in this regard was made by Colonel V. Larionov as late as November 1968: 'The danger of local wars to peace lies in their possible escalation to a world war, if the nuclear powers are drawn into the conflict.'[2]

What was emphasised was not just that a local war started by the US could escalate into a world war, but that local wars in general could do so. In other words, while American involvement in Vietnam was dangerous enough, for the USSR to become as involved would increase that danger. Thus, the Soviet Union would not become heavily involved militarily in the Vietnam conflict. More broadly, even though the United States might not recognise the danger of local war, the USSR did, and thus the Soviets would not militarily confront the US in any local war in which the US had become heavily involved.

As during the Khrushchev era, the Soviets wanted to let it be known that if the United States threatened Soviet vital interests through involvement in a local war, the Soviets could threaten the US with the possibility of nuclear war. By repeating this formula throughout the American buildup in Vietnam without actually threatening such a war, the Soviets admitted that the outcome of the Vietnam war was not worth the risk of a wider conflict. It was apparent that the USSR was willing to do very little on behalf of the Vietnamese communists beyond the shipment of arms. Again, as during the Khrushchev era, local war was considered a military option open only to the imperialists, and not to the Soviet Union. The Soviets repeated the warning about the danger of local war escalating during the 1964-68 period in the hope that the US would take heed, but this quite obviously did not work.

The Nature and Types of Conflict in the Third World

While the Soviet military had criticised Khrushchev's revision of the traditional military view of the nature and types of wars during the former First Secretary's own reign, they criticised his classification system much more openly afterwards. Shortly after his fall from power, Khrushchev was directly criticised for formulating a classification system based on scale of warfare; this type of classification was seen as not adequately taking into account the concept of 'justness' in war.[3] The fourth edition of *Marksizm-Leninizm o voine i armii* published in 1965 reasserted the traditional Soviet military classification of types of war: '(1) world war between opposing social systems; (2) civil wars; (3) national liberation wars; (4) wars between bourgeois states'.[4] The main difference between this classification and the one in the third edition of 1962 was that now wars between opposing social systems were referred to as world wars. However, the authors made it clear that although such a war would be on a larger scale than the other types, this had no effect on how the justness of each side in any type of war was to be judged:

> Any war which is waged by a people in the name of freedom and social progress, for the liberation from exploitation and national suppression or in defense of state independence and against aggressive attack is a just war.
> Conversely, any war begun by the imperialists in the aim of capturing foreign territory, or enslaving and plundering other peoples is an unjust war.[5]

Khrushchev's classification did not make this point clear. He considered world wars and local wars unjust as types of wars. This did not please the military, who believed that the progressive side always fought a just war no matter what the scale of the conflict might be. Indeed, a world war between socialism and imperialism was the most just war that socialists could fight.

Given the four types of war and the concept of justness in the traditional Soviet military formulation, the just side in any conflict could be quickly and unambiguously determined. In each case, the just side was the one whose victory would either maintain, establish, or improve the chances for the establishment of socialism.[6] Both sides could be unjust in a war (wars between bourgeois states), but no more than one side could be just; it was not conceivable that socialist nations could fight each other. Further, the concept of justness did not bear any relationship to which side attacked first in a war. Being attacked did not make the defending side necessarily just:

> In appraising the nature of foreign policy and of wars, Marxists also encountered the criterion of 'defensiveness', which is widely employed in bourgeois literature. However, the founders of Marxism-Leninism identified this criterion as one of the many synonyms of 'justness' and pointed out its inaccuracy when applied to social relations, because a just war does not exclude offensive action, similarly as an unjust war does not exclude defensive action.[7]

Thus, even if a socialist nation initiated hostilities by attacking another country, the cause of the war still rested with imperialism. Except in the case of a weak bourgeois nation defending itself against attack from a large imperialist one,[8] it was considered impossible for an imperialist nation to fight a just war. Similarly, it was impossible for a socialist nation to fight an unjust war. What this traditional Soviet military view of the nature and types of war provided was a justification for the Soviet Union to support the progressive side in any war solely on the basis of the class or sociopolitical nature of the conflict without reference to any other factors such as which side started the war, scale of conflict, or anything else. This did not necessarily mean that the USSR would support the just side militarily, but at least that it would do so politically, diplomatically, and perhaps economically.

However, this traditional Soviet military view that allowed an unambiguous judgement to be made about which side the USSR should support in any given conflict contained one crucial assumption. It was implicitly assumed that all wars could be classified into the four Marxist-Leninist types of war that had been accepted by the Soviet military. A war that did not fit into one of these categories could present difficulties as to how it should be viewed by the Soviet Union. It was this assumption that would later be challenged by theorists in the Soviet military itself.

Returning to the period right after the fall of Khrushchev, Soviet military thinking was devoted primarily to the consideration of wars between socialism and imperialism. In some treatments of war in general, conflict in the Third World was not even mentioned.[9] Nevertheless, more attention was devoted to this question than during the Khrushchev era.

As during the Khrushchev era, the Soviet military saw national liberation wars as the only type of war that took place in the Third World. Civil wars were seen as taking place only between the proletariat and the bourgeoisie in advanced capitalist countries. In addition, national liberation wars were usually led by the national bourgeoisie. While the victory of this class over the colonialists was progressive, the result was not socialism but only better conditions for socialism to develop later. Significantly, though, the possibility of national liberation wars being led by the proletariat was now acknowledged.[10] This had occurred in North Vietnam and appeared to be taking place in recently decolonised nations with anti-Western, anti-capitalist leaders.

Accepting the premiss that only the category of national liberation wars was applicable to the Third World, Colonel S. Malyanchikov attempted to explain the diversity of Third World conflicts by dividing the national liberation war category into three sub-categories:

> The local wars of the post-war period may conditionally be divided into three groups. In first place (by number) are wars of imperialists against weak countries recently freed from colonial dependence. Approximately the same number of wars are unleashed against colonial and dependent countries which are fighting for their independence. There have been wars or attempts of imperialists to carry out aggression against countries which have chosen the socialist way of development.[11]

Thus it was recognised that Third World countries might fight Western industrialised ones both as colonies and as independent nations. Yet while wars unleashed by imperialists against colonies and independent nations in the Third World could easily be seen as national liberation wars, it would seem that the third sub-category (wars against socialist countries) would be more serious. On the face of it, this would involve conflict between capitalism and socialism. While this might have been true about a Western attack on Eastern Europe, the socialist countries being referred to here were ones in the Third World, such as North Vietnam. It was obvious that the Soviets had no intention of allowing even such a serious conflict to be transformed into a world war. This was clearly signalled through including this sub-type under the category of national liberation wars. While Malyanchikov admitted that this was the most serious type of war in this category, the only support he could offer socialist nations in the Third World was the thought that eventually the imperialists would lose any war with them.[12]

This basically was the extent of Soviet military thinking about the nature and types of conflict in the Third World during the early Brezhnev years. The military rejected the revision in the categories of war made by Khrushchev and instead reasserted the traditional military view that was more compatible with determining the just and unjust side in wars on strictly ideological grounds. Yet, since national liberation wars were the only type of war seen as taking place in the Third World, the Soviets were somewhat sceptical about them. Even when the socialists were fighting the imperialists in the Third World, the Soviets made it clear that their support to the national liberation forces would be limited.

From this assessment, the conclusion may be drawn that the Soviet military did not perceive Soviet involvement in Third World conflicts as beneficial to the interests of the USSR. Even with over a half million American troops in Indochina, the Soviets would do little beyond shipping arms. In addition to the risk of confrontation with the United States, conflict in the Third World was not seen as something that the USSR could use to its advantage. Despite the progressive nature of the national liberation forces, their victory did not necessarily mean the immediate advance of socialism, especially when the national bourgeoisie led the struggle. This also undoubtedly served to limit Soviet willingness to aid such groups.

In the late 1960s, however, the traditional Soviet military view of conflict in the Third World began to change within the Soviet military itself. In a major article published in the February 1968 *Voyennaya Mysl'*, Major General K. Stepanov and Lt. Colonel Ye. Rybkin challenged the traditional fourfold classification of types of war by adding two new types that particularly concerned conflict in the Third World. Rybkin's co-authorship of this article was especially significant. One Western analyst has noted that his 'articles appeared to establish guidelines that other writers would follow' in the 1960s and 1970s concerning nuclear war.[13] As shall be seen both in this and subsequent chapters, Rybkin's writings on the subject of conflict in the Third World have often set forth new formulations that would later become generally accepted in Soviet military thought, though sometimes in modified form. Since this was the first article in which Rybkin expressed his views on conflict in the Third World, it merits particularly close attention.

National liberation wars were the only type of war that occurred in the Third World, according to the traditional Soviet military view. The kind of war this category envisioned was one between Third World nations or groups and the Western imperialist nations. By the time this 1968 article was written, though, it was evident that a growing number of conflicts were taking place between and within Third World nations which did not necessarily involve Western nations. One type was civil war within Third World nations concerning the kind of regime that was in power (not ones in which regions attempted to secede from an existing nation). These wars, however, were not civil wars between the bourgeoisie and the proletariat. Although Soviet military thought had long predicted this latter type of civil war would occur in the developed capitalist nations, it stubbornly refused to occur there. This new type of civil war was one between the people and a regime of extreme reaction. Included under the term 'the people' were the proletariat and the bourgeoisie, who fought together against the reactionary regime.[14] Stepanov and Rybkin emphasised the difference in the manner in which these two different types of civil war were fought and the goals they could achieve:

Their distinction from civil wars of the aforementioned type lies in the fact that, firstly, they are waged either for purposes of democratic revolution or for anti-fascist purposes, pursuing the mission of repulsing the advance of the most reactionary forces and maintaining bourgeois democracy; secondly, they are waged, on the one hand, by all or a great part of the working classes and, in some cases, by a part of the national bourgeoisie, and, on the other hand, by the most reactionary strata of the bourgeoisie, supported either by foreign imperialists or by a part of the deceived petty bourgeoisie, but most frequently by the former and latter together; thirdly, in such wars the proletariat does not always lead the struggle on the part of the people. It usually shares the leadership with the other classes, even though it is the most active power. The political content and results of these wars may be quite different — from defense of a bourgeois-democratic republic from fascism to creation of conditions for the development of a democratic revolution into a socialist one.[15]

Unlike the type of civil war predicted for the West, which has not occurred, this newly designated type has occurred frequently in the Third World. The aim, for the most part, appears to be the overthrow of dictatorships. This type of civil war might not be 'directly connected with the struggle for socialism', and is generally anti-fascist in character. However, it might also lead to the 'creation of conditions for the development of a democratic revolution into a socialist one', although this will not always occur.

Stepanov and Rybkin did not envision this type of civil war taking place in Western industrial democracies, but in the underdeveloped regions of the world instead:

In our time there have been a significant number of such wars: the anti-fascist uprising in Bulgaria (1923); the first and second civil wars in China; the war in Spain (1936-1939); civil war in Greece (1946-1949); civil war in Cuba (1956-1959); the revolutionary uprising in Iraq (1958); civil war in Laos, the war in South Vietnam, and others. Such civil wars on the part of the working masses are unquestionably just.[16]

Three civil wars between the people and a regime of extreme reaction did take place in Europe (Bulgaria, Spain and Greece). However, they took place in three of the least developed European nations and in none of them did the proletariat come to power by means of such a civil war.

This type of civil war in Third World nations, however, led to more congenial results for the cause of socialism. Even in those Third World nations where socialism actually succeeded in coming to power, it did so through the second type of civil war and not through the more traditional civil war between proletariat and bourgeoisie. Of course, even if the side considered just won a civil war between the people and a regime of extreme reaction in a Third World nation, this did not mean that socialism would automatically come to power, but only that the conditions for socialism would be enhanced (Iraq). On the other hand, victory by the just side in a civil war between the proletariat and the bourgeoisie would definitely mean socialism coming to power:[17]

It should be noted that civil wars of the type we have cited are not usually distinguished from wars between the proletariat and the bourgeoisie, and this is hardly right. As has already been stated, they differ according to their social basis, causes, aims, and the nature of the classes waging them, and frequently they lead to other social results.[18]

This new category of civil war between the people and a regime of extreme reaction did not present any problems in terms of applying the concept of justness. The people were always just and the regime of extreme reaction always unjust. 'The people', of course, could be led either by the bourgeoisie or the proletariat. Unlike the traditional military view of national liberation wars in which the bourgeoisie, and not the proletariat, was seen as coming to power, Stepanov and Rybkin believed that either of them could come to power in this type of civil war. In one sense, whether the bourgeoisie or the proletariat led the people appeared to be a matter of indifference to the authors. If either of them defeated a regime of extreme reaction that was supported by the imperialists, the Soviet Union would benefit. American support to the reactionary regime would promote hostility on the part of the people toward the US even if led by the bourgeoisie. This in turn would lead the revolutionary forces to seek the support of the USSR. Thus, the Soviet Union stood to gain an ally if the just side won such a civil war notwithstanding whether the bourgeoisie or the proletariat actually came to power.

In another sense, though, the possibility of either bourgeois-democracy or socialism resulting from the victory of the people in this type of civil war gave the Soviet Union an opportunity that it did not have in national liberation wars. In national liberation wars, the bourgeoisie was

expected to come to power; the Soviet Union really could not do anything to change this. However, in civil wars between the people and a
regime of extreme reaction, the possibility of either the bourgeoisie or
the proletariat coming to power meant that the Soviet Union might be
able to influence which one actually did. Thus, unlike the traditional
Soviet military view of conflict in the Third World, this new category of
war allowed (indeed, almost called for) some form of Soviet involvement
in such conflicts. Stepanov and Rybkin did not specify how the USSR
should help the proletariat come to power in this type of civil war,
though they did lay the theoretical basis for the USSR to play such a
role. Nevertheless, it must be emphasised that even if the proletariat did
not come to power in a civil war between the people and a regime of
extreme reaction, Stepanov and Rybkin were still satisfied if the
bourgeoisie did, since the overthrow of the reactionary regime alone
was seen as harmful to American interests and helpful to Soviet ones.
Besides, even with the bourgeoisie in power, socialism would have a
better chance of eventually replacing it at some point in the future.

Equally important in this article as the division of civil wars into two
types was the description of an entirely different category of war. This
was introduced somewhat elliptically by a quotation from Lenin
describing three types of war that were not directly class based (such as
civil war or war between imperialists), but that took place between states.
These included, first, 'the relationship of an oppressed nation to an
oppressor nation' (national liberation war), secondly, 'the relationship
between two oppressor nations' (wars between imperialist states), and

> (III) The third type. The system of equal rights nations. The problem
> here is much more complex!!!! Especially if tsarism has an equal
> position with civilized and comparatively democratic nations. This
> was (approximately) the situation in Europe from 1815 to 1905.
> (*Complete Works,* vol. 49, pp. 369-70)[19]

While Stepanov and Rybkin were referring to 'types of wars that
involve conflicts between states' here, Lenin in this quotation was
actually discussing 'the three types of social contradictions which give
rise to such wars'[20] (hence the use of the words 'relationship' and
'system'). This classification by Lenin is curious; it is difficult to understand how a true Marxist could consider capitalist bourgeois-democracy
equal to feudal autocratic monarchy.[21] Even if they were equal, however, it is not clear why contradictions and wars between them would
not be included in the second category of wars between oppressor nations.

In any event, Lenin considered this unusual system to have come to an end in 1905. Not so Stepanov and Rybkin: 'Does this thesis have any significance for the modern day, or has the phenomenon fixed by it irrevocably faded into the past? In our opinion this thesis (although in a different situation) is applicable to the modern epoch.'[22] The different situation to which this thesis now applied was the '. . . several dozen non-socialist and non-imperialist states having equal rights in their relationship with each other'.[23] This type of conflict occurred between Third World nations and was caused by imperialism drawing artificial boundaries and the inherent turmoil of the region.[24] As a result of these problems, conflicts between equal nations in the Third World frequently arose:

> All these processes, in a number of cases, lead to military conflicts between countries which are equal in their relations. Suffice it to cite such cases as the Indo-Pakistani military conflicts over Kashmir (1947-1948 and 1965), the Arab-Israeli wars, the military conflict between Yemen and Saudi Arabia, the Moroccan aggression in Algeria (1963), the military conflict between Ethiopia and Somalia (1964), and others . . .[25]

The creation of this new category resolved the problem of trying to fit this type of conflict into categories where it did not belong. This new category also drew attention to the fact that conflicts between Third World nations were taking place. However, its creation also caused one important problem: how were conflicts between equal states to be classified in terms of just versus unjust? In wars between imperialist states, both sides were condemned as unjust; the Soviets clearly did not want to brand all participants in Third World conflicts as unjust. If an imperialist power were involved in such a war, then the side it supported would presumably be unjust. However, which were the just and unjust sides in wars between equal non-socialist but also non-capitalist nations? Indeed, if both sides in a conflict were equal, how was it possible to call one just and the other unjust? If they were equal, they should have an equal claim to justness, but Soviet military thinking would not permit both sides in a conflict to be just, nor did the Soviets want to think of both sides as unjust.

How was this dilemma to be resolved? Stepanov and Rybkin sidestepped this question by blaming this type of conflict on imperialism in general which either deliberately inspired conflicts between Third World nations or caused them through having drawn contentious boundaries between them.[26] Having said this, though, Stepanov and Rybkin admitted that wars between Third World nations were not caused solely by the imperialists: 'it is impossible to consider that in this type of conflict political contradictions between the conflicting countries play no role whatsoever'.[27] Further, in individual Third World conflicts, the authors were able to judge which side was just and which unjust. For example, in the 1967 Middle East war, Israel was unjust and the Arabs were just, and in the Saudi-Yemeni war, Saudi Arabia was unjust and Yemen was just.[28] Yet even though they were able to make this judgement in individual cases, Stepanov and Rybkin were not able to formulate a general rule for deciding which side was just and which unjust in conflicts between equal nations. This was completely different from every other category of war in which the just nature of the participants could be judged from the ideological basis of the conflict. There was no ideological difference between equal Third World nations fighting one another that could be identified in the abstract. This could only be done by examining the merits of each side in each individual conflict.

This problem was more than an ideological one. The difficulties created by this category of war did not arise merely from Stepanov and Rybkin having invented it, but from the actual occurrence of conflict between Third World nations. The inability to formulate a general rule to decide which side was just and which unjust in these conflicts reflected the inability of the Soviet Union to have a general policy applicable to them all. The Soviet Union wished to consider itself the ally of all the Third World. This was not difficult so long as the Third World fought only the West. When Third World nations fought each other, though, the USSR was faced with difficult choices. If it sided with some states against others, it risked making permanent enemies within the Third World (if the states the Soviets sided against were US allies, though, this might not be so important). But if the Soviet Union did nothing, it risked losing an opportunity to extend its influence in the Third World. Since these conflicts were usually territorial ones, the issue was not one of socialism versus capitalism. How the USSR should act in each of these conflicts, then, could only be decided on an individual basis. Though Stepanov and Rybkin did not formulate a general rule to guide Soviet actions in conflicts between Third World nations, the implicit one which emerged was that the USSR should act in whatever way would further its own foreign policy interests. In other words, the USSR should support that country whose victory would benefit the USSR, or should support neither side if Soviet support to either would damage Soviet interests.

The significance of the Stepanov and Rybkin article was that for the first time Soviet military thinkers gave some recognition to the possibility that a form of conflict existed within the Third World that could not be easily explained in traditional Marxist-Leninist military terms. Conflicts between equal nations were not necessarily caused by class conflict. Instead, the source of these conflicts lay within the politics of the Third World itself. Neither the capitalist nor the socialist camps created these conflicts, and so their outbreak could not be controlled by the superpowers. Yet while the cause of conflict existed within the Third World itself, this did not mean that the Soviet Union could not take advantage of their occurrence for its own purposes. These conflicts might not have their source in the larger East-West conflict at all, being essentially local in nature. Nevertheless, it was possible for the USSR to use these local conflicts for its own benefit in the larger East-West conflict.

The Stepanov and Rybkin article was also significant because it was the first example of Soviet military thinking about conflict in the Third World being modified by the military itself, and not by the Party. Indeed, unlike the Khrushchev era, the Party had nothing to say about the nature and types of war during the Brezhnev era. Pronouncements on this subject were left completely to the military. Ironically, the basis upon which the Soviet military criticised Khrushchev's pronouncements on the nature and types of war was that they introduced non-ideological factors into the categorisation of conflict, and yet Stepanov and Rybkin, military thinkers themselves, sought to modify Soviet military thinking by introducing the category of wars between equal nations which did not involve class struggle, but territorial disputes in a specific region of the world instead.

The ideas expressed by Stepanov and Rybkin, however, did not by any means gain full or immediate acceptance by other Soviet military thinkers. The fifth edition of *Marksizm-Leninizm o voine i armii* listed the following types of wars as occurring at the present time:

(1) wars between opposing social systems; (2) civil wars between the proletariat and the bourgeoisie; (3) civil wars between the popular masses and reactionary forces, supported by the imperialists of other countries; (4) wars between colonialists and nations fighting for their independence; (5) wars between capitalist states. Along with them in our time can occur military conflicts and wars between underdeveloped countries, provoked by the imperialists and internal reactionaries (the conflict between India and Pakistan in 1965).[29]

In this highly influential book, it can be seen that the category of civil wars between the people and a regime of extreme reaction was readily accepted by the Soviet military since it was listed here as a regular category with its own number. What was referred to here as wars between underdeveloped countries, though, was not treated as well. This category was not included with the others and not given a number, but simply acknowledged as a special type of conflict. Further, these were blamed on the imperialists and internal reactionaries here, unlike in the Stepanov and Rybkin article which emphasised that these were often territorial disputes without a distinct class character. Even then, the authors of this book were more generous to this theoretical innovation than other Soviet military writers. Colonel V. Larionov, for example, accepted the new category of civil war between 'the exploited classes against the ruling classes' in addition to the traditional civil wars between the proletariat and the bourgeoisie, but made no mention of wars between equal nations, thereby indicating that he did not accept this category as a valid one.[30]

It was not difficult to understand why the category of civil wars between the people and a regime of extreme reaction was more readily accepted than the category of wars between equal nations. While the former category lent itself easily to the concept of just versus unjust due to the class nature of the conflict, the latter did not at all. That a category of war was being propounded for which a general rule to determine the just nature of each side could not be formulated must have been repugnant to many Soviet military thinkers. Acceptance of the category of wars between equal nations occurring in the Third World meant acceptance of the proposition that there were types of conflict that existed independent of the class struggle and Marxist-Leninist doctrine. In all other types of war the forces of reaction fought the forces of progress; although setbacks might occur, socialism was seen as triumphing throughout the world. These conflicts between Third World nations had nothing to do with this struggle for socialism. What would they eventually lead to? Was it possible that Marxism-Leninism was irrelevant to even a part of the Third World's struggles and concerns? Such an idea was unthinkable, and so many Soviet military writers tended to downplay or ignore this new category of war.

And yet Stepanov and Rybkin were certainly not saying anything like this. The point they were attempting to make was that while the traditional Soviet military view regarded national liberation wars as the only type of war that occurred in the Third World, other types of war were in fact taking place of which Soviet military thought had to take account if Soviet foreign policy was to be made intelligently and successfully. The publication of this article signalled the beginning of a debate within the Soviet military between the traditional view that was ideologically orthodox but could not fully explain reality and a revisionist view which sought to explain reality accurately but could not do so in orthodox ideological terms.

Peaceful Coexistence

At the 23rd Party Congress held in 1966 (the first Party Congress held during the Brezhnev era), the new Soviet leaders reaffirmed their commitment to peaceful coexistence which had originally been made by Khrushchev. A theme that continued in Party statements from the Khrushchev era was that peaceful coexistence was necessary in order to avoid a world war.[31] However, another theme also emerged in Party writings during the early years of the Brezhnev era that concerned the relationship between peaceful coexistence and the national liberation struggle in the Third World.

Party writers began to argue that the policy of peaceful coexistence with the West pursued by the Soviet Union actually benefited the national liberation movements. If the imperialists were made to pursue peaceful coexistence, they would not be able to intervene in national liberation wars without risking the end of peaceful coexistence, and thus conflict with the USSR. Peaceful coexistence could, in effect, 'paralyze' the forces of imperialism from undertaking aggression; in this atmosphere, national liberation wars would be able to flourish much more easily.[32] Thus, national liberation forces should favour Soviet efforts at peaceful coexistence since Soviet success in bringing it about would lead also to the success of the national liberation movements.

As during the Khrushchev era, the Soviet military rarely mentioned peaceful coexistence during the early years of the Brezhnev era. The declaration that the USSR would pursue a policy of peaceful coexistence made by the Party at the 23rd Party Congress was virtually ignored by the military during this period. In an important article on the question of local wars published in September 1968, Major General V. Matsulenko noted that American intervention in the Third World affected Soviet foreign policy interests and that, 'The Soviet Union cannot allow imperialist circles to perpetuate unpunished any sort of aggression against freedom loving peoples.'[33] Then, instead of quoting from the 23rd Party Congress which was the most recent one, Matsulenko quoted a passage from the 22nd Party Congress held in 1962 to the effect that the USSR must support national liberation movements.[34] While it was not unusual for military writers to quote from Party Congresses preceding the most recent one, it was unusual that Matsulenko ignored the most recent Party Congress altogether here. Such a step would indicate his disagreement with the policies of the 23rd Party Congress.

It is quite understandable why Matsulenko and the Soviet military did not readily accept the Party's argument that peaceful coexistence would benefit the national liberation movements. The early years of the Brezhnev era saw the huge American military buildup in Southeast Asia. Further, despite all claims to the contrary, the Soviet military could not be at all certain that the US would be defeated in Vietnam. Thus, the policy of peaceful coexistence that the Party followed to avoid world war must have appeared to the military as serving only to signal to the United States that it could engage in local war anywhere in the Third World with impunity since the Party displayed such an obvious aversion to potential conflict between the superpowers.

Since the Party and the military would vocally agree on the policy of peaceful coexistence after the 24th Party Congress in 1971, the silence of the Soviet military on this subject before then may definitely be interpreted as disagreement with the views expressed by the Party. This was another example of the military formulating a position independent from the Party on questions related to conflict in the Third World, though the military expressed its opposition only indirectly by not repeating the Party position. Also noteworthy was that while the military may have disagreed with the Party on this issue, it was the Party's policy that the Soviet Union pursued.

Indigenous Third World Forces

The optimism of the Khrushchev era that radical leaders in the Third World could guide their countries to socialism was dispelled in the early Brezhnev years when many of these radical leaders were overthrown and replaced by conservative military juntas (as in Indonesia, Ghana and Mali). This was a setback on the road of progress to socialism that had not been foreseen. The problem facing the Soviet Union was that of finding the best way to maintain a Third World country on the path toward socialism. Both military and civilian authors proposed solutions to this problem — solutions which differed markedly from one another.

The lesson that the military learned from the conservative military coups in the Third World was that the army was the most highly organised and most powerful element in these underdeveloped societies. The class orientation of Third World armies, then, was crucial in determining whether a country would pursue capitalism or socialism. As the coups of the mid-1960s demonstrated, a capitalist-oriented army could overthrow a socialist-oriented government. However, if the army was socialist-oriented, it could guide the rest of the nation toward socialism as well. The key to maintaining a Third World country on the path toward socialism, then, was to have a progressive army which could defeat all domestic enemies of socialism. Without a progressive army to protect it, socialism could be easily struck down by a bourgeois army.[35] Thus, a progressive army was the most important element in ensuring that Third World countries maintained the path toward socialism.

The lesson that some civilian writers learned, though, was quite different from this. They believed that the downfall of radical Third World leaders could be traced to the unscientific ideologies of 'Asian', 'African', or 'national' socialism that these leaders espoused. What was needed in the Third World was scientific socialism and the formation of a Marxist-Leninist vanguard party in order to protect it. A vanguard party in power would be the most vigilant guardian of the path toward socialism; once it was formed, the party could transform all other institutions in society as well. Neither of these functions could be performed by a party espousing 'unscientific' socialism. Thus, during the early Brezhnev era, civilian writers inveighed heavily against 'national socialism' that deviated from Marxism-Leninism.[36] To them, a vanguard party was the key to bringing socialism to the Third World.

G. Mirskiy, who had been optimistic during the Khrushchev era about the ability of radical Third World leaders to lead their nations to socialism, became extremely pessimistic following the conservative military coups of the mid-1960s about Third World nations achieving socialism unless a vanguard Marxist-Leninist party led the revolutionary struggle. He was particularly pessimistic about Third World armies. He felt that although they might oppose foreign capitalists, they usually favoured domestic ones. Third World armies consisted primarily of bourgeois and petty bourgeois elements. Thus, they could not be trusted to adhere to a proletarian ideology which would inevitably clash with their class interests. Only a dedicated Marxist-Leninist party could succeed in consistently following scientific socialism.[37]

These differing views held by military and civilian thinkers had differing policy implications. The favourable view of progressive Third World armies that the Soviet military took meant that the Soviet Union should support progressive military regimes in the Third World, while the unfavourable view of them held by some civilian writers meant that the USSR should not support such military regimes, but should help true Marxist-Leninists come to power instead. The high Soviet Party leadership did not comment upon this dispute. In practice, the Party tended to support progressive Third World military regimes but attempted to persuade them to form a vanguard party in order to ensure the continued course of their nations toward socialism.

Regarding guerrilla armies in the Third World, the Soviet military appraisal of them during the early Brezhnev years had not changed significantly from the Khrushchev era. In his 1968 article, Major General Matsulenko divided local wars into two types based on the means of armed struggle: (1) wars in which regular troops fought regular battles, as in the Second World War; and (2) irregular, guerrilla wars.[38] The author made it clear, though, that he considered the first type to be more important. He portrayed guerrilla warfare as a means of armed conflict that was resorted to only through weakness. Once guerrilla forces had gained sufficient strength they would form a conventional army to fight a conventional war.[39] Further, while guerrilla warfare might provide useful battle experience, guerrilla officers tended not to be sufficiently grounded in Marxism-Leninism;[40] this the author regarded as highly detrimental to the outcome of the war.

Little during the early years of the Brezhnev era would have caused the Soviet military to have a more optimistic view of guerrilla warfare. Not only was the success of the Vietnamese communists very much in doubt in the Indochina war at this time, but also guerrilla movements following the theories of the Cuban revolution had been defeated in Bolivia and Colombia. Thus, guerrilla wars undoubtedly appeared to be losing prospects that were not helped through peaceful coexistence pursued by the USSR. Even if the USSR did assist them to a greater extent, this would only provoke an American response without promising victory.

Unlike the Khrushchev era, the military had its own independent position on indigenous forces in the Third World. The Soviet military's pessimism about guerrilla armies contrasted with its optimism about established progressive Third World armies in bringing about socialism despite the fact that many of the drawbacks of guerrilla armies — such as their propensity to form governments independent of the USSR once they came to power — could also apply to Third World armies. They saw progressive armies in the Third World as a means by which socialism and a Soviet ally could be secured permanently, and thus they wanted to seize the opportunity by extending Soviet support. It would only be later that the Soviet military would realise that even progressive Third World armies could abandon the road toward socialism.

American Ideas and Actions in Local Wars

The Soviet view of American ideas about local war during the early Brezhnev years continued along the same lines as during the Khrushchev era. Soviet military writers expressed the belief that the increase in the power of socialism prevented the US from unleashing world war and forced it to resort to local war. The imperialists assumed that local war could be kept localised, but here they were mistaken; local war could grow into world war.[41] As during the Khrushchev era, Soviet criticism of American ideas about local war was based on the Soviet view of the relationship between local war and world war.

Unlike the Khrushchev era, though, the increasing American military involvement in the Vietnam war forced Soviet military writers to pay more attention to American actions in local wars. The basic comment that they made was that no matter what the US might do militarily in Vietnam, its actions were doomed to failure.[42]

What was significant was *why* Soviet military thinkers believed the US would lose. During the Vietnam war, it was recognised that the US was more powerful militarily in Vietnam. However, even though the Vietnamese communists were weaker in this regard, they possessed a high moral spirit based on the justness of their cause. The Americans lacked this because theirs was an unjust cause. This was the crucial factor that prevented the US from achieving its aims in Vietnam, as Matsulenko pointed out:

> the interventionists use any barbarous means in local wars — right up to the cruellest and most destructive — not only against the national liberation armies, but also against the peaceful population. But, as indicated by the experience of recent decades, the imperialists have been unable to retard, and even less so to suppress, the national liberation movement and social progress. The enemy armed with the most modern means of battle has been opposed by the high moral spirit and inflexible will of peoples defending their freedom and independence with the fraternal support of the socialist countries and by the flexibility and many-sided military art of their armies. A shining example of this is the inability of the American aggressors to gain victory over the Vietnamese people. On Vietnamese soil they

are suffering one defeat after another . . .[43]

During the Vietnam war itself, then, Soviet military thinkers saw the conflict largely in ideological terms. The American armed forces were viewed as more technologically capable than those of the Vietnamese communists, but this only served to make American actions more barbaric. Despite this technological superiority, the Americans could not win; at best, they could only postpone defeat, though even this would hurt the Americans more than it would the Vietnamese. What was crucial was the moral factor and the fact that the war was more important for the Vietnamese than it was for the Americans. This allowed the Vietnamese communists to endure any hardship that American technological superiority might inflict upon them and to survive and strike back. Their ability to attack the Americans was not as great, but the immoral nature of the war for the Americans made them suffer much more keenly from the just reprisals of the Vietnamese. This moral factor, which so heavily influenced the morale, and consequently, the fighting effectiveness of the armed forces on each side of the conflict, was based solely on the sociopolitical nature of the conflict. Because the Vietnamese communists were the just side in this war, they would eventually prevail over the militarily superior but thoroughly unjust Americans. In this conflict, military superiority simply was not a relevant factor to the final outcome.

In addition, because their ideological justness meant that the Vietnamese communists would eventually triumph, large-scale Soviet military support to Vietnam was not needed. Thus, the Vietnamese could win without the Soviet Union risking a military confrontation with the United States. It was obvious, though, that the US did not fear Soviet warnings of a local war escalating to world war. In their discussion of Vietnam, the Soviets tacitly admitted that they were not prepared to raise the level of the conflict. Instead of the fear of world war, the Soviet Union could only hope to persuade the US that its actions in Vietnam were 'doomed to failure', and to withdraw. While the US would later become convinced of this, during the early Brezhnev years the Soviets really could not be sure that this would happen. Soviet statements that the US eventually would leave Vietnam must have been of very little comfort to the Vietnamese communists at a time when American forces were growing and the Soviet Union was providing relatively little support.

The Soviet Role in Third World Conflicts

During the early years of the Brezhnev era, the Party at first backed
away from Khrushchev's promises to send arms. Instead of explicitly
mentioning arms, more vague means of Soviet support were often
mentioned. Phrases were used such as 'active aid' or 'all-round support'
which did not necessarily mean military support, but often only economic support instead.[44] By 1968, though, the Party strongly advocated
the shipment of arms to progressive forces in Third World conflicts,
especially to the Vietnamese communists and to the Arab states con-
fronting Israel.[45]

Military thinking about the Soviet role in Third World conflicts
developed in a similar pattern. One of the most striking examples of the
Soviet military expressing how little military support the USSR would
give to the Third World was made in 1965 when the greatest factor
contributing to the efforts of liberated countries against military danger
was described as 'universal peace'.[46] The USSR would unselfishly
struggle to achieve peace for the benefit of the national liberation
movements. This was, of course, a virtual acknowledgement that little
in the way of military support was being given to the Third World at
that time. With regard to Vietnam as well, only 'fraternal support and
increasing aid' were acknowledged.[47] In April 1968, though, an article
reporting on the Warsaw Pact Conference of the Political Consultative
Committee held in Sofia the previous month announced specific forms
of military assistance to Vietnam:

> True to the principles of proletarian internationalism, the socialist
> countries will continue to extend to the fraternal Democratic
> Republic of Vietnam, to the Vietnamese people, the full support
> and all of the necessary aid, including economic, and with the means
> for the defence, technology and specialists. The member nations of
> the Warsaw Pact again affirmed the readiness of providing the
> opportunity of sending their volunteers to Vietnam, if the government
> of the DRV would express the request.[48]

Although this offer appeared relatively generous, it actually was not.
'Full support and all of the necessary aid' would only be given in the
economic area. For its defence, Vietnam would receive 'specialists', but
no soldiers. 'Technology' did not necessarily mean arms, but only the
advice of the specialists. Finally, only if Hanoi requested would 'volunteers' be sent. Even then, since these were volunteers, they would not

include units of the regular armed forces.

A more active role in Third World conflicts was envisioned by Matsulenko. He stated that 'Local wars cannot help directly or indirectly affecting the political interests of the Soviet Union,' and that the USSR would 'henceforth come out against each and every usurpatory war', including wars against people fighting for national liberation.[49] Matsulenko both acknowledged and defended Soviet arms transfers as a form of military assistance:

> Soviet military aid differs fundamentally from the military 'aid' of the United States and other imperialist states. In helping the peoples of Asia, Africa, and other regions of the world the Soviet Union is pursuing no selfish ends. It proceeds from a feeling of international fraternal solidarity. Soviet weapons are not intended for attacking other countries to take them over, but to repulse the imperialist export of counterrevolution. Such military help reinforced the socialist commonwealth, the common front of world revolutionary forces in the battle against international imperialism.[50]

This appeared to be an open offer to send arms to peoples fighting national liberation wars, though the examples of this policy that he cited (North Korea during the Korean War and Egypt in the 1956 Suez crisis) were not ones in which Soviet arms supplies were particularly generous. Regarding Vietnam, he only stated that the USSR would give it complete support, 'right up to the dispatch of volunteers', though nothing was said about the dispatch of arms.[51] Still, this description of Soviet arms transfers was significant as arms transfers were to be cited as one of the means of Soviet military support in almost all subsequent statements about the role of the USSR in Third World conflicts.

Despite these relatively circumspect statements about arms transfers, by 1968 the Soviet Union was indeed shipping large amounts of arms to Vietnam and certain Arab states. The Soviet Union had even gone a step beyond this in Egypt where it had begun to send a large number of military advisers to retrain the Egyptian army so that it could more effectively use Soviet weapons.[52] The policy of sending Soviet military advisers had not been discussed at this time; as with arms transfers, discussion of sending military advisers took place only after the Soviets had implemented the policy. As in the Khrushchev era, the USSR was more involved in conflicts than Party and military statements indicated. However, while the transfer of arms was the extent to which the USSR became involved in Third World conflicts then, the USSR was now willing to become more involved in certain conflicts by sending a large number of military advisers.

Nevertheless, even though the policy of arms transfers had been (and would be henceforth) advocated and the policy of sending military advisers had been undertaken in practice, the role envisioned by the Soviet military for the USSR in Third World conflicts was still a limited one. Through arms transfers, progressive forces would be given the means to defeat reactionary ones. Through sending military advisers, the progressive forces would be trained to use these weapons effectively. The Soviet Union itself, though, was not seen to have a more direct role in Third World conflicts; armed forces from neither the Soviet Union nor other socialist countries would become directly involved in conflict, unless the conflict actually involved a socialist nation as in Vietnam. Even here Soviet and other socialist country armed forces would not become involved. Through these statements and actions, the Soviets signalled that the primary responsibility for the victory of the progressive forces in the Third World over their opponents rested with the progressive forces themselves, and not with the Soviet Union, though the Soviets were now more willing to help these forces than they were previously.

Conclusion

One significant change that occurred during the early Brezhnev years was that the Party no longer dominated military thinking about conflict in the Third World the way it had done during the Khrushchev era. The main concern of Party writers at this time was change in the Third World through economic and political means; for the most part they gave little attention to military means.[53] On both peaceful coexistence and indigenous forces in the Third World, the military and the Party expressed differing opinions. In each case, the Soviet military appeared more willing to become involved in the Third World, as indicated by its dissatisfaction with peaceful coexistence and its desire to support radical military regimes. The Party was in favour of peaceful coexistence and certain civilians were sceptical about radical military regimes. Most striking of all was that while previously Khrushchev had unilaterally revised the traditional Soviet military view of the nature and types of war in the Third World, the Party made no pronouncements on this subject at all during the Brezhnev era. This was left completely to the military, which even began to change its own traditional views on the nature and types of war. What this indicated was that unlike the Khrushchev era, the Party was now willing to allow the Soviet military to formulate and express independent military views on the question of conflict in the Third World. The Party might not necessarily put the military's views into practice, but at least they would be considered in the formation of policy.

Regarding the relationship between military thought and actual Soviet foreign policy, it was again evident that the Soviets were more active militarily than their statements would indicate. The Soviet Union made large-scale arms shipments to the Third World during these years, especially to North Vietnam and certain Arab states. The Soviets also began to send a large number of military advisers to Egypt after the 1967 war. Yet little was said at first about specific forms of Soviet military assistance during the early years of the Brezhnev era. By 1968, the transfer of arms was acknowledged as a means of assisting progressives in the Third World, but sending advisers was not.

During the 1960s, both military and Party writers held the belief that there were progressive forces in the Third World who would act to fulfil the Marxist-Leninist prediction of socialism spreading worldwide as well as to further Soviet interests. Until the right-wing coups of the mid-1960s, radical Third World leaders were seen to play this role. Through them, Soviet interests would be furthered with little effort expended by the USSR itself. Following these coups both the Party and the military had to reassess this judgement. Radical Third World leaders could no longer be completely relied upon, but there were others who could. For the military these were radical Third World armies while for some civilians these were vanguard parties. It was apparent, though, that these groups needed some assistance if socialism was to be victorious. Thus, while it was realised that Soviet military assistance was necessary, it was hoped that a limited amount would be sufficient and that the USSR would not have to become further involved.

Not only was the increasing military strength of the Soviet Union a factor in the growing Soviet role in Third World conflicts, but also the Soviets began to realise that indigenous progressive forces could not further the interests of socialism and the USSR completely on their own. This was a more pessimistic view of the prospects for socialism in the Third World than that held during the Khrushchev era. The politics of the Third World were also a source of confusion since they did not appear to be following Marxist-Leninist predictions. Thus, the early years of the Brezhnev era saw the beginning of a reassessment of conflict in the Third World made by Stepanov and Rybkin to elucidate both the problems and the opportunities faced by the USSR there. Yet while Soviet military thought about the military involvement in the Third World had grown from the level of the Khrushchev era, it still remained relatively limited during the early Brezhnev years. The middle years of the Brezhnev era, though, would see significant changes in the level of Soviet military involvement in the Third World which would be accompanied by concomitant changes in Soviet military thinking.

Notes

1. Adam B. Ulam, *Expansion and Coexistence: Soviet Foreign Policy, 1917-73*, 2nd edn (Praeger, New York, 1974), p. 716.

2. Colonel V. Larionov, 'Politicheskaya storona sovetskoy voyennoy doktrini', *Kommunist Vooruzhennykh Sil*, no. 22, November 1968, p. 16. For similar statements, see Lt. Colonel T. Kondratkov, 'Kharakter i osobennosti sovremennoy voini', *Kommunist Vooruzhennykh Sil*, no. 19, October 1967, p. 81, and Major General K. Stepanov and Lt. Colonel Ye. Rybkin, 'The Nature and Types of Wars of the Modern Era', *Voyennaya Mysl'*, no. 2, February 1968, CIA FB FPD 0042/69, p. 73.

3. Colonel I. Sidel'nikov, 'V.I. Lenin o klassovom podkhode k opredeleniyu kharaktera voin', *Krasnaya Zvezda*, 22 September 1965. Sokolovskiy also abandoned even the outward acceptance of Khrushchev's classification system and declared that both national liberation wars and civil wars were local wars; they were not unjust *per se*, but only for the reactionary forces that fought in them. See Marshal of the Soviet Union V.D. Sokolovskiy (ed.), *Voyennaya strategiya*, 3rd edn (Voyenizdat, Moscow, 1968), p. 222.

4. Major General N. Sushko and Colonel S. Tyushkevich (eds.), *Marksizm-Leninism o voine i armii*, 4th edn (Voyenizdat, Moscow, 1965), p. 80.

5. Ibid., pp. 70-1.

6. K. Sergeyev, 'O kriteriyakh v otsenke kharaktera voin i vneshney politiki', *Voyenno-Istoricheskiy Zhurnal*, no. 9, September 1966, p. 105.

7. Ibid.

8. Major General N. Bochkarev, Colonel I. Prusanov and Colonel A. Babukov, *Programma KPSS o zashchite sotsialisticheskogo otchestva*, 2nd edn (Voyenizdat, Moscow, 1965), p. 32.

9. See, for example, Colonel P. Trifonenkov, 'Ob"yektivniye zakoni voini i printsipi voyennogo iskusstva', *Kommunist Vooruzhennykh Sil*, no. 1, January 1966, pp. 8-16, and V. Baskakov, 'Ob osobennostyakh nachal'nogo perioda voini', *Voyenno-Istoricheskiy Zhurnal*, no. 2, February 1966, pp. 29-34.

10. Bochkarev, Prusanov and Babukov, *Programma KPSS o zashchite sotsialisticheskogo otchestva*, pp. 32-3.

11. Colonel S. Malyanchikov, 'On the Nature of Armed Struggle in Local Wars', *Voyennaya Mysl'*, no. 11, November 1965, CIA FDD trans. no. 953, pp. 12-13.

12. Ibid., p. 13.

13. William F. Scott, *Soviet Sources of Military Doctrine and Strategy* (Crane Russak, New York, 1975), p. 18.

14. Stepanov and Rybkin, 'The Nature and Types of Wars of the Modern Era', p. 76.

15. Ibid.
16. Ibid.
17. Furthermore, this type of civil war was generally expected to result in the victory of the proletariat; perhaps this is why Bulgaria, Spain and Greece were included under the other category. Of course, it was possible for the proletariat to achieve power through peaceful means avoiding civil war. See ibid., pp. 75-6.
18. Ibid., p. 76.
19. Ibid., p. 77.
20. Ibid.
21. Perhaps only a Russian Marxist such as Lenin could have considered them as equal.
22. Ibid., p. 79.
23. Ibid.
24. Ibid.
25. Ibid.
26. Ibid.
27. Ibid.
28. Ibid.
29. S.A. Tyushkhevich, N. Ya. Sushko and Ya. S. Dzyuba, *Marksizm-Leninism o voine i armii*, 5th edn (Voyenizdat, Moscow, 1968), p. 86.
30. Larionov, 'Politicheskaya storona sovetskoy voyennoy doktrini', pp. 14-15.
31. A.A. Gromyko, *The International Situation and Soviet Foreign Policy (Speech of June 27, 1968)* (Novosti, Moscow, 1968), pp. 9-15.
32. See G. Starushenko, 'Bor'ba s neokolonializmom – delo vsekh narodov', *Kommunist*, no. 3, February 1966, p. 116; V. Korionov, 'Mezhdunarodnoye znacheniye XXIII sy"ezda KPSS', *Kommunist*, no. 6, April 1966, p. 16; and N. Inozemtsev, 'Leninizm – nauchnaya osnova sovetskoy vneshney politiki', *Kommunist*, no. 7, May 1966, p. 19.
33. Major General V. Matsulenko, 'Lokal'niye voini imperializma (1945-1968 gg)', *Voyenno-Istoricheskiy Zhurnal*, no. 9, September 1968, p. 37.
34. Ibid.
35. Colonel Ye. Dolgopolov, 'Armii osvobodivshikhsya stran', *Krasnaya Zvezda*, 19 May 1968. See also Charles C. Petersen, 'Third World Military Elites in Soviet Perspective', Center for Naval Analyses Professional Paper 262, November 1979, pp. 11-22.
36. See K. Brutents, 'Voprosi ideologii v natsional'no-osvoboditel'nom dvizhenii', *Kommunist*, no. 18, December 1966, pp. 37-50; K. Bogdanov and V. Rumyantsev, 'Nasushchniye voprosi revolyutsionnogo dvizheniya v Afrike', *Kommunist*, no. 3, February 1967, pp. 80-92; and R.Ul'yanovskiy, 'Nauchniy sotsializm i osvobodivshiyesya strani', *Kommunist*, no. 4, March 1968, pp. 92-106.
37. G. Mirskiy, 'O kharaktere sotsial'nikh sil v Azii i Afrike', *Kommunist*, no. 17, November 1968, pp. 89-102.
38. Matsulenko, 'Lokal'niye voini imperializma', p. 41.
39. Ibid., pp. 47-8.
40. Ibid., p. 51.
41. See, for example, Colonel N. Ponomarev, 'Avanturizm voyenno-politicheskikh kontseptsiy imperializma', *Kommunist Vooruzhennykh Sil*, no. 1, January 1966, pp. 42-8, and Captain 1st Rank V. Kulakov, 'Proiskhozhdeniye i sushchnost' strategii "gibkogo reagirovaniya"', *Voyenno-Istoricheskiy Zhurnal*, no. 3, March 1968, pp. 40-9.
42. See Colonel N. Ponomarev, 'Avanturizm voyenno-politicheskikh kontseptsiy imperializma', p. 48, and Matsulenko, 'Lokal'niye voini imperializma', p. 39.
43. Matsulenko, 'Lokal'niye voini imperializma', p. 47.
44. See A.N. Kosygin, *Zayavleniye pravitel'stva SSSR ob osnovnikh voprosakh*

vnutrenney i vneshney politiki (Politizdat, Moscow, 1966), p. 21; Boris Ponomarev, 'Istoricheskiye uroki VII kongressa kominterna i sovremennost'', *Problemi Mira i Sotsializma*, no. 12, December 1965, p. 5; N. Inozemtsev, 'Leninizm', p. 19; and V. Zelentsov, 'Pravoye delo v'etnamskogo naroda vostorzhestvuet', *Kommunist*, no. 10, July 1966, pp. 115-16.

45. See L.I. Brezhnev, *Leninskim kursom: rechi i stat'i*, vol. 2 (Politizdat, Moscow, 1970), pp. 126-8, and Gromyko, *The International Situation and Soviet Foreign Policy*, pp. 5-6.

46. Bochkarev, Prusanov, and Babukov, *Programma KPSS o zashchite sotsialisticheskogo otchestva*, p. 53.

47. Colonel N. Ponomarev, 'Avanturizm voyenno-politicheskikh kontseptsiy imperializma', p. 48.

48. 'Pod znamenem proletarskogo internatsionalizma', *Kommunist Vooruzhennykh Sil*, no. 7, April 1968, p. 33.

49. Matsulenko, 'Lokal'niye voini imperializma', p. 37.

50. Ibid., pp. 40-1.

51. Ibid., p. 40.

52. Jon D. Glassman, *Arms for the Arabs: The Soviet Union and War in the Middle East* (Johns Hopkins University Press, Baltimore, 1975), p. 67.

53. See Richard Lowenthal, *Model or Ally? The Communist Powers and the Developing Countries* (Oxford University Press, New York, 1977), pp. 260-7.

3 THE MIDDLE BREZHNEV YEARS: 1969-1975

The middle Brezhnev years were ones of growing optimism concerning the success of Soviet foreign policy in the Third World. Obstacles that had previously hindered the spread of Soviet influence appeared to fall away. While after the Cultural Revolution, the Sino-Soviet rift still continued as strong as ever, China was no longer as fervent about bringing Maoist revolution to the Third World. Chinese competition for the leadership of the world revolutionary movement became less important, though growing Chinese friendship with the United States was disturbing to Moscow. Regarding the US, the Soviet Union was finally able to catch up with America in nuclear weapons capabilities. Arms control agreements were signed, détente grew, and the threat of nuclear war between the US and the USSR receded.

In the Third World, one of the most significant events was the withdrawal of American forces from Indochina and the fall of the Saigon government which the US had supported for so long. The US suffered a major defeat while communist forces had scored a major victory. Not only had the US lost a war, it had also lost the will to become militarily involved in other Third World conflicts. Another significant event was the fall of the Portuguese Empire. The Portuguese colonies in Africa were the last major European colonies to become independent. The governments of both Guinea-Bissau and Mozambique grew out of Marxist guerrilla armies. A three-way power struggle emerged in Angola, but eventually the Soviet and Cuban supported MPLA became the dominant force there. Ethiopia also experienced a Marxist revolution.

Nevertheless, not all went well for the USSR. Egypt, with which the Soviet Union had signed a treaty of friendship and co-operation, expelled Soviet advisers in 1972. While the USSR gave Egypt much greater assistance in the 1973 war than it had in 1967, relations between the USSR and Egypt soon after deteriorated. In Latin America, the Soviets had seen the prediction that socialism could come to power by peaceful means fulfilled when Allende was elected president of Chile in 1970. When Allende was overthrown by a military coup in 1973, it appeared that the peaceful road to socialism was not possible in the Third World after all.

In general, though, the reasons for the Soviets to be optimistic about the prospects for spreading Soviet influence in the Third World outweighed the setbacks that may have led to pessimism. The United States was increasingly regarded less and less important as a factor hindering Soviet actions or harming Soviet interests in the Third World. The Third World as a whole was perceived as the natural ally of the Soviet Union against the imperialist West and chauvinist China. Disputes were occurring between and within Third World nations frequently; conflicts between Jordan and Syria, India and Pakistan, Iran and Iraq, the Arabs and Israel were just some of them. The USSR found that it was not in a position to settle these conflicts itself; it usually could neither force the belligerents to make peace nor persuade them to do so. More and more, the USSR sought to spread its influence through supporting one side in a conflict. However, this policy risked permanently alienating the other side in the conflict, or even alienating the side that the USSR was supporting, as in the case of Egypt.

During these years, both the military and the Party devoted much more attention to conflict in the Third World than they had previously. Almost all aspects of Soviet military thought on this subject changed during the middle Brezhnev years. These changes reflected both the changing circumstances of world politics and the fact that the military had begun seriously to study the complexity of the Third World now that the Soviet Union played a larger military role there; it could no longer afford to rely on the same simplistic ideas as when the Soviet role in the Third World was relatively small.

The Relationship of Local War to World War

During the middle years of the Brezhnev era, the Soviet view of the relationship of local war to world war underwent significant change. A first step in this change was made, not by the military, but by the Party at the International Conference of Communist and Workers' Parties held at Moscow in June 1969. At this conference, the Soviet Union sought to legitimise its pursuit of arms control and peaceful co-existence through obtaining the approval of these policies by other communist parties. One of the conference documents declared that the combined efforts of the progressive forces could prevent a world war from occurring:

> The main link of united action of the anti-imperialist forces remains the struggle against war for world peace, against the menace of a thermonuclear war and mass extermination which continues to hang

over mankind. A new world war can be averted by the combined effort of the socialist countries, the international working class, the national liberation movement, all peace-loving countries, public organizations and mass movements.[1]

This statement, though, was an ambiguous one. The relationship between local war and world war was not actually mentioned. The socialist forces were viewed as being able to prevent world war, but how this could be done was unclear. Would world war be prevented because the Soviet Union and others were making such strong efforts to ensure peace through détente and arms control, or because the Soviet Union now had enough military power to frighten the imperialists from expanding a local war into a world war? Indeed, was the Soviet Union now so strong that even if it was involved in a local war, world war could be prevented? No comment was made by the Party on any of these questions at the 1969 conference.

In 1972, though, V.M. Kulish did discuss the relationship between local war and world war. While admitting the possibility that local war could lead to world war, he also believed that this would not necessarily occur:

Any local war, any aggressive act of imperialism in greater or lesser degree contains the danger of developing into a wider international conflict. Such a danger took place in the period of the war in Korea, in which the United States succeeded in drawing in fourteen allies or dependent states with it. Having unleashed the war against Vietnam, American imperialism is striving to spread it into all Southeast Asia.

Inasmuch as world war can arise as the consequence of extremely aggravated economic, political, social and other basic contradictions in the world, and before all the contradictions between international systems and the leading powers of these systems, in it can be used the most effective weapons of armed struggle, up to nuclear missiles. However, since a world war can be simultaneously a nuclear-missile one, and consequently, extremely dangerous for humanity, the probability of its unleashing is limited.[2]

In other words, while Kulish believed that local war could grow into world war, the catastrophic nature of world war might be enough to prevent a local war from escalating. Thus, it was the devastating threat of escalation into a world war that would prevent local war from expanding; Kulish did not say that the Soviet Union itself was so strong that it could by its own strength prevent local war from becoming a world war.

What V.M. Kulish did not say in 1972, however, Colonel G. Malinovskiy did appear to say in 1974:

Characteristic of today's local wars are the expansion of their scale and the involvement in their orbit of new territories and countries. For example, the war unleashed by the imperialists in South Vietnam involved an additional three countries of Indochina: the DRV, Laos, and Cambodia. The area of imperialist aggression in the Near East has also been expanded, having covered not only Egypt, Syria and Jordan, but even Lebanon. The escalation of military operations and the involvement therein of new states increases the danger of their developing into a world war. However, with the change in the balance of forces in the international arena in favor of socialism, another possibility is also increasing more and more – that of preventing the development of local wars into an enormous clash on a worldwide scale. 'A new world war can be averted by the combined effort of the socialist countries, the international working class, the national liberation movement, all peace-loving countries, public organizations and mass movements,' it was stressed at the International Conference of Communist and Workers' Parties held in 1969.[3]

Local wars were capable of expanding, as in Southeast Asia and the Middle East. However, with the increase in the strength of socialist forces, socialism itself was now strong enough to prevent local wars from escalating. Malinovskiy's quotation from the 1969 conference appeared to put a more definite meaning on a sentence that was originally an ambiguous one. Whereas in the original 1969 statement, the 'effort' on the part of the socialist countries *et al.* in preventing world war did not refer to anything in particular, in Malinovskiy this 'effort' seemed to consist of military force. Further, Malinovskiy considered this ability on the part of socialism to prevent the escalation of local war into world war to be beneficial.

Continuing this theme, General of the Army I. Shavrov (commandant of the General Staff Academy) in March 1975 defined in relatively neutral terms local war as a war which, unlike world war, could be successfully limited:

In terms of scope and weapons employed, a local war [lokal'naya voina] is a local [mestnaya], small war. In comparison to world war, it can be limited by the number of participant countries and the limits of a defined geographic region of military actions and, as a rule, is waged with conventional weapons.[4]

These statements were quite different from the dominant Soviet military view of the 1960s. Previously, the Soviet military saw local war as posing for the Soviet Union the choice between two evils: the risk of world war if the imperialists were opposed by the USSR in a local war, or the risk of the imperialists winning if not opposed. If, as Malinovskiy and Shavrov believed, the risk of local war growing into world war could be removed through the ability of the forces of socialism to prevent it, the Soviet Union was left free to concentrate on whether the forces of socialism or imperialism would win in a local war.

This change in thinking about the relationship between local war and world war had a major effect on other Soviet ideas about conflict in the Third World. The ability to prevent the outbreak of world war through the increased strength of socialism meant not only that the USSR could play a greater role in aiding progressive forces to counter a local war launched by the imperialists, but also that the Soviet Union could itself make foreign policy gains through local wars without fear of world war. Previously, local wars had been thought of as a means through which only the imperialists could gain. Now it was recognised that the USSR could gain from local wars as well, as both Vietnam and Angola demonstrated.

The Nature and Types of Conflict in the Third World

The search for a more accurate means of defining the nature and types of war in the Third World (which Stepanov and Rybkin had begun in 1968) than the traditional Soviet military view offered continued during the middle Brezhnev years. This subject aroused the interest of several major thinkers within the Soviet military who set forth several different theories about it. This discussion was less of a debate between purely traditional and purely revisionist points of view (though there were in certain cases disagreements along these lines) than it was an attempt to truly understand the different kinds of conflict occurring in the Third World, what their causes were, and ultimately, what Soviet attitudes toward them should be. What emerged from this discussion was a consensus that while ideological factors were important in defining the nature and types of wars in the Third World, non-ideological factors were also important.

One of the most significant theorists of those who argued for a change from the traditional Soviet military view was Ye. Rybkin, who continued to publish the views that he and Stepanov first set forth in 1968.[5] The argument that Rybkin made was basically the same as before; to the traditional four categories of war, Rybkin added civil wars between the people and a regime of extreme reaction and wars between Third World nations. This last category had been referred to as wars between equal states in 1968. Rybkin also referred to it as 'military clashes between developing countries',[6] and 'military conflicts . . . which cannot be assigned to one of the above types'.[7] Whereas wars between Third World nations had been emphasised previously, Rybkin now also included in this category civil wars within Third World nations between regions, tribes and other non-class divisions.[8] The just nature of these conflicts had to be determined on an individual basis; no general rule for them could be formulated.

In 1972 Rybkin went further than he had previously in describing the complexity of conflict between and within Third World nations. Socialist, capitalist, feudal, peasant and primitive societies were all seen to exist alongside one another in the Third World. In addition, 'Various groups, some progressive and others reactionary, replace one another in many countries as in a kaleidoscope.'[9] No explanation was offered as to why, but the implication was that sociopolitical relations in the Third World operated somewhat differently than Marxism-Leninism envisioned. All this led Rybkin to conclude that traditional class-based analysis alone was not sufficient for understanding the complexity of conflict in the modern era — especially in the Third World.

This was an extreme point of view. The suggestion that class principles operated differently in the Third World from what Marxist-Leninist ideology regarded as a universal law was something that other Soviet military writers would not repeat. Indeed, Rybkin himself retreated from this position the following year in an article declaring that the just nature of *all* wars could be determined from the underlying class conflict.[10] Significantly, because he stressed the class nature of all wars in this 1973 article, he was unable to say anything about wars between and within Third World nations except to acknowledge their existence. The contradiction between this article and Rybkin's earlier ones illustrated extremely well the revisionists' dilemma: if conflict within and between Third World nations was to be described accurately, Marxist-Leninist ideology would have to be modified. On the other hand, if

Marxist-Leninist ideology was to remain unmodified, then Third World conflict could not be understood accurately.

This dilemma, then, applied to traditionalists as well as to revisionists. One Soviet military thinker, Lt. Colonel N. Khmara, attempted to explain conflict in the Third World at the present time while retaining unchanged the traditional Soviet military view of the nature and types of war, including the traditional Soviet military categorisation that recognised only four types of conflict. Khmara rejected even the category of civil wars between the people and a regime of extreme reaction which Soviet military thinking in general had accepted. Instead, Khmara viewed all civil wars at the present as civil wars between the proletariat and the bourgeoisie.[11] Khmara mentioned several civil wars that had occurred in the Third World in which the side favoured by the imperialists had won. The imperialists need not win, however, if the civil war could be transformed into a war of national liberation. This would happen if the imperialists became involved militarily. The bourgeoisie would then join the proletariat to fight against the imperialists. Once the imperialists had been defeated and had withdrawn, the national liberation war could be transformed into a civil war between the bourgeoisie and the proletariat. The proletariat, though, would be much stronger now and would be able to defeat the bourgeoisie as well as bring about socialism.[12]

This formulation may have been more in line with traditional Marxist-Leninist ideology, but it contained certain glaring inconsistencies. First, Khmara saw civil wars between the proletariat and the bourgeoisie as occurring in the Third World while the traditional military view saw them as occurring only in developed capitalist nations. Secondly, Khmara's scheme contained an illogical element. This was that the imperialists would only intervene in a civil war between the bourgeoisie and the proletariat in order to support the bourgeoisie. Yet once the imperialists intervened, Khmara expected the bourgeoisie to join the proletariat in order to fight against the imperialists. Such a scenario was hardly plausible. Khmara might have avoided this difficulty, though, if he had accepted the category of civil wars between the people and a regime of extreme reaction. Here, the imperialists would intervene to support the reactionary regime against the people (both the proletariat and the bourgeoisie). Once the imperialists had been defeated, the proletariat and the bourgeoisie would then fight each other.

Another problem with Khmara's formulation was that, according to him, the proletariat had the best chance of ultimate success if the imperialists first intervened militarily against it. The implication of this

was that the Soviet Union should encourage the United States to intervene militarily in as many civil wars as possible. This, however, was
exactly what the Soviet military did not want to encourage. Surely the
proletariat had a better chance of defeating the local bourgeoisie than it
did of defeating the most powerful imperialists. Thus, while Khmara's
formulation did not challenge traditional Marxism-Leninism, the
logical inconsistencies in it were such that no other Soviet military
thinker wished to repeat or defend it.

Other Soviet military writers attempted to make a compromise
between the extreme revisionist and extreme traditionalist positions in
order to arrive at an accurate understanding of Third World conflict
while retaining the Marxist-Leninist notion of conflict being based on
class struggle. One of these was Colonel G. Malinovskiy, whose important
statements concerning the relationship of local war to world war have
already been discussed. In the same article, Malinovskiy claimed that all
Third World conflicts fell under the category of national liberation wars,
exactly as the traditional Soviet military view had regarded them. This
category, however, was divided into three sub-categories: (1) wars by
imperialists against colonies; (2) wars by imperialists and puppet regimes
against the people; and (3) wars by imperialists against independent Third
World nations.[13] In addition, there was a special sub-category of wars
between and within Third World nations caused by the imperialists.[14]
What he had done, of course, was simply place Rybkin's two new
categories of civil wars between the people and a regime of extreme
reaction and wars between and within Third World nations under the
heading of national liberation wars.

The advantage of Malinovskiy's formulation was that wars of national
liberation in the traditional Soviet military view had a wider variety of
acceptable outcomes; anyone who fought against the imperialists was
progressive. Malinovskiy thus gave a more definite ideological aspect to
all Third World conflicts, even conflicts between and within Third
World nations. This was more acceptable than Rybkin's 1972 suggestion
that traditional Marxist-Leninist notions of class struggle did not apply
to the Third World. The disadvantage of his formulation, though, was
that, unlike Rybkin, Malinovskiy portrayed the imperialists as the
direct cause of all Third World conflicts. Even in wars between Third
World nations where the potential for conflict already existed between
them, Malinovskiy insisted that actual conflict was initiated directly by
the imperialists and the Maoists.[15] This, of course, was simply contrary
to fact. Third World conflicts often arose from purely Third World disputes, as Rybkin had earlier pointed out. Thus, even though Malinovskiy

attempted to take into account the increasing complexity of conflict in the Third World, his unwillingness to modify ideological orthodoxy prevented him from more fully and accurately describing conflict in the Third World as Rybkin's less orthodox discussion had done.

Another major Soviet military thinker, Colonel T. Kondratkov, sought to resolve the problem in a different way. Kondratkov believed that while the categorisation of types of war should be made on an ideological basis, he felt that non-ideological factors such as scale of warfare and means of conflict should also form part of the categorisation.[16] Kondratkov, however, proceeded no further than this. While saying that ideological and non-ideological factors should be used to form categories of war, he did not say how this should be done. Nevertheless, Kondratkov did make a major contribution to formulating a general rule to determine the just side in a conflict that could be applied to wars between and within Third World nations that had little or no class basis. The new formulation was that 'The just and progressive nature of a modern war can be established only from the standpoint of the interests of socialism and communism . . .'[17]

This was quite different from previous Soviet military thinking which determined the just nature of a war according to its 'objective' type. In other words, in a civil war between the bourgeoisie and the proletariat, the proletariat was just because it was progressive while the bourgeoisie was unjust because it was reactionary. Rybkin showed that such a general rule could not be applied to conflicts between and within Third World nations; their unusual class basis (often none at all) demanded individual appraisal for each such conflict. Kondratkov's formulation, though, could apply to all conflicts. That side in any type of conflict whose victory would further the interests of socialism (the USSR) was just.

The problem of finding a formula that would adequately explain the nature and types of wars occurring in the Third World was authoritatively resolved by General of the Army I. Shavrov. While Malinovskiy had sought to describe the complexity of conflict in the Third World under the constraints of the category of national liberation wars and Kondratkov stated that non-ideological factors should be included in any classification of wars but did not construct such a classification, Shavrov in 1975 boldly introduced a systematic classification of Third World conflicts that included non-ideological factors.

To begin with, Shavrov saw all conflict in the Third World as local wars. All wars to be classified in terms of three factors: (1) sociopolitical, (2) scale and (3) nature of the weapons and forces employed.[18] Having established these criteria, Shavrov then classified local wars into tabular form (see Table 1). Local wars between imperialist states and individual socialist states fighting in defence of the socialist fatherland were wars such as those fought by already established Third World socialist states (North Korea, North Vietnam) against imperialist attack on their own territory. The two standard components of the national liberation war category (imperialists versus young non-capitalist states, imperialists versus colonies) were listed as separate types. The note with regard to civil wars referred to the Malinovskiy article of May 1974; although Shavrov did not explicitly state it, this was an acknowledgement that both civil wars between the proletariat and the bourgeoisie and between the people and a regime of extreme reaction existed. The category 'local wars between individual capitalist states' was unusual because it was the only one that did not refer to 'imperialists'. Obviously, wars between imperialists had to be included in this category, but Shavrov must also have meant wars between Third World nations, since he listed local wars between two states of one geographic region and wars within one country as classifications of scale. Further, he specifically referred in the text of the article to conflicts between Third World nations, as well as to conflicts even smaller than those which could be called local war.[20]

An unusual aspect of the classification of wars by types of weapon used was that not only were conventional wars distinguished from nuclear wars, but also from wars in which only the threat of using nuclear weapons existed. In addition, conventional wars were divided into ones where regular armies alone did the fighting and those in which irregular forces also participated. Finally, Shavrov saw each type of war as transformable into another type (a concept that Khmara had earlier applied to civil wars and national liberation wars).

General Shavrov did more than any other Soviet military writer to expand the classification of types of war to include factors other than sociopolitical ones. His sociopolitical categories were not new and the breakdown in scale of war and means of combat was not extraordinary by itself. What was original, however, was Shavrov's view that each war could be classified according to three criteria simultaneously: sociopolitical, scale, and means of combat. This was quite different from Soviet military thinkers during and after the time of Khrushchev who objected to the First Secretary's inclusion of non-ideological factors in the classification of wars, insisting that types of war be categorised on the basis of sociopolitical factors alone. Still, Shavrov's formulation differed from Khrushchev's, who lumped all factors together in his simple classification: world wars, local wars and wars of national liberation.

Table 1: Classification of Local Wars[19]

Classification Features	Criteria for Evaluating the Wars	Types of Wars
Sociopolitical	Social composition of the participants.	Local wars between individual imperialist states and individual socialist states fighting in defence of the socialist fatherland.
	Political aims of each side.	Local wars between imperialist states and young non-capitalist-type sovereign states fighting for their national independence.
		Local wars between imperialist states and nations fighting for their national liberation.
		Local wars between individual capitalist states.
		Civil wars between antagonistic classes within one state with or without overt interference by a major imperialist power.[a]
Scale	Number of participating states. Territory enveloped by military actions. Number of participating troops. Duration.	Local wars between two states of one geographic region.
		Local wars between one [sic] or several states of different regions of the world.
		Wars within one country.
Nature of participating armies and weapons used in the war	Regular or irregular armies.	Conventional local wars with the participation of regular armies.
		Conventional local wars with the participation of regular and irregular formations.
	Conventional weapons or weapons of mass destruction.	Conventional local wars with the threat of employment of nuclear weapons or escalation into nuclear war.

Note: a. This type of local war may be subdivided in turn into subtypes. (For more details on this see *Voyenno-Istoricheskiy Zhurnal*, 1974, no. 5, p. 93.

Shavrov kept his criteria separate from one another; the scale of war and the means of combat were determined without reference to the determination of sociopolitical character.

Another important difference between Khrushchev and Shavrov was that while Khrushchev made a distinction between local wars (which were to be avoided) and national liberation wars (which were to be supported), Shavrov included national liberation wars (as well as other types) within the framework of local wars. Significantly, Shavrov did not mention anything about avoiding local wars, as Khrushchev did. Khrushchev feared that local wars could grow into world wars. Shavrov, on the other hand, thought that world war could be avoided and even included wars involving nuclear weapons as a type of local war. Thus, although Shavrov may have included some of the same non-sociopolitical factors in his classification of types of wars that Khrushchev did, his ideas about conflict in the Third World were much less restrictive than the former First Secretary's.

Because Shavrov kept the criteria for classifying types of wars separate, his use of non-sociopolitical factors did not adversely affect the determination of just versus unjust. Each war had to be evaluated in terms of sociopolitical factors, scale, and means of combat; no war could be classified in terms of the second two criteria alone without the first. Further, since the second two criteria did not affect the sociopolitical factors, the justness of each war could be judged solely in terms of the first criterion.

Yet while justness versus unjustness could be easily applied to each participating side in Shavrov's sociopolitical categories of types of local war, justness versus unjustness could less easily be applied to the concept of local war as a whole. Whereas Khrushchev considered local war to be unjust, Shavrov appeared to consider the concept as a whole to be neutral. Although Khrushchev's formulation of local war mixed sociopolitical and other factors, he believed that it was 'objectively' unjust as a type of war. Referring to any of Shavrov's sociopolitical types of local war, an 'objective' determination of the just nature of each side in the war could be made, but not for the concept of local war as a whole. What this meant was that Shavrov did not consider local war something that the Soviet Union should reject *per se*. Instead, local war was a means through which all types of nations could make foreign policy gains, including socialist nations.

What was the importance of all these varying descriptions of the nature and types of conflict in the Third World made by Soviet military writers? First of all, it signified the importance of Third World conflict to the Soviet military. The two new categories introduced by Stepanov and Rybkin as well as all the other different formulations on the nature and types of war concerned only conflict in the Third World. Such a large-scale reassessment was not being made about other types of war (world war, war in Europe) at this time. This discussion marked the change between the previous period when Third World conflicts were only of secondary interest to the Soviet military and the middle Brezhnev years when they became of primary interest.

In addition to an increasing interest in Third World conflicts, this discussion showed that the Soviet military was earnestly struggling to find an acceptable means of explaining and evaluating these conflicts. This was essential if the Soviet military was to understand the new types of conflict that were emerging – types that had not been envisioned in the Marxist-Leninist classics. Equally important, this understanding was necessary if the Soviet Union was to formulate a foreign policy toward these conflicts that would succeed in enhancing Soviet interests.

The change in evaluating the just nature of wars from the traditional means by ascertaining the type of war to the determination of what would be in the best interests of socialism (the USSR) was especially important in evaluating Third World conflicts. As was pointed out earlier, this allowed the Soviets to make judgements about conflicts between and within Third World nations that did not have a clear class basis, but were caused by territorial or tribal disputes. In addition, a type of conflict was beginning to occur during this period of the Brezhnev era that had not been seen earlier. This was conflict in which progressive forces battled each other. In Ethiopia, for example, the Soviets had given a certain amount of support to the Marxist guerrillas in Eritrea fighting for independence from the feudal government in Addis Ababa. After the Ethiopian revolution, Marxist Eritrean guerrillas fought against the now Marxist government in Addis Ababa. How was the USSR to decide which side to support? Similarly, how would the USSR decide whom to support in the territorial dispute between Marxist Somalia and Marxist Ethiopia? The determination of the type of conflict these were would not help, especially since it was not recognised that two just sides, or two socialist groups, would fight one another. The only way the USSR could choose between rival Marxists was by referring to its own foreign policy interests. Thus, the change in the means of judging the just and unjust sides in a conflict was also an adjustment to the uncomfortable reality of Marxists increasingly fighting other Marxists, and not the imperialists.

Further, the decision to include non-ideological factors in the consideration of the nature and types of war indicated a willingness to consider more active Soviet involvement in local wars. When the Soviet military rejected Khrushchev's mixture of non-ideological factors in determining the categories of war, they were rejecting his absolute pessimism about Soviet ability to counter American actions in local wars. At that time, non-ideological factors pointed to Soviet weaknesses rather than strengths. The US was able to intervene in the Third World while the USSR was not. Similarly, the US had a much greater nuclear capability than the USSR possessed then. Khrushchev pointed to these non-ideological factors as a reason for the USSR not to become involved in Third World conflicts. The Soviet military did not agree with the degree of pessimism of this assessment; they expressed their desire for limited Soviet involvement in national liberation wars by stressing ideological factors alone and ignoring non-ideological ones. Now, though, the non-ideological factors could be used as an argument for a greater Soviet role in Third World conflicts. The USSR had a nuclear weapons capability roughly equal to the US, and a greater conventional capability that could be used in the Third World including more sophisticated weapons that could be transferred, and more transport that could ship weapons, Soviet advisers, and (to Angola) Cuban troops. Greater Soviet conventional capability allowed the USSR to be less fearful of American efforts to oppose Soviet actions. Finally, the US had withdrawn from the Vietnam war without achieving its goal of preventing the communists from taking power. Thus, Soviet military thinkers who favoured a greater Soviet role in Third World conflicts could hardly fail to take notice of these encouraging non-ideological factors.

Indeed, these non-ideological factors must have appeared more encouraging than did the ideological ones in conflicts that were becoming increasingly confused in terms of the traditional Soviet view of the types of conflict that existed. What was important, though, was that the Soviet military did not abandon class analysis in examining Third World conflicts. Rybkin's 1972 suggestion that the traditional Marxist-Leninist view of class struggle might not be applicable to the Third World was not accepted by any other Soviet military writer; indeed, Rybkin himself rejected it in 1973. Instead, the Soviet military attempted to improve class analysis by adding new categories to the traditional Soviet military classification of types of wars. The Soviet military was committed not just to enhancing the interests of the Soviet Union, but also the interests of socialism. This would have an increasingly important effect on foreign policy. It meant that the Soviet Union would rush to support Marxist-Leninists whose hold on power was relatively weak, such as in Ethiopia and Afghanistan, even at the expense of alienating established Soviet allies that were not as committed to Soviet ideology (such as Somalia), or of requiring a vast Soviet military effort to keep the Marxist-Leninists in power when the non-communists previously in office had co-operated with the Soviet Union (as in Afghanistan). Thus, while non-ideological factors became increasingly important in Soviet military discussions of the nature and types of war in the Third World during the middle Brezhnev years, they did not by any means displace the importance of ideological factors to the Soviet military.

Peaceful Coexistence

A major change occurred in the Soviet military view of peaceful co-existence during the middle Brezhnev years. While previously the Soviet military had not been enthusiastic about it, from the time of the 24th Party Congress in 1971, military writers made statements that were strongly in favour of peaceful coexistence. The purpose of peaceful co-existence was to prevent nuclear war and to create an atmosphere of peace in which national and social liberation in the Third World could more easily take place. This was what the Party had advocated since Khrushchev. Now, however, there was one important change: while pursuing peaceful coexistence with the West, the USSR would actively help the struggle for national and social liberation in the Third World. The USSR would not just be satisfied with creating more peaceful conditions in which progressive forces in the Third World would struggle on their own. The Soviet military was in favour of this change.[21]

The Soviet military argued that world war between opposing social systems was something that both the US and the USSR had an equal interest in preventing. However, the maintenance of the *status quo* in the Third World of governments dependent on the West was an artificial situation. Without the support of the West, these governments would not be able to prevent the popular forces of socialism from gaining power. Since the US exercised an undue influence on events in the Third World, the USSR was justified in extending its influence in counterbalancing the US by supporting wars of national and social liberation in the Third World.[22]

To American objections that Soviet support of revolutionary change in the Third World was not in accord with peaceful coexistence, the Soviet military responded that peaceful coexistence extended only to preventing military conflict between states with differing social systems.

The USSR did not interpret peaceful coexistence as the end to all class struggle. This struggle continued in the ideological, political, diplomatic and economic realms. Further, the Soviet Union would support progressive forces in the Third World that were struggling for national and social liberation through military means. If the Soviet Union did not do so it would mean that the USSR supported the imperialists.[23]

Yet while the Soviet military regarded Soviet military support of revolutionary groups in the Third World as being compatible with peaceful coexistence, they also saw peaceful coexistence as a means to try to prevent the US from militarily assisting the counter-revolutionary forces. Peaceful coexistence could serve to paralyse the US in exercising military force in Third World conflicts. Nevertheless, the Soviets did not see American military actions in the Third World as actually being incompatible with peaceful coexistence. Certainly they opposed such actions on the part of the US, but this did not make them willing to give up the advantage of peaceful coexistence. Instead, they appeared to consider the Third World an area where Soviet and American interests were likely to be opposing and where local conflicts would arise as a result; indeed, they viewed this as being the natural course of events.

This sanguine view of American actions was based on a fundamental change that occurred in world politics during the middle years of the Brezhnev era: by the mid-1970s the US was no longer as willing to become militarily involved in Third World conflicts as it had been previously. On the other hand, the Soviet Union was now more willing than before to become involved in them. Whereas during the early Brezhnev years, peaceful coexistence held out only the vague promise of eventual success for the progressive forces in the Third World while the American military involvement in Vietnam grew larger and larger, now peaceful coexistence was actually seen to fulfil its promise. The US had withdrawn from Vietnam and the communists came to power. Further, during the Angolan crisis, the US showed little inclination to intervene militarily against the MPLA, which through Soviet and Cuban support was able to come to power. The US truly appeared to be paralysed from exporting counter-revolution to the Third World. The Soviet military recognised that the policy of peaceful coexistence could help to keep the US in this state. Thus, in order to keep the US from becoming once again more active militarily in the Third World and in order to reduce the possibility of major conflict between the US and the USSR, the Soviet military now became a strong advocate of peaceful coexistence.

Indigenous Third World Forces

While during the early Brezhnev years, several leftist civilian regimes were overthrown by rightist military coups, during the middle Brezhnev years, several rightist regimes were overthrown by leftist military coups. This occurred in Iraq, the Congo (Brazzaville), and Peru all in the last half of 1968, Somalia in 1969, Dahomey (now Benin) in 1972, and Ethiopia in 1974.[24] These events confirmed the Soviet military in the belief of the early Brezhnev years that a progressive army could act as the vanguard of socialist development in Third World countries. Soviet military writers emphasised that the dominant position a Third World army had gave it the possibility of shaping the rest of society in conformity with its own ideological outlook.[25] Progressive military regimes, then, deserved the support of the Soviet Union. This view of radical Third World armies was an extremely optimistic one. In effect, the Soviet military believed that the Third World could be launched on the path toward socialism through them with little effort on the part of the Soviet Union. Soviet interests would be advanced by political actors independent of the Soviet Union.

Several Party/civilian writers shared the optimistic view of radical Third World armies that the Soviet military held.[26] This was not surprising since it appeared at this time that radical military regimes were more successful in maintaining Third World nations on the path to socialism than were radical civilian regimes. Many other Party/civilian writers, though, continued to hold a pessimistic view of radical Third World military regimes.[27] They argued that no matter how radical a Third World army might be, its class origins were primarily petty bourgeois. Becoming a privileged group through its seizure of power, the army soon found that a true socialist revolution would destroy this position. Further, there was nothing to prevent a leftist army from sliding to the right and becoming an exploitative force itself. Thus, Third World armies could not be entrusted with the task of leading developing societies to socialism; only a Marxist-Leninist vanguard party could do this.

In the early 1970s, though, Party/civilian writers were optimistic about the success of another route to socialism in the Third World. This was the peaceful route, such as occurred in Chile. Pointing to the Chilean experience, they saw the Cuban model of violent revolution through guerrilla warfare as not necessarily applicable.[28] Even after the rightist military coup of 1973 in Chile, when the applicability of the peaceful road to socialism appeared to be in grave doubt, the Cuban *foco* theory was still criticised since it called for the revolutionary armed forces to create the vanguard party rather than the other way around.[29]

The Soviet view of guerrilla armies in the Third World did, however, undergo a major change during the middle Brezhnev years. Previously, Soviet military thinkers did not look upon guerrilla armies with particular favour. A victorious guerrilla army, even if it were socialist, could establish its own power base independent of the Soviet Union, as occurred in Yugoslavia and China. Yet while the Soviet military did not care to see socialist guerrilla armies come to power only to break away from Moscow's influence, the Vietnam war demonstrated that guerrilla armies allied to the Soviet Union could be successful. It was this ability to succeed that now made guerrilla armies worthy of favourable consideration by the Soviet Union.[30] Guerrilla warfare also had the advantage of being able to arise almost anywhere under almost any conditions.[31] The expectations that the Soviet military had of guerrilla armies in the Third World had thus risen considerably. There was, however, one condition that a guerrilla army had to meet in order to be acceptable to the USSR: 'guerrilla activities must be carried out under party control and supervision'.[32]

Even though the Soviet military was now optimistic about guerrilla armies, this qualification was deemed necessary to avoid the lapses in socialist solidarity evidenced by earlier guerrilla armies that had come to power. It was noteworthy that the Soviet military did not insist on party control of ordinary Third World armies; perhaps this was because a radical Third World army that disappointed the Soviet Union had not yet been experienced, though this would soon change. Despite this qualification insisting on party control, the Soviet military also viewed guerrilla armies as it did radical Third World armies: independent actors that would further Soviet foreign policy interests with little effort necessary on the part of the USSR.

Indeed the Soviet military was most optimistic about indigenous Third World forces finding their way to socialism during the middle Brezhnev years. All forces working for change in the Third World were seen as the natural ally of the Soviet Union — even guerrilla armies, which the Soviet military had previously been sceptical about. During this period, everything appeared to be going well for the Soviet Union in the Third World, especially since little was going well for the United States. It was natural, then, for the Soviet military to hold such an optimistic view. Compared to its view, the pessimism of some Soviet Party/civilian writers, such as Mirskiy, must have appeared almost defeatist. However, the events of the late Brezhnev era would soon demonstrate that the pessimism of the latter had been justified while the optimism of the former had not.

American Ideas and Actions in Local Wars

During the Khrushchev and early Brezhnev years, Soviet military thinkers had criticised American ideas about local war for assuming that such a conflict could be kept localised; the Soviets emphasised that local wars could escalate into world wars. However, once Soviet military thinkers themselves accepted the proposition that local war could be prevented from growing into world war, this criticism of American ideas ceased completely. Indeed, from the middle Brezhnev years onward, there was very little discussion by the Soviet military of American ideas about local war at all except to note that the increasing might of the Soviet Union prevented the United States from unleashing world war and forced it to resort to local war.[33]

Soviet military discussion about American actions in local wars, however, increased during the middle Brezhnev years, particularly with regard to Vietnam. During the Vietnam war itself, Soviet military writers continued to describe the conflict in purely ideological terms, as they had during the early Brezhnev years. While the US was militarily stronger than the Vietnamese communists, the Vietnamese communists were fighting a just war and therefore were morally superior to the US. While the war in Vietnam was a limited one for the Americans, it was not for the Vietnamese. Thus, American actions in Vietnam were doomed to failure.[34]

Soon after the Vietnam war was over, however, Soviet military thinkers began to change their assessment of American actions in Vietnam. This started with statements that examined relatively objectively, and sometimes favourably, specific functions of the American armed forces. In 1973, for example, a Soviet Navy officer wrote an article portraying American amphibious forces as being relatively effective, though the article was written in a vitriolic style. The author concluded:

> The people of the world are demanding that the United States halt its intervention in the affairs of other states, that it remove its troops from foreign territories, and withdraw American military ships and transports with the Marines from foreign shores.[35]

What was noteworthy about this conclusion was that the author did not describe the US Marines as being defeated anywhere by the forces of socialism and national liberation; instead, the US was asked to withdraw them voluntarily, since their effectiveness would not allow the Marines to be defeated easily. Similarly, in 1972, even before American involvement in the war had ended, a book was published on aircraft carriers that contained a chapter discussing how these vessels could be used to accomplish several important missions in local wars and citing the Korean and Vietnam wars as examples of how the Americans had done this.[36] Others discussed fairly objectively US bombing missions against North Vietnam, the results of North Vietnamese air defence measures to counter them, and then the results of US efforts to counter the Vietnamese air defence measures; in 1975, Colonel V. Babich actually concluded that US air defence neutralisation methods in Vietnam had been relatively successful.[37]

These statements indicated there were certain aspects of the American local war capability that the Soviet military found interesting enough to give some praise. These were capabilities that the Soviet military may have thought the Soviet Union should possess as well. They also indicated that with the end of the Vietnam war, Soviet military writers were willing to judge the American involvement more on its military merits than on its ideological merits alone. This was a trend that would continue much more strongly in the late Brezhnev years.

The Soviet Role in Third World Conflicts

During the middle years of the Brezhnev era, the policy of arms transfers was judged to have been successful by the Soviet military, especially with regard to Vietnam. Soviet military assistance to the Vietnamese communists was seen as having prevented the US from achieving a military victory in Vietnam. The failure to achieve a military victory led to an erosion of American political will to continue the struggle which in turn further hindered the US from fighting effectively.[38] In other words, if Soviet military assistance could prolong a conflict in which the US was involved, domestic support in the US for the war would decline, causing pressure for American forces to be withdrawn. Thus, only a relatively small degree of Soviet involvement in a Third World conflict (arms transfers) was considered to be extremely effective in halting a large-scale American military operation.

However, during the middle years of the Brezhnev era, a form of more direct Soviet military involvement in Third World conflicts began to be discussed: the training of revolutionary forces by Soviet military advisers.[39] It was recognised that guerrilla and other Third World armies fighting for just causes might not be able to triumph over the imperialists even after receiving Soviet arms transfers. Often, it was necessary for Soviet military advisers to train progressive forces how to use Soviet weapons effectively. Sometimes, the need for training was so great against a perceived imperialist threat that a vast number of Soviet military advisers were required, as in Egypt. For the most part, though, the role of Soviet military advisers was not one of direct participation in combat on behalf of progressive Third World forces. The actual fighting was to be done mostly by these forces, while the Soviet role remained primarily one of aiding and assisting them. Thus, while the advocacy of dispatching Soviet military advisers reflected a willingness for the USSR to become more directly involved in Third World conflicts, this involvement had its limits.

However, the Soviet military had become relatively optimistic about the ability of national and social liberation to succeed in the Third World with only a limited amount of Soviet military involvement. As Colonel Malinovskiy put it in 1974:

the possibility of the triumph of the progressive forces in national liberation wars is increasing. Of decisive significance here is the all-round assistance of the USSR and all the countries of the socialist commonwealth to the struggling peoples. The practise of the liberation struggle of the oppressed nations shows that it is impossible to defeat a people who consistently struggle against imperialism and for freedom and independence, and who are supported by the Soviet Union, all the countries of the socialist commonwealth and the progressive forces of the entire world.[40]

Saying that no one could be defeated who had the support of the Soviet Union was indeed an optimistic point of view, though, as was mentioned earlier, the Soviet military had reason to be optimistic about the Third World during this period.

It was also during the middle Brezhnev years that the Soviet Navy began to envision a greater role for itself than it had before. Previously, the tasks of the Navy were seen primarily as protecting the Soviet coastline and supporting ground forces in coastal areas. In a series of articles that appeared in *Morskoy Sbornik* during 1972 and 1973, though, Admiral Gorshkov redefined the role of the Soviet Navy. He saw the Soviet Navy as an ocean-going force with the responsibility of supporting socialist forces worldwide.[41] This included a greater role for the Soviet Navy in patrolling the Third World.[42]

In comparison to actual Soviet military involvement in the Third World, Soviet military thinkers once again were unwilling to acknowledge in writing all that the Soviet Union did in practice. In addition to Soviet weapons and Soviet military advisers sent to the Third World the Soviet Union also acquired military base facilities, most notably in Egypt and Somalia (though the USSR would only enjoy these temporarily). In addition, the Soviet Union threatened to send combat forces to Egypt during the 1973 Middle East War, though this threat was not carried out. Most spectacular of all, however, was the shipment of Cuban armed forces to Angola in 1975 to participate directly in combat on behalf of the MPLA. With the help of the Cubans, the MPLA was able to come to power in Luanda, though its control of Angola has never been complete due to the continued guerrilla warfare against it conducted in the south by UNITA.[43]

Even by adding Soviet advisers to their discussion of the Soviet role in Third World conflicts, the Soviet military expressed a greater willing-ness for the USSR to become more heavily involved in these conflicts than previously. It indicated a greater willingness to manage events in Third World conflicts. Nevertheless, the fighting itself was to be under-taken primarily by indigenous forces. Even in Angola where Cubans participated in the fighting, the Soviets themselves did not. Thus, while the Soviet Union developed an increased role in Third World conflicts during the middle Brezhnev years, the extent of this role was still limited.

Conclusion

During the middle Brezhnev years, the interest of Party/civilian writers in the Third World also grew. The concerns of these writers were similar to those of the Soviet military, but they differed somewhat in emphasis. One of the main themes that the Party/civilian writers discussed was non-capitalist economic development in the Third World;[44] the usual recommendation being that the Third World should follow the example of the Soviet Central Asian republics. As Rybkin had, some civilian writers noted the tendency toward fragmentation and conflict between and within Third World nations. In order to prevent this, they urged the formation and strengthening of Marxist-Leninist parties throughout the Third World, which they saw as being able to overcome these conflicts.[45] In addition, 'national' or 'non-scientific' socialist ideology was criticised for not adhering to Marxism-Leninism; only errors and mistakes were seen to result from this type of ideology in the Third World.[46] Chinese foreign policy was also heavily criticised for working against the interests of socialism in the Third World.[47]

Party/civilian writers also made statements about the military aspect of the struggle for socialism in the Third World during the middle Brezhnev years. Like the military, they did not see peaceful coexistence with the West as being incompatible with Soviet assistance to national and social liberation movements in the Third World.[48] They also acknowledged Soviet military assistance to the Third World.[49] Little was said, however, beyond this by civilians.

There was, though, one important exception during this period. This was V.M. Kulish, who was a retired colonel but who edited a book on military force and international relations that was published by the civilian Institute of World Economy and International Relations (IMEMO). In this book, Kulish called for a Soviet 'military presence' in the Third World similar to that which the US enjoyed.[50] More strikingly, this book advocated the separate consideration of military-political problems of international relations from all other aspects of international affairs.[51] This presumably meant separation from ideological considerations as well. Thus, Kulish appeared to be saying that military-political considerations should be the sole basis upon which decisions about conflicts ought to be made.

This statement was an extreme one. It could be interpreted as a rejection of Marxist-Leninist ideology as a guide for Soviet foreign policy and its replacement with principles by which a traditional great power might be guided. This view was never repeated either by military or Party/civilian writers. Further, shortly after the publication of this book, Kulish's employment with IMEMO was terminated. Some Western analysts, though, viewed the publication of this book as a decisive turning point in Soviet military thinking that signalled the complete abandonment of Marxist-Leninist ideology from military considerations.[52] However, in light of the significant ideological element in military and Party/civilian writing both before and after the book was published, this conclusion was unwarranted.

In fact Kulish never did explicitly call for the abandonment of ideological considerations or for the military to make decisions about Third World conflicts without reference to the Party. The rejection by the Party and the military of the formula that military-political considerations should be examined separately from all other considerations, which Kulish hinted at but did not actually make, was highly important in showing the relationship that existed between the Party and the military. While the military may have had a greater knowledge about conflict in the Third World, the military did not formulate policy toward the Third World by itself nor did it formulate positions in opposition to the Party. Military writers discussed in greater detail than the Party conflict in the Third World, but it must be remembered that all Soviet military writing (indeed, all Soviet writing) has to be approved by the censorship process, which is controlled by the Party. The Party would not tolerate serious opposition to its policies on the part of the military, nor would the military ever oppose the Party this way. The one area during the middle Brezhnev era where military and Party writers explicitly disagreed — the role of indigenous forces in the Third World — did not disprove this since the Party writers who were pessimistic about the reliability of radical Third World military regimes were primarily academicians of the various international institutes of the Academy of Sciences and not high Party officials. The Soviet Union did, after all, support radical Third World military regimes as the military had advocated. If anything, it was these academicians who opposed both the military and the Party in this regard, though the fact that their views continued to be published indicated that they received some sort of high level support within the Party. What this showed was that within the highest levels of the Communist Party itself there was disagreement over the reliability of radical Third World military regimes, and thus, the extent to which the USSR should support them.

In addition, while the military did disagree with the policies of the Party leadership in the past (over the nature and types of war, and peaceful coexistence), the military expressed its opposition with extreme circumspection. It is possible that the military expressed even this much disagreement only because part of the Party leadership which shared these misgivings encouraged the military to do so. After all, Khrushchev's policies were extremely controversial within the Party itself (so much so that the Party eventually ousted him), and it is doubtful that peaceful coexistence had the unanimous support of leaders used to thinking of capitalism as their bitter enemy.

With regard to the relationship between military thought and actual Soviet behaviour, the military did not acknowledge all that was being done in practice. Arms transfers and sending Soviet advisers were acknowledged after they had taken place, but not before. Discussion of the use of Cuban troops in local conflicts was not made at this time, though Cubans had been sent to Angola. The pattern of discussing the

Soviet role in Third World conflicts that existed in the Khrushchev and early Brezhnev years continued into the middle Brezhnev years. More of a Soviet role in Third World conflicts was acknowledged during this period than before: for the first time, discussion of the role of Soviet advisers in the Third World took place.

Other changes in Soviet military thought also signalled a change in attitude that was more favourable to greater Soviet involvement in the Third World. Among these new changes were the belief that the Soviet Union could now prevent local war from becoming world war, that peaceful coexistence with the West was not incompatible with Soviet military assistance to national and social liberation movements, and that guerrilla armies (though only those under Party control) could successfully bring about socialism. All these changes reflected the change in the correlation of forces between East and West at this time during which the West appeared to be on the retreat, especially after Vietnam. American opposition to Soviet involvement was no longer as forceful, and so the USSR did not fear the possibility of US-Soviet military confrontation arising from Soviet involvement in Third World conflicts.

Thus, as was mentioned before, this was a period of growing optimism concerning the change in the Third World toward socialism. During these years, Marxism had come to power throughout all of Indochina and important parts of eastern and southern Africa. In the Horn of Africa, both Ethiopia and Somalia had by 1975 Marxist-oriented governments; the Soviet Union hoped to reconcile the two nations' border dispute and form a large Marxist federation with them and South Yemen. The one serious setback of this period was Egypt, which ordered its large number of Soviet advisers to leave in 1972. Although Soviet aid came to Egypt in the 1973 Middle East War, their relations soon deteriorated seriously. In 1976, Egypt would abrogate the treaty of friendship and co-operation that had been signed with Moscow. Egypt was a country that had been ruled by a Third World military leader (Nasser) who did not institutionalise socialism by creating a vanguard Marxist-Leninist party or by creating a radical Marxist army. Because of this, there were no strong internal forces to prevent Nasser's successor Sadat from leading the army away from socialism. What happened in Egypt after Nasser died resembled what happened to the rule of radical Third World leaders who were overthrown in the early Brezhnev era. Had there been a strong vanguard party or a Marxist army in command, this situation might not have taken place.

However, in addition to the optimism expressed by the Soviet military about the Third World becoming socialist, albeit with a greater amount of Soviet military support than had been previously thought necessary, Soviet military thought during this period reflected a concerted effort to understand the causes for different types of conflict in the Third World. This was particularly noticeable in the discussion of the nature and types of war in which several different points of view were put forward concerning what types of conflict existed and how the attitude of the Soviet Union toward them should be formed. Through acceptance of the new categories of civil war between the people and a regime of extreme reaction and of wars between and within Third World nations (the latter possessing a more diverse class basis than other wars), it was clear that the Soviet military did not see these types of conflict as only being contests between communist and imperialist forces, but recognised their often complicated local origins within the Third World itself. Through an accurate understanding of the local basis of a conflict, the USSR could formulate a policy toward it that would, in turn, assist the Soviet Union in gaining in the larger East-West contest. Yet while this may have contributed during the middle Brezhnev years to Soviet optimism that the USSR could make foreign policy gains in the Third World through involvement in local conflicts, during the late Brezhnev years Soviet views would become more pessimistic in this regard.

Notes

1. *Dokumenti mezhdunarodnogo sobeschaniya kommunisticheskikh i rabochikh partii* (Politizdat, Moscow, 1969), p. 33.

2. V.M. Kulish (ed.), *Voyennaya sila i mezhdunarodniye otnosheniya* (Izdatel'stvo 'Mezhdunarodniye Otnosheniya', Moscow, 1972), p. 47. At the time this book was written, Kulish was a retired Soviet military officer. This volume was written under the auspices of the Institute of World Economy and International Relations (IMEMO), making it a part of Party/civilian literature, and not military. The significance of this book will be discussed later in this chapter.

3. Colonel G. Malinovskiy, 'Lokal'niye voini v zone natsional'no-osvoboditel'nogo dvizheniya', *Voyenno-Istoricheskiy Zhurnal*, no. 5, May 1974, p. 97. In the final sentence, Malinovskiy quoted from the 1969 conference cited above (see note 1).

4. General of the Army I. Shavrov, 'Lokal'niye voini i ikh mesto v globalnoy strategii imperializma' (part 1), *Voyenno-Istoricheskiy Zhurnal*, no. 3, March 1975, p. 61.

5. See Colonel Ye. Rybkin, 'Voini sovremennoy epokhi i ikh vliyaniye na sotsial'niye protsessi', *Kommunist Vooruzhennykh Sil*, no. 11, June 1970, pp. 9-16, and Colonel Ye. Rybkin, 'Leninskiye printsipi sotsiologicheskogo analiza

voin i sovremennost',' in Major General A.S. Milovidov and Colonel V.G. Kozlov (eds.), *Filosofskoye naslediye V.I. Lenina i problemi sovremennoy voini* (Voyenizdat, Moscow, 1972), pp. 31-52.

6. Rybkin, 'Voini sovremennoy epokhi i ikh vliyaniye na sotsial'niye protsessi', p. 12.

7. Rybkin, 'Leninskiye printsipi sotsiologicheskogo analiza voin i sovremennost'', p. 46.

8. Rybkin, 'Voini sovremennoy epokhi i ikh vliyaniye na sotsial'niye protsessi', p. 13.

9. Rybkin, 'Leninskiye printsipi sotsiologicheskogo analiza voin i sovremennost'', pp. 46-7.

10. Colonel Ye. Rybkin, 'Leninskaya kontseptsiya voini i sovremennost'', *Kommunist Vooruzhennykh Sil*, no. 20, October 1973, pp. 24-5.

11. Lt. Colonel N. Khmara, 'Nekotoriye osobennosti grazhdanskikh voin v sovremennuyu epokhu', *Kommunist Vooruzhennykh Sil*, no. 16, August 1971, pp. 17-18.

12. Ibid., pp. 23-4.

13. Malinovskiy, 'Lokal'niye voini v zone natsional'no-osvoboditel'nogo dvizheniya', p. 93.

14. Ibid., pp. 94-5.

15. Ibid., p. 95.

16. Lt. Colonel T. Kondratkov, 'Organichennaya voina – orudiye imperialisticheskoy agressi', *Kommunist Vooruzhennykh Sil*, no. 8, April 1969, pp. 25, 30; and Colonel T. Kondratkov, 'Problema klassifikatsii voin i ee otrazheniye v ideologicheskoy bor'be', *Kommunist Vooruzhennykh Sil*, no. 11, June 1974, pp. 20-4.

17. Kondratkov, 'Problema klassifikatsii voin i ee otrazheniye v ideologicheskoy bor'be', p. 20.

18. Shavrov, 'Lokal'niye voini i ikh mestolv globalnoy strategii imperializma', p. 62.

19. Ibid., p. 63.

20. Ibid., pp. 62-3.

21. See Colonel V. Serelrayannikov and Colonel M. Yasyukov, 'Mirnoye sosushchestvovaniye i zashchita sotsialisticheskogo otechestva', *Kommunist Vooruzhennykh Sil*, no. 16, August 1972, p. 10; M. Avakov and S. Chernichenko, 'Zhizennaya sila leninskikh printsipov mirnogo sosushchestvovaniya', *Kommunist Vooruzhennykh Sil*, no. 23, December 1973, p. 25; and Colonel D. Volkogonov, 'The Ideological Struggle at the Present State', *Voyennaya Mysl'*, no. 12, December 1973, FBIS FPD 0048, pp. 16-17.

22. Serelrayannikov and Yasyukov, 'Mirnoye sosushchestvovaniye i zashchita sotsialisticheskogo otechestva', pp. 15-16.

23. Colonel N. Vetrov, 'Problems of War and Peace and the World Revolutionary Process', *Voyennaya Mysl'*, no. 8, August 1971, FBIS FPD 0011/74, p. 18.

24. Charles C. Petersen, 'Third World Military Elites in Soviet Perspective', Center for Naval Analyses Professional Paper 262, November 1979, p. 19.

25. Colonel Ye. Dolgopolov, 'Razvivayushchiyesya strani Azii, Afriki i Latinskoy Ameriki', *Kommunist Vooruzhennykh Sil*, no. 16, August 1973, pp. 72-9; P. Golub, 'Revolyutsiya i demokratizatsiya armii', *Voyenno-Istoricheskiy Zhurnal*, no. 3, March 1974, pp. 3-13; and Colonel Ye. Dolgopolov, 'Armii razvivayushchiksya stran i politika', *Kommunist Vooruzhennykh Sil*, no. 6, March 1975, pp. 76-81.

26. See Ye. S. Sherr (ed.), *Somali v bor'be za sotsialisticheskuyu orientatsiyu* (Nauka, Moscow, 1974), pp. 211-17; A. Trepetov, 'Latinskaya Amerika: revolyutsionniy protsess i vooruzhenniye sili', *Kommunist*, no. 2, January 1974,

pp. 124-7; and A.E. Shul'govskiy, 'Ideologicheskiye i teoreticheskiye aspekti revolyutsionnogo protsess v Peru', *Latinskaya Amerika*, no. 4, July-August 1975, pp. 8-28.

27. See Georgiy Mirskiy, *Armiya i politika v stranakh Azii i Afriki* (Nauka, Moscow, 1970), esp. pp. 320-41; Z. Tikhmenev, 'Leninizm i revolyutsionniy protsess v Latinskoy Amerike', *Kommunist*, no. 3, February 1971, pp. 114-19; and A. Bel'skiy, 'Natsional'no-osvoboditel'naya revolyutsiya: zakonomernosti i perspektivi', *Aziya i Afrika Segodnya*, no. 3, March 1975, p. 29. See also Petersen, 'Third World Military Elites', pp. 25-30. Petersen portrayed pessimism about Third World military regimes as being limited primarily to Mirskiy while most of the Party was optimistic about them, as was the Soviet military. It appears to me, though, that more of the Party shared Mirskiy's view than Petersen indicated.

28. See Gabor Kartsag, 'O razvitii revolyutsionnogo protsessa v Latinskoy Amerike', *Latinskaya Amerika*, no. 1, January-February 1972, pp. 6-24, and I. Rybalkin, 'Chiliyskiy opit: obshchiye zakonomernosti i svoeobraziye revolyutsionnogo protsessa', *Kommunist*, no. 8, May 1972, pp. 120-7.

29. L.L. Kruglov (ed.), *Vooruzhennaya bor'ba narodov Afriki za svobodu i nezavisimost'* (Nauka, Moscow, 1974), pp. 64-6.

30. Colonel V. Andrianov, 'Partizanskaya voina i voyennaya strategiya', *Voyenno-Istoricheskiy Zhurnal*, no. 7, July 1975, p. 29.

31. Ibid., p. 32.

32. Ibid., p. 31.

33. Captain 1st Rank I. Potapov, 'Evolutsiya strategicheskikh kontseptsiy imperializma v poslevoyenniy period', *Voyenno-Istoricheskiy Zhurnal*, no. 5, May 1971, pp. 42-50.

34. See Lt. Colonel T. Kondratkov, 'Organichennaya voina – orudiye imperialisticheskoy agressi', p. 28; Major General V. Zemskov, 'Characteristic Features of Modern Wars and Possible Methods of Conducting Them', *Voyennaya Mysl'*, no. 7, July 1969, CIA FP FPD 0022/70, p. 25; V. Perfilov, 'Limited Warfare in U.S. Foreign Policy', *Voyennaya Mysl'*, no. 4, April 1971, FBIS FPD 0019/74, pp. 108-11; and Lt. Colonel D. Volkogonov, 'The Moral Factor in Local War', *Voyennaya Mysl'*, no. 12, December 1971, FBIS FPD 0003/74, pp. 26-7.

35. Captain 1st Rank I. Potapov, 'Morskiye desantnyiye sili SShA v poslevoyenniy period', *Voyenno-Istoricheskiy Zhurnal*, no. 1, January 1973, p. 46.

36. I.M. Korotkin, Z.F. Slepenkov and B.A. Kolyzayev, *Avianostsy i vertolet-onostsy* (Voyenizdat, Moscow, 1972), Ch. VIII.

37. See Colonel A. Krasnov and Lt. Colonel A. Koryuk, 'Primeneniye aviatsiy v lokal'nikh voinakh', *Voyenno-Istoricheskiy Zhurnal*, no. 8, August 1972, pp. 87-92; Colonel V. Babich, 'Strategicheskaya aviatsiya i takticheskiye zadachi', *Aviatsiya i Kosmonavtika*, no. 2, February 1974, pp. 46-7; and Colonel V. Babich, 'Taktika ognevogo vozdeystviya', *Aviatsiya i Kosmonavtika*, no. 9, September 1975, pp. 46-7.

38. Colonel S. Tyushkhevich, 'Politicheskiye tseli i kharakter voini', *Kommunist Vooruzhennykh Sil*, no. 7, April 1969, p. 37; and Rybkin, 'Voini sovremennoy epokhi i ikh vliyaniye na sotsial'niye protsessi', p. 16.

39. See Khmara, 'Nekotoriye osobennosti grazhdanskikh voin v sovremennuyu epokhu', p. 23; Colonel A. Leont'yev, 'Istoricheskaya pobeda V'etnama', *Kommunist Vooruzhennykh Sil*, no. 6, March 1973, p. 84; Dolgopolov, 'Razvivayushchiyesya strani Azii, Afriki i Latinskoy Ameriki', p. 79; Dolgopolov, 'Armii razvivayushchiksya stran i politika', pp. 76-81; and Captain 2nd Rank Yu. Morozov, 'Klassoviy kharakter sovetskoy vneshney politiki', *Kommunist Vooruzhennykh Sil*, no. 19, October 1975, p. 14.

40. Malinovskiy, 'Lokal'niye voini v zone natsional'no-osvoboditel'nogo

dvizheniya' p. 98.

41. Sergei G. Gorshkov, *Red Star Rising at Sea* (US Naval Institute, Annapolis, Md., 1974), p. 134.

42. For an analysis of the significance of Gorshkov's work, see Michael MccGwire, 'The Rationale for the Development of Soviet Seapower', *US Naval Institute Proceedings,* 106:5 (May 1980), pp. 173-9.

43. See John A. Marcum, *The Angolan Revolution,* vol. 2 (MIT Press, Cambridge, Mass., 1978), Ch. 6.

44. See V. Rumyantsev, 'Arabskiy vostok na novom puti', *Kommunist,* no. 16, November 1969, pp. 90-101; D. Kunayev, 'V.I. Lenin i natsional'no-osvoboditel'noye dvizheniye', *Kommunist,* no. 17, November 1969, pp. 50-60; V. Solodovnikov, 'Leninizm i osvobozhdayushchayasya Afrika', *Mirovaya Ekonomika i Mezhdunarodniye Otnosheniya (MEiMO),* no. 4, April 1970, pp. 67-78; S. Tikhvinskiy, 'Klyucheviye problemi sovremennogo natsional'no-osvoboditel'nogo dvizheniya', *Kommunist,* no. 16, November 1972, pp. 110-12; V. Tyagunenko, 'Mirovoy sotsializm i natsional'no-osvoboditel'niye revolyutsii', *Kommunist,* no. 8, May 1973, pp. 42-54; G. Mirskiy, 'Vazhniye problemi natsional'no-osvoboditel'nogo dvizheniya', *Kommunist,* no. 9, June 1974, pp. 124-8; and A. Kiva, 'Aziya i Afrika: glubokiye peremeni', *Aziya i Afrika Segodnya,* no. 11, November 1975, pp. 18-22.

45. See Ye. Zhukov, 'Natsional'no-osvoboditel'noye dvizheniye narodov Azii i Afriki', *Kommunist,* no. 4, March 1969, p. 34; R. Ul'yanovskiy, 'Osvoboditel'naya bor'ba narodov Afriki', *Kommunist,* no. 11, July 1969, p. 40; Boris Ponomarev, 'Mezhdunarodnoye znacheniye obrazovaniya i razvitiya SSSR', *Problemi Mira i Sotsializma,* no. 10, October 1972, p. 8; Petr I. Manchkha, *Avangardniye otryadi revolyutsionnoy bor'bi v Afrike* (Politizdat, Moscow, 1971), pp. 47-8; and L.D. Yablochkov, *Printsipy vneshney politiki afrikanskhikh gosudarvst* (Nauka, Moscow, 1974), pp. 205-7.

46. See Mikhail Suslov, 'Leninizm i sovremennaya epokha', *Problemi Mira i Sotsializma,* no. 5, May 1969, p. 14; R. Ul'yanovskiy, 'Nekotoriye voprosi nekapitalisticheskogo razvitiya', *Kommunist,* no. 4, March 1971, pp. 103-12; and Ye. S. Troitskiy and V.D. Agafonov, 'Ideologiya sovremennoy revolyutsionnoy demokratii', *Nauchniy Kommunizm,* no. 4, 1973, pp. 55-64.

47. T. Deych, '"Noviy kurs" Pekina i Afriki', *MEiMO,* no. 2, February 1974, pp. 39-49; V.G. Dolgin, 'Mirnoye sosushchestvovaniye i faktori ego uglubleniya i razvitya', *Voprosy Filosofii,* no. 1, 1974, p. 67; A. Krasil'nikov, 'Politika Pekina i razvivayushchiyesya strani', *Aziya i Afrika Segodnya,* no. 1, January 1975, pp. 44-7; and L. Shurin, 'Solidarnost' po-pekinski', *Aziya i Afrika Segodnya,* no. 2, February 1975, pp. 38-40.

48. See V. Khvostov, 'V.I. Lenin o printsipakh vneshney politiki sovetskogo gosudarstva', *Kommunist,* no. 9, June 1969, pp. 79-89; V. Stepanov, 'Mirovaya sistema sotsializma – vedushchaya revolyutsionnaya sila sovremennosti', *Kommunist,* no. 10, July 1969, p. 27; D. Tomashevskiy, 'Leninskiy printsip mirnogo sosushchestvovaniya i klassovaya bor'ba', *Kommunist,* no. 12, August 1970, pp. 108-10; Professor G. Tunkin, 'Leninskiy printsip mirnogo sosushchestvovaniya i ego protivniki', *Pravda,* October 9, 1970; V.V. Zagladin (ed.), *Mezhdunarodnoye kommunisticheskoye dvizheniye* (Politizdat, Moscow, 1970), pp. 123-33; V.V. Kortunov, 'Mirnoye sosushchestvovaniye i ideologicheskaya bor'ba', *Voprosy Istorii KPSS,* no. 7, 1972, p. 66; 'Mirnoye sosushchestvovaniye gosudarstv i klassovaya bor'ba', *Problemi Mira i Sotsializma,* no. 3, March 1974, pp. 40-1, 43; S.L. Agayev, 'Razryadka mezhdunarodnoy napryazhennosti i kommunisticheskoye dvizheniye', *Rabochiy Klass i Sovremenniy Mir,* July-August 1974, p. 24; and Boris Ponomarev, 'Rol' sotsializma v sovremennom mirovom razvitii', *Problemi Mira i Sotsializma,* no. 1, January 1975, p. 5.

49. L.I. Brezhnev, 'Kommunisticheskoye dvizheniye vstupilo v polosu novogo pod"ema', *Problemi Mira i Sotsializma*, no. 8, August 1969, p. 8; L.I. Brezhnev, *Leninskim kursom: rechi i stat'i*, vol. 3 (Politizdat, Moscow, 1972), p. 218; Boris Ponomarev, 'Slavnaya godovshchina v istorii kommunisticheskogo dvizheniya', *Problemi Mira i Sotsializma*, no. 2, February 1969, p. 16; 'Leninskaya vneshnyaya politika sovetskogo soyuza', *Kommunist*, no. 14, September 1970, p. 12; G. Drambyants, 'Politika internatsional'noy solidarnost'', *Kommunist*, no. 5, March 1972, pp. 84-95; Valeria Benke, 'Sovetskiy Soyuz s chest'yu vipolyaet internatsional'niy dolg', *Kommunist*, no. 17, November 1972, pp. 47-8; I.V. Dudinskiy, 'Internatsional'niye i natsional'niye interesi sotsialisticheskikh gosudarstv', *Voprosy Filosofii*, no. 10, 1973, p. 70; and A.A. Gromyko, 'Predisloviye', in I.D. Ovsyaniy *et al.*, *Vneshnyaya politika sovetskogo soyuza* (Politizdat, Moscow, 1975), p. 14.

50. Kulish, *Voyennaya sila i mezhdunarodniye otnosheniya*, pp. 136-9.

51. Ibid., pp. 7-8.

52. C.G. Jacobsen, *Soviet Strategic Initiatives: Challenge and Response* (Praeger, New York, 1979), pp. 15-16.

4   THE LATE BREZHNEV YEARS: 1976-1981

During the late Brezhnev years, détente with the United States reached its limits, as symbolised by the refusal of the Senate to ratify the SALT II treaty, forcing President Carter to withdraw it from consideration. Soviet-American relations began to take on a more confrontational edge. In addition, the Sino-Soviet rift remained even after Mao Tse-tung died in 1976 and more pragmatic leadership came to power. Further, that the PRC had moved closer to the United States and the West was evidenced by the normalisation of relations between Washington and Peking and the signing of the Sino-Japanese Treaty of Friendship and Co-operation. Yet while Moscow's relations with its two major opponents worsened, and relations between those opponents improved, the Soviet Union appeared to be making spectacular foreign policy gains in the Third World. Following close on the victory of the MPLA in Angola through Soviet and Cuban support, the USSR and Cuba aided Marxist Ethiopia in defeating the Somali attempt to acquire the Ogaden and the Eritrean effort to separate from the rest of Ethiopia. The USSR's ally, Vietnam, invaded Kampuchea, drove out the Pol Pot government that had been allied to China, and set up the Heng Samrin government in Phnom Penh. The Iranian revolution overthrew an important American ally on the USSR's southern border. A Marxist coup took place in Afghanistan, and when domestic insurgency threatened to topple it, the Soviet Union sent 85,000 soldiers to prop up the Kabul government. Even as geographically close to the United States as Central America, the Marxist Sandinistas overthrew a government allied to the US in Nicaragua. By 1981, civil war raged in El Salvador and threatened to do so in Guatemala and Honduras too. Finally, the Soviet Union signed treaties of friendship and co-operation during this period with Angola, Ethiopia, Mozambique, Afghanistan, South Yemen, Syria and (in May 1981) the Congo.

However, the Soviet Union also suffered serious setbacks in the Third World during this period. Both Egypt and Somalia abrogated their treaties of friendship and co-operation earlier signed with Moscow, and both became allies of Washington. The four conflicts in which either Soviet allies or the Soviet Union itself have become involved in actual combat (Angola, Ethiopia, Cambodia and Afghanistan) have not yet ended. Large numbers of Cuban troops are still in Angola fighting UNITA and in Ethiopia fighting Somalis. Vietnam has eliminated neither the Khmer Rouge nor other Cambodian insurgent groups. The USSR itself has become bogged down in a guerrilla war in Afghanistan which the Soviets do not appear likely to win in the near future. The Iranian revolution has given rise to Islamic fundamentalism; while the Iranian government is anti-American, it is also strongly anti-Soviet and anti-communist. The guerrilla war in Zimbabwe, through which the Soviet Union hoped a Marxist government would come to power, was settled relatively peacefully. Indeed, Zimbabwe's constitutionally elected government led by the former guerrilla leader Robert Mugabe has been distinctly unfriendly to the USSR. The USSR has also lost allies in Peru, Uganda and Guinea-Bissau. Finally, events in Latin America have led the United States to become somewhat more assertive than it has been since the end of the Vietnam war; a small number of American military advisers have been sent to El Salvador, along with a large amount of military aid, to help defeat the Marxist guerrillas there.

Although the Soviet Union became more directly involved in Third World conflicts during this period than it was at any time previously, it was apparent that even this increased level of involvement was not sufficient to fully achieve Soviet goals. Angola, Ethiopia, Cambodia and Afghanistan have not yet been subdued. Instead of serving as stepping stones to further conquests, these conflicts have served primarily to drain the resources of the USSR and its allies. The Marxist regimes in these countries maintain their power only through the presence of large numbers of troops from other communist powers. Without this external support, it is doubtful any of them could remain in power for long. Thus, the armed forces of the USSR, Cuba and Vietnam are, in effect, trapped in these conflicts for a prolonged period since their withdrawal would probably mean the collapse of the local Marxist governments.

In these later years of the Brezhnev era, then, it is not surprising that a note of pessimism has entered into both military and Party/civilian thinking about conflict in the Third World. Particularly pessimistic has been their assessment of the ability of a Third World nation that has entered onto the path of socialist development to maintain that path. Since the time of the Iranian revolution and the Afghan war, there has arisen the fear that the forces of change in the Third World are not the natural friends of the USSR as had earlier been assumed, but perhaps the Soviet Union's natural enemies.

The Relationship of Local War to World War

Acceptance of the idea that the Soviet Union was becoming more able to prevent local wars from escalating into world war through increasing Soviet military might was signalled through its expression by Colonel G. Malinovskiy in a volume of the *Sovetskaya voyennaya entsiklopediya* published in 1978:

> The tendency toward the broadening of the scale of local war and the intensification of the struggle in them increases the danger of transforming local war into world war. At the same time, with the growth of the economic and military might of the countries of the socialist commonwealth, grows the possibility of preventing the transformation of local wars into a conflict of worldwide scale.[1]

It must be emphasised that the Soviet military never proclaimed that local war would under no circumstances become a world war. The danger of escalation still existed. However, the growing military might of socialism was a key factor in preventing the growth of local war into world war.

The Soviet position that local war could be prevented from becoming world war was very close to the position that as late as 1969 the Soviets had criticised the Chinese for having.[2] The intervening decade saw both the Soviets and the Chinese change their earlier positions on the question of world war. In 1979, Major General S. Tyushkevich (one of the editors of the later editions of *Marksizm-Leninizm o voine i armii*) criticised the Chinese not for saying that world war was impossible, but for saying that it was inevitable.[3] During the 1950s and 1960s, the Chinese had seen national liberation struggles as something that would benefit the PRC by driving American influence from the Third World while the USSR feared them due to the possibility of their provoking a larger Soviet-American conflict. In the 1970s, China often opposed such local conflicts that were now seen as benefiting the Soviet Union, whereas the USSR favoured them for the same reason. After Vietnam, neither the USSR nor China saw the United States as playing an aggressive role in the Third World.

In admitting the possibility that local war could still grow into world war, the Soviet military recognised that a local conflict in which the United States and the Soviet Union directly confronted each other could escalate. At no time has the Soviet military expressed a willingness to confront the US itself in the Third World. Where the US did not become involved, though, the Soviet Union now had a greater ability both to become involved militarily and to keep the conflict localised. Thus, the escalation of local war to world war was not inevitable. In contrast to the 1960s, when the possibility of local war growing into world war was emphasised as the US became more militarily involved in Third World conflicts and the USSR less so, now the possibility of keeping local wars localised was emphasised when the US was less involved in Third World conflicts and the USSR was more so.

The Nature and Types of Conflict in the Third World

The acceptance of the classification of the nature and types of war made by General of the Army Shavrov in 1975 could be seen in an article on the classification of wars by Colonel Malinovskiy and Colonel Rybkin that appeared in the *Sovetskaya voyennaya entsiklopediya*. Both of these writers had made innovative, though somewhat differing contributions to the development of the classification of wars previously. In this article, the categories of wars between equal nations and civil wars between the people and a regime of extreme reaction were mentioned.[4] In addition, the classification of wars both by ideological and non-ideological factors simultaneously was discussed. Non-ideological factors specifically cited were scale (world or local), means of armed struggle (nuclear or conventional), duration (short or protracted), and conduct of military operations (war of manoeuvre or war of positioning).[5]

Soviet military thinking about the nature and types of war, however, did not stop here. In 1978, Colonel Rybkin introduced yet another type of war into the system of ideologically based categories. This new type of war was a war of a nation on the path of socialist development in defence of socialism. This category referred to Third World nations such as Angola, Ethiopia and Afghanistan which had experienced Marxist revolutions and were beginning to develop socialism, but which faced internal and/or external military opposition.[6]

This new category of war differed from the existing six in several important respects. It was not a national liberation war since the unjust side was not one of the major imperialist states fighting to retain a colony or to conquer a Third World nation. Although the major imperialists might support this conflict, the main opponents were local forces based internally or externally. Yet these wars were not civil wars either. Civil wars between the bourgeoisie and the proletariat were seen as taking place in the developed capitalist nations; neither a developed bourgeoisie nor a developed proletariat existed in Third World nations. Rybkin did not see the category of civil wars between the people and a regime of extreme reaction as applicable here either. This was not a case of the people fighting against a right-wing dictatorship. Instead, internal and external groups were fighting against a left-wing dictatorship. They were not wars between and within Third World nations either since these were wars in defence of socialism against internal and external opponents backed by imperialism; in these there was no question about which side was just. And yet even though these were wars in defence of socialism, Rybkin did not elevate them to the category of wars between opposing social systems. By not doing so, Rybkin indicated that the USSR was not willing to risk escalating such conflicts into world war, as the category of war between opposing social systems implied. Thus, although these were wars in defence of socialism, they were fought only by nations on the path of socialist development; these were not fully-fledged socialist nations whose socialist form of government the USSR was more strongly committed to protect, as in Eastern Europe.

This new category of war reflected the fact that for the first time since the German invasion of the USSR in the Second World War and the UN drive north of the 38th parallel in the Korean War, socialist forces were fighting a kind of war in which, instead of being on the offensive, they were on the defensive. It did not matter that the forces of socialism may at one time have been on the offensive, nor that the defence of socialism involved an offensive Soviet military action, as in Afghanistan. The fact remained that Marxist governments had been established in Angola, Ethiopia, Cambodia and Afghanistan, but that each of them faced armed opposition. In Angola, UNITA continues to fight against the MPLA government. Ethiopia faces opposition not only from Somali-backed rebels in the Ogaden, but also from Eritrean rebels and liberation movements in some of the provinces of Ethiopia proper. The Vietnamese have been unable to defeat both the socialist and non-socialist guerrilla forces in Cambodia. The Marxist government in Afghanistan faces strong Moslem opposition which even the intervention of 85,000 Soviet soldiers has failed to crush. In each of these wars, Marxist governments are on the defensive, though their primary opponents are not the major Western powers (despite all Soviet claims to the contrary), but indigenous forces within the Third World itself. Even though the formulation of this new category of wars of nations on the path of socialist development in defence of socialism was an innovation on Rybkin's part, surely he and the rest of the Soviet military would have preferred this type of war not to occur at all.

Yet while Soviet military thinkers did acknowledge this new type of conflict which they undoubtedly would have preferred not to see occur, there was another type of conflict that they would not acknowledge at all. It was stated earlier that the Soviet military did not regard as possible that both sides in a conflict could be just. Because of this, two socialist states would never fight each other. However, in 1978 socialist Vietnam invaded socialist Cambodia, and in 1979 Vietnam fought a brief war with the People's Republic of China.

The Vietnamese invasion of Cambodia did not cause an ideological problem for the Soviets since Cambodia under Pol Pot was not regarded as a socialist state by Moscow. It was not regarded as one under Heng Samrin either; at the 26th CPSU Congress, Brezhnev described both Vietnam and Laos as countries belonging to the socialist community, but not Cambodia.[7] Cambodia appeared to be a nation that was on the path of socialist development under the Heng Samrin government; under Pol Pot, Cambodia had not even achieved this state, and so there was no question of there having been a war between two socialist states.

The war between Vietnam and China was different, though, since the Soviet Union had in the past acknowledged China as a socialist state. Thus it was for this reason that the Sino-Vietnamese war of 1979 provoked a denial on the part of Major General Tyushkevich that this conflict was an example of a war between socialist states. Peking's attack on Vietnam proved to him that China could no longer be considered socialist:

> It is no secret that China's unprovoked aggression against socialist Vietnam gave bourgeois propaganda an excuse for a broad campaign with the objective of 'proving' that wars are born not only of imperialism, but also of socialism. But this ideological diversion is built on sand. The truth is that socialism, both as a teaching and as a political system, cannot bear responsibility for the attack on Vietnam by Chinese forces. This aggression was prepared and carried out by Peking for the sake of anti-socialist, great power predatory goals and was sanctified by the ideology of chauvinism, great power politics and hegemonism, which is alien to Marxism-Leninism.[8]

Yet while Tyushkhevich was insistent that this was not an example of a war between socialist states, he did not specify what type of conflict the Sino-Vietnamese war actually was. It would be interesting to speculate on what category he might have put it in. It did not belong to either of the two types of civil war or to the category of war between imperialist states. It was not a war between 'equal' Third World nations either, since Vietnam was a socialist nation and was unambiguously the just side in Soviet eyes. Since Vietnam was already a full-fledged socialist state, this would exclude the war from being classified in Rybkin's new category of wars of nations on the path toward socialist development in defence of socialism. The category of war between opposing social systems did not seem to apply either; while China's goals might be anti-socialist, its social system could not be called capitalist. In any event, the Soviet Union made it obvious that it would not raise the level of conflict, as this category called for, by attacking China in order to protect Vietnam. The one remaining category, wars of national liberation, would appear more applicable than all the others, but this category was meant to describe the struggle between a weak underdeveloped nation against an advanced capitalist state; China was clearly not the latter. Although Tyushkevich would disagree strongly, the category of war between socialist states appears to most accurately describe the type of conflict that Vietnam and China engaged in. However, whatever category of conflict this was, it was also a type that the Soviets would definitely have preferred not to take place at all.

Two things are noteworthy about the Soviet military view of the nature and types of conflict in the Third World during the late Brezhnev years. First, ideological factors remained highly important in the discussion of the types of conflict that were occurring. Rybkin's new category of wars of nations on the path of socialist development in defence of socialism was more purely class based than his earler innovation of wars between and within Third World nations. Though non-ideological factors played a greater role now in defining the nature and types of wars than they did in the early Brezhnev years, non-ideological factors by no means displaced ideological ones, but were complementary to them instead. Even then, ideological factors remained of primary importance.

Second, the late Brezhnev years saw types of conflict emerge in which the socialist community led by the USSR was defending, instead of expanding, its existing position. Both wars of nations on the path of socialist development in defence of socialism and wars between socialist states (the latter, of course, were not acknowledged as existing) showed that the socialist community faced internal and external opponents in addition to the major imperialist nations. Indeed, these types of conflict demonstrated that the socialist world was subject to the same kind of centrifugal forces that the Soviets had thought were present only within the imperialist world. Yugoslavia, China, Albania, and even Romania on some issues had all been examples of socialist nations rejecting Soviet leadership, though remaining socialist. Now, however, socialism itself was facing military conflict with non-Marxist forces in the Third World. Further, these non-Marxist forces were not being defeated. This was a trend which the Soviet military certainly did not regard with optimism.

Peaceful Coexistence

The Soviet military continued to hold the same view of peaceful co-existence during the late Brezhnev years that it developed during the middle Brezhnev years.[9] Reducing the threat of nuclear war with the United States through peaceful coexistence was not viewed as incompatible with Soviet support (even military support) for wars of national and social liberation. Further, peaceful coexistence was a useful means of discouraging the United States from exporting counter-revolution, though if the US did become involved in a Third World conflict, the USSR would not give up the benefits of peaceful coexistence in Soviet-American bilateral relations.

During this period, Soviet military thinkers objected to American charges that the USSR was using peaceful coexistence in order to lull the United States into a false sense of security while it exported revolution to the Third World. The 'export of revolution' by the USSR was denied vehemently by the Soviets, although Soviet military assistance to wars of national and social liberation was at the same time admitted.[10] Indeed, one writer went to such lengths to assert that the USSR never exported revolution that he insisted that even in Eastern Europe after World War II socialist revolutions were carried out by indigenous local forces; the Red Army present in these countries played only a minor role ensuring that the imperialists did not intervene to assist the counter-revolutionaries.[11] The statement that the USSR did not export revolution to Eastern Europe, being false, did not give credibility to statements that the USSR was not exporting revolution to the Third World now. In general, though, the point that the Soviet military wanted to make was that even when the USSR became involved in a Third World conflict, the USSR did not cause the conflict; instead, the cause of the conflict was in the local situation. While they may not have caused the conflict, this did not mean that the Soviets would refrain from assisting the progressive forces by military means.

Finally, peaceful coexistence was seen not only as providing the possibility of socialist gains in the Third World, but also as having concretely done so. In February 1979, Major General D. Volkogonov viewed peaceful coexistence as having blocked to some extent American interests in the Third World while at the same time as having furthered Soviet interests:

> Stepping forth as peaceful competition between the two systems, peaceful coexistence permits restructuring and blocking to a certain extent the manifestations of the chief reasons for wars of modern times which is rooted in the economic depths of the exploiter system.
>
> At the same time, it is known that Marxist-Leninists do not come out against all and any wars in general, but only against aggressive, imperialist wars. Peaceful coexistence does not mean 'prohibiting' revolutionary, civil wars of workers for social liberation or national liberation wars against imperialist aggression. The Soviet Union's decisive support of socialist Vietnam, revolutionary Ethiopia, people's democratic Yemen, new Angola, and the progressive forces of Kampuchea in no way contradicts our adherence to a policy of peaceful coexistence despite what our class enemies sometimes declare.[12]

In June 1979, B. Vesnin expressed the idea that a direct relation existed between peaceful coexistence and socialist success in Third World conflicts:

> Revolutionary and democratic forces have succeeded in achieving new and significant successes under conditions of détente. The war of the Vietnamese peoples against US imperialism ended in victory. The Vietnamese people not only became totally free but also succeeded in reuniting their country. The socialist revolution in Laos was victorious. The people of Kampuchea became liberated first from reactionary pro-American forces and subsequently from the tyrannical pro-Peking regime of the Pol Pot clique as well.[13]

In sum, Soviet military thinkers regarded peaceful coexistence not only as a means through which it was possible for socialism to make gains through Soviet military support of groups it favoured in Third World conflicts, but also as a policy through which socialism, with the aid of the USSR, had actually succeeded in making such gains, as well as avoiding a wider confrontation with the United States. Co-operating with the United States in reducing the possibility of a world war between the two superpowers (a policy that both the US and the USSR had an equal interest in pursuing) did not mean that the Soviet Union would refrain from supporting militarily groups it favoured in Third World conflicts. Indeed, it was the reduction of the likelihood of world war through peaceful coexistence that made Soviet involvement in local conflicts less risk prone. Further, while the Soviet Union, of course, opposed American involvement in Third World conflicts, such involvement was not necessarily regarded as incompatible with peaceful coexistence in other aspects of Soviet-American relations, such as co-operation in arms control and other bilateral issues.

Indigenous Third World Forces

At the beginning of this latest period of the Brezhnev era, the difference of opinion persisted between civilian and military writers over the reliability of radical Third World military regimes in maintaining their nations on the path of socialist development. In 1976, G. Mirskiy published another book expressing deep pessimism about radical Third World military regimes, and describing Marxist-Leninist parties as the surest instruments for maintaining socialism.[14] The same year, Colonel Ye. Dolgopolov, one of the most vocal military advocates of Soviet support to radical Third World military regimes, criticised Mirskiy as having written an 'unsatisfactory book', and stated that progressive military elements could exercise revolutionary power for a relatively prolonged period of time.[15] The military was still optimistic about them at this point.

However, with the dramatic abrogation in 1977 of the Soviet-Somali Treaty of Friendship and Co-operation that had been signed only in 1974 by the 'progressive' Somali military regime following a similar action by Egypt in 1976, as well as the *volte-face* of the Peruvian military regime which had up to then been friendly with the USSR, the Soviet military became considerably less optimistic about the ability of radical Third World military regimes to maintain socialism in their countries. Soon after these events, even Colonel Dolgopolov stressed the importance of developing vanguard parties in the Third World since radical Third World armies could not substitute for them.[16] Neither military nor civilian writers would ever again express such optimism about progressive military regimes. Strong emphasis was placed on the need for vanguard parties to rule in socialist Third World countries in order for socialism to survive in them.[17] Without a vanguard party in power, the revolutionary gains made in Third World countries could easily be lost. Because of this, the Marxist government of Ethiopia has come under Soviet pressure to transform its government based on a radical military into one based on a vanguard party.[18] So far, the Ethiopian government has resisted this, and has only formed a centre for the study of the creation of a Marxist-Leninist party. This is undoubtedly a disappointment to the Soviets, who do not wish to see Ethiopia follow the path of Egypt and Somalia.

With regard to guerrilla armies, while Soviet military thinkers came to approve of them under the direction of a Marxist-Leninist party, their approval did not extend to guerrilla armies without such leadership, or guerrilla armies that dominated the socialist parties supposed to be in control of them. In March 1979, one military author described unguided guerrilla armies as a form of Maoism:

> Mao Tse-tung and his supporters frequently absolutized a partisan war as practically the only form of people's war . . . In this way the Maoists ignored such an important question for the national liberation movement as the creation of an army of a new type in order to accomplish the tasks facing it. It is appropriate here to recall V.I. Lenin's attitude toward partisan war. He said, 'that never can the party of the proletariat consider a partisan war to be the only or even the chief means of struggle: that this means has to be subordinated to others and has to be commensurate with the chief means of struggle, ennobled by the enlightening and organizing influence of socialism'.[19]

This statement pointed out a problem the USSR faced to a greater extent during the late Brezhnev era than ever before – that guerrilla armies in the Third World either ignored Soviet interests, as in Zimbabwe, or fought directly against them, as in Angola, Ethiopia, Cambodia and Afghanistan. The Soviets had become used to seeing guerrilla armies fight against Western interests (sometimes effectively as in Vietnam, and sometimes not as in Malaya and Oman). A guerrilla leader calling himself Marxist, such as Robert Mugabe, who came to power and promptly ignored the USSR while making overtures to the West must have disappointed the Soviets, who probably envisioned Zimbabwe under the guerrillas as being similar to Angola under the MPLA or Mozambique under FRELIMO. That guerrilla armies, which the USSR had regarded as representing the forces of change, actually fought against established Marxist governments in the Third World must have been disturbing to them indeed – especially since these guerrilla armies were not being defeated. The Soviets tended to see these armies as extensions of imperialism or Maoism, and not as the locally based opposition to Third World Marxist regimes that they were.

However, the Soviets were not pessimistic about all guerrilla armies. In 1980, the journal of the Latin American Institute of the USSR Academy of Sciences gave a highly favourable review of them. What was especially noteworthy was that after the victory of the Sandinistas in Nicaragua, the Soviets have for the first time begun to praise the Cuban revolutionary model in which a Marxist guerrilla army and not a communist party serves as the vanguard force. S.A. Mikoyan, the editor of *Latinskaya Amerika,* concluded in an article expressing the consensus of participants in a discussion of Central America that, 'As yet only the armed path has led to the victory of revolutions in Latin America. And the Nicaraguan experience affirms what had been considered refuted by some after the death of Che Guevara and the defeat of a number of other guerrilla movements.'[20] The reason for this change in the Soviet view of the Cuban revolutionary model was that while the peaceful path to socialism was demonstrated by Chile to be a failure, a revolution similar to the Cuban one for the first time succeeded in another country (Nicaragua), and presented the possibility of success in others as well (most notably in El Salvador). Mikoyan noted, however, that the Cuban model was not the only armed path to socialism and that what might be a vanguard force at one point in time might also become a reactionary force at a later point.[21] This was an admonition that the vanguard guerrilla army must form and surrender authority to a Marxist-Leninist party after coming to power to prevent the army from eventually eroding socialist gains. Thus, there was a note of caution even in the optimistic Soviet assessment of the Nicaraguan revolution.

Much less optimism has been expressed about the Iranian revolution. The Soviets welcomed the revolution in Iran because it overthrew a government closely allied to the United States. This revolution, however, did not follow a pattern that Marxism-Leninism envisioned. Instead of more progressive class-based forces coming to power, the religiously inspired mullahs have come to rule Iran. This has given rise to a mixed assessment of events in Iran. At the 26th Party Congress, Brezhnev described the revolution in Iran as having a 'special' character which was fundamentally anti-imperialist; at the same time he warned that Islam can be a reactionary force as well as a revolutionary one.[22] Colonel Rybkin noted that 'revolutions of the Iranian type . . . are unbelievably complex in their social substance',[23] indicating that he found it extremely difficult to express what had happened in Iran in traditional ideological terms. Increasingly, though, the Soviets have come to condemn the notion of Islamic revolution for being anti-communist in nature.[24] The reason for this is because Islamic forces threaten the existence of the Marxist government of Afghanistan and the allied government of Syria (where the Sunni Moslem Brotherhood is leading widespread opposition against the Alawite and Soviet-oriented Assad government). Further, the danger exists that the ideology of Islamic revolution might spread to the Moslem population of Soviet Central Asia; should Soviet Moslems ever decide to follow the example of their brothers in Iran or Afghanistan, the territorial integrity of the Soviet Union itself would be threatened. Thus, the revolutionary potential of Islamic revivalism that is taking place so near to the USSR is a cause for pessimism rather than optimism to the Soviets.[25]

An important change in the Soviet view of indigenous Third World forces during the late Brezhnev era has been, as Seweryn Bialer has pointed out, the shift in emphasis from non-capitalist development in the Third World at the 23rd and 24th Party Congresses (held in 1966 and 1971 respectively) to an emphasis on socialist development at the 25th Party Congress (held in 1976).[26] This emphasis on socialist development has continued through to the 26th Party Congress (held in 1981).[27] This change reflected the desire of the Soviet leadership to have Third World allies who would more closely follow the foreign policy lead of the Soviet Union. At the same time, this emphasis on socialist development reflected the fact that left-wing Third World governments that were not actually Marxist-Leninist could not be relied upon to do what the USSR desired them to do, or even to remain as Soviet allies for more than a short period of time. This change in emphasis from non-capitalist development to socialist development was also reflected in an article by the important Soviet military theorist Colonel G. Malinovskiy who discussed how the reverses that socialism was experiencing in the Third World could be prevented. Noting that such reverses were occurring, and not even describing them as being temporary, Malinovskiy formulated two conditions that he felt were necessary for the survival of socialism in the Third World: (1) internally, 'the presence in the country of a revolutionary-democratic authority relying on a broad alliance of the working classes', and (2) externally, reliance on 'the comprehensive support of world socialism'.[28]

Ideally, Malinovskiy regarded the fulfilment of the first condition occurring through the formation of a vanguard party:

The convergence of revolutionary democracy with the theory and practise of scientific socialism has become noticeably stronger. This is manifested in particular in the creation of vanguard parties of a new type in a number of countries (Angola, Mozambique, Benin, South Yemen), which base their programs on principles of scientific socialism. Such a party is now being set up in Ethiopia. Meanwhile, experience shows that the evolution of revolutionary democracy toward scientific socialism is a complex, lengthy process which often is accompanied by opposition between its left and right wings.[29]

Of all the radical and revolutionary regimes in the Third World that did not actually belong to the socialist camp, only four were seen as having vanguard parties. Even in Ethiopia, which was so closely allied to the USSR, this condition had not been fulfilled. Further, the evolution of revolutionary democracy was regarded as having many pitfalls; this was hardly an encouraging assessment for the success of other vanguard parties.

The second condition for socialist development in the Third World was reliance on the support of world socialism. This was not only of great importance during the struggle for national and social liberation, but afterward as well through the establishment of treaties of friendship and co-operation:

> There is inestimable importance in the support provided by socialist states to peoples who are forced to fight for their independence or defend it with guns in hand . . . Treaties of friendship and cooperation have been concluded between the Soviet Union and Angola, Afghanistan, India, Iraq, Mozambique, Ethiopia, and South Yemen.[30]

Malinovskiy did not mention that both Egypt and Somalia had abrogated such treaties with the USSR. Even the signature of a treaty of friendship and co-operation, then, did not guarantee that a nation would become fully socialist or remain an ally of the USSR. It was only those nations that fulfilled both conditions which provided the best hope for this. In looking at Malinovskiy's lists of nations that fulfilled each condition, it may be seen that both of them were fulfilled only by Angola, Mozambique and South Yemen (had this article been published only a month later, Afghanistan would also have been described as having a vanguard party and would also have met both conditions). With the Marxist governments of Angola, Ethiopia and Afghanistan all facing strong insurgencies, only two nations — Mozambique and South Yemen — appeared to be securely on the road to socialism (even

Mozambique, though, is fighting a small anti-Marxist insurgency).

Thus, while imperialism was in part responsible for the deviation of Third World nations from the socialist path, internal forces were responsible as well. Indeed, the indigenous Third World opposition to socialism appeared to be an even greater obstacle to Soviet interests in this region than imperialism. With the exception of Nicaragua, about which the Soviets were not completely optimistic, the Soviet view of indigenous forces throughout the Third World became relatively pessimistic. This was in marked contrast to the middle Brezhnev years when the Soviets generally saw indigenous Third World forces as favouring the USSR.

While the Soviets had previously learned that indigenous Third World forces were useful in defeating the interests of the West, they were now becoming aware that Soviet interests would not benefit in the long run unless such movements were brought under Marxist-Leninist control. However, Marxist-Leninist control was difficult both to establish and to maintain since indigenous Third World forces adhered to it of their own volition and could reject it with as little difficulty as they had in adopting it. Hence arises the pessimism with which the Soviets have regarded the willingness of Third World nations on the path of socialism to stay on that path. This pessimism was also in contrast to the optimism with which they regarded peaceful coexistence with the West in allowing the pursuit of Soviet interests in the Third World. But if the West did not present great obstacles to the pursuit of Soviet interests in this region, it was obvious to Soviet military thinkers by the late 1970s that there were indigenous forces within the Third World itself that did.

American Ideas and Actions in Local Wars

During the later years of the Brezhnev era, as during the middle years, the discussion of American ideas about local war virtually ceased. Having accepted that local war could be kept localised instead of escalating into world war, the basis of criticism of American ideas fell away. Instead, the Soviet military focused on American actions in local wars. The trend toward evaluating American actions in Vietnam more in military terms than in ideological terms after the war ended continued in the late Brezhnev years.

One aspect of the Vietnam war that was evaluated differently by Soviet military thinkers after the US withdrew were the factors of time and surprise. Among others, Colonel Rybkin noted during the war that the more prolonged the conflict was, the more likely that domestic unrest in the US would grow making continued prosecution of the war increasingly difficult for the US.[31] Nor did the use of tactical surprise help the imperialists, for, as Lt. Colonel Volkogonov pointed out, the morally superior forces could overcome this:

> Subjected to the effect of new weapons, libertarian forces develop a high capability to stand up against the element of surprise and seek to find effective methods of struggle. In Indochina this has been expressed in the employment of tunnels, night actions, stepped-up military activities in the rainy season, etc.[32]

In short, no matter what the imperialists did militarily, they could not overcome the forces which were just. After the Vietnam war, this view changed. In December 1978, Colonel N. Nikitin described both US operations in the Vietnam war and Israeli operations in the 1973 Middle East War in generally favourable terms. Indeed, he took care to note when their operations had been particularly effective. He said that local wars often began with surprise attacks, but also observed that, 'The longer the war dragged on the stronger the position of the national liberation forces.'[33] The implication made was that if a surprise attack led to immediate victory, surprise could obviously be a crucial factor for an attacker in a local war, whereas if it did not, a prolonged war would become more difficult for an attacker to win.

In April 1979, Major General V. Matsulenko indicated that there was a direct relationship between the effective use of surprise and success in warfare.[34] In this article, he discussed the use of surprise in four instances: by the US in Korea and in Vietnam and by Israel in 1956 and 1967. Matsulenko described Israel as making extremely effective use of surprise both in 1956 and 1967; Israel was also described as having achieved its war aims in 1967 and as being about to do so in 1956 but stopped only by the actions of the Soviet Union.[35] The United States was seen as making only relatively good use of surprise in Korea (really just once at Inchon) and as being only partially successful in this war. Finally, the US was regarded as having made relatively poor use of surprise in Vietnam (indeed, never on a strategic scale at all) and also as having failed to achieve its aims in this conflict. Factors other than sociopolitical ones were now seen to make a difference in the outcome of a conflict. Surprise, then, could be crucial to the outcome, Matsulenko concluded. This was quite different from the belief Volkogonov held during the Vietnam war that the just side could overcome any form of military surprise undertaken by the unjust side.

In addition, while during the Vietnam war the US was seen as failing due to sociopolitical factors, after the war the US was seen as having failed due to military ones, especially the lack of a unified command of the armed forces. In October 1975, Colonel P. Maslennikov wrote that the American failure to consolidate the South Vietnamese and other allied forces under US military command led to immense difficulties in conducting joint operations to the point where the allied forces often worked at cross purposes from one another. He saw the lack of unity of command as greatly contributing to military failure and did not mention sociopolitical factors at all.[36]

In March 1980, Matsulenko made an even stronger statement concluding that unity of command led to success in local wars. Discussing both the Korean and the Vietnam conflicts, he observed that in Korea, the United States established a unified UN (really US) command over all the allied forces. He concluded that, 'On the whole . . . this system for direction of coalition armed forces made it possible to control the military operations of interventionist forces efficiently and rather purposefully . . .'[37] Matsulenko noted, however, that in the allied advance through North Korea, little co-ordination was established between the eastern and western wings of the allied forces, causing great confusion when the socialist forces counterattacked. In general, though, unity of command helped the US achieve many of its goals.

In Vietnam, by contrast, the US was not able to achieve unity of command. While troop control over different branches of American armed forces was effective, Vietnamese and other allied forces were not integrated into the American command. As a result, 'It was constantly necessary to coordinate the joint actions by American and Saigon forces as well as those of other countries allied with the United States, which sometimes took a great deal of time.'[38] In sum, unity of command and troop control by the Americans in Korea was relatively good, and in that conflict the Americans were partially successful; in Vietnam unity of command and troop control was not acheived over all the allied forces, and the Americans failed in this conflict. That these conclusions applied to the Soviet Union as well was indicated by Matsulenko in the final sentence of the article: '. . . a thorough study of the experience of local wars by military cadres . . . will make it possible for them to improve questions of troop control creatively based on scientific-technical progress'.[39]

This view that unity of command and effective troop control were crucial to the success of local wars expressed by Matsulenko was especially significant since Matsulenko himself in 1968 expressed the very different view that while the Americans were superior militarily, the moral superiority of the Vietnamese, based on the justness of their cause, would prevent the US from achieving victory.[40] This change in the basis of criticism of American actions in Vietnam from the socio-political and moral level to the purely military one implied that if the US had not committed these military errors, it might not have lost the war despite whatever the sociopolitical factors of conflict were.

Finally, there have recently appeared statements by Soviet military thinkers favourably evaluating certain types of combat operations conducted by American armed forces in Vietnam, particularly air mobile operations featuring helicopters.[41] In June 1979, Colonel A. Sinitskiy summarised what certain American experts concluded about this type of operation:

> Based on the combat experience of American forces in the mountain-ous regions of South Vietnam certain specialists in the United States believe that air mobile forces organized in a division and equipped with helicopters and vertical takeoff-and-landing airplanes will be used extensively in mountainous theaters. They will be able to seize and hold mountain passages, passes, peaks, and villages and wage offensive and defensive actions, striking the enemy in the flank and the rear.[42]

Significantly, Sinitskiy did not dispute the opinion of these specialists; indeed, he appeared to endorse it. It would seem, then, that air mobile operations came to be regarded as a successful means of conducting operations in a local war against an enemy waging guerrilla warfare.

The change by Soviet military thinkers in the evaluation of American actions in local wars from an emphasis on sociopolitical factors during the Vietnam war to an emphasis on military ones after it represented an important progression of ideas. No longer was the outcome of local war seen as being determined solely by sociopolitical factors involved in it. Indeed, such wars were won or lost depending on the degree of military skill each side exercised.

Further, the appraisal of the success and failure of various military actions from the American side in Korea and Vietnam would appear to indicate that Soviet military thinkers have over time begun to picture themselves as being in a position similar to that which the Americans were in — interveners in a local conflict against insurgent forces. In this sense, the praise of those actions in which the US was successful was a call to adopt them in the Soviet armed forces while criticism of American failures was a warning for the Soviets to avoid committing the same errors. Soviet military thinkers, then, have become somewhat optimistic about the ability of the Soviet Union to succeed in local wars; by learning from American mistakes, the Soviets were in a better position to win militarily even though they might be fighting the same basic kind of war against insurgents that the Americans did. However, they were not so optimistic as to conclude that because they were Marxist-Leninists, they would succeed where the imperialists failed. A local war had to be won militarily — sociopolitical factors were no longer seen as predetermining the outcome.

The Soviet Role in Third World Conflicts

While previously the Soviet military mentioned only arms transfers and Soviet advisers in discussing the role of the USSR in Third World conflicts, in the late Brezhnev era, more direct means of involvement were acknowledged. One of these was the use of Cuban armed forces in certain conflicts. In December 1977, Major General M. Yasyukov praised the military aid given to Angola by both the USSR and Cuba in order to thwart 'infringements by imperialism, the racists of South Africa, and domestic infringements'.[43] Malinovskiy, in December 1979, appeared to regard the Cuban military effort in Angola as being as important as direct Soviet aid there, in addition to proving to be of critical importance in Ethiopia:

> Timely assistance by the socialist countries, and the USSR and Cuba above all, played a decisive role in the victory of the People's Republic of Angola over foreign interventionists and local dissidents, and it disrupted the threat of dismemberment to revolutionary Ethiopia.[44]

Treaties of friendship and co-operation were also regarded as an important means of Soviet military support of Third World nations. One military writer underlined the importance of these treaties in an article intended for political study group leaders: 'Such treaties create a firm basis for augmenting mutual efforts in the struggle for independence of the liberated countries, for the final elimination of colonialism and for strengthening the peace.'[45]

Finally, no references were made by the Soviet military to the use of

Soviet armed forces themselves in actual conflict in local wars in the Third World as a general policy. However, there have been some recent indications that Soviet military thinkers are not averse to such a development. For example, in discussing the role of the Red Army in national liberation struggles before 1945, not only is the Soviet Army praised for its role in Eastern Europe, but also for its actions in Mongolia and China.[46] In addition, as mentioned in the previous section, Soviet military thinkers have also favourably evaluated certain actions of American armed forces in Vietnam. Nevertheless, the direct use of Soviet armed forces at the present time in the Third World has not (yet) been discussed by Soviet military thinkers.

However, an article appearing in the Party weekly, *New Times,* shortly after the Soviet invasion of Afghanistan expressed the determination of the USSR to protect Marxist revolutions in the Third World by military means if necessary. The unsigned article asked rhetorically whether the internationalist solidarity of revolutions required the USSR to extend only moral and diplomatic support to Marxist governments, such as Afghanistan, fighting to remain in power, or whether the USSR should extend military assistance as well. Noting Soviet military assistance to China and Spain before the Second World War, the answer given to this question was, 'To refuse to use the possibilities at the disposal of the socialist countries would signify virtually evading performance of the internationalist duty . . .'[47] An even blunter statement calling for Soviet military assistance was also made:

> The experience of the revolutionary liberation struggle of the peoples shows that at critical moments solidarity with a victorious revolution calls not only for moral support, but also for material assistance, including, under definite circumstances, military assistance. To deny support to the Afghan revolution, to leave it face to face with the forces of imperialist reaction would have been to doom it to defeat, which would have been a serious blow to the entire communist and national liberation movement.[48]

This article was described by a *New York Times* reporter as an extension of the Brezhnev doctrine enunciated shortly after the Soviet invasion of Czechoslovakia in 1968.[49] However, whereas the Brezhnev doctrine of 1968 called for Soviet intervention to prevent full-fledged socialist nations in Eastern Europe from leaving the socialist community, this new article was seen as calling for the USSR to prevent Marxist Third World governments that had not yet achieved socialism from leaving the socialist community as well. It must be noted, though, that this article was intended primarily as a justification for Soviet actions in Afghanistan. Further, while calling for Soviet military assistance to endangered Marxist regimes, the article did not actually call for the intervention of Soviet armed forces. Indeed, references to the Soviet armed forces in Afghanistan always stress the limited and temporary nature of its mission, as Brezhnev reiterated in his 26th Party Congress speech.[50] In other words, even though 85,000 Soviet troops have been sent to Afghanistan, the Party has not yet advocated direct Soviet military intervention as a general policy toward Third World conflicts.

In the light of Soviet actions in Third World conflicts, once again the pattern emerges that the Soviet military would not acknowledge actual Soviet behaviour as a general policy until (1) a new policy action had already been undertaken in practice and (2) that policy action proved to be successful. The use of Cuban armed forces in Angola and Ethiopia was only praised after the MPLA government had been established in Luanda and the Somalis had been driven out of most of the Ogaden. As military intervention in Afghanistan has yet to prove successful, direct Soviet military intervention has not yet been acknowledged as a policy. However, such a statement might occur in the future if the Soviets succeed in subduing the Afghan rebels, though this will be an extremely difficult task for the Soviets to accomplish.

What this trend has meant during the late Brezhnev era is that the protection of Soviet interests has been acknowledged as requiring more and more direct Soviet involvement in Third World conflicts. No longer would it suffice for the USSR to play an indirect role while local forces undertook most of the fighting. Without a greater degree of direct Soviet involvement, the local forces whose victory the Soviets desire might instead be defeated. This is a result of the trend for indigenous Third World forces to have interests that not only differ from, but also conflict with Soviet interests. Thus, the protection of Soviet interests in the Third World must increasingly be borne by the USSR itself. The manifestations of this trend (in the form of more treaties of friendship and co-operation with military clauses and the use of Cuban and even Soviet armed forces in the Third World) are frightening to many nations both in the West and the Third World. However, the Soviets cannot be satisfied with the trend of growing opposition by indigenous Third World forces to Soviet foreign policy in this region that forces the USSR to become more directly involved militarily in order to protect its foreign policy interests, which action in turn evokes even greater indigenous Third World opposition to Soviet policies.

Conclusion

Party/civilian interest in the Third World was strong in the late Brezhnev years as well. The change in emphasis from non-capitalist development at the 23rd and 24th Party Congresses to socialist development at the 25th and 26th Party Congresses was evident in other Party/civilian statements during this period that called for Third World nations to follow the Soviet model of development.[51] To this end, the importance of adopting scientific socialism as an ideology and not 'national' socialism was strongly emphasised.[52] To a greater extent than before, Party/ civilian writers discussed the military aspect of Third World conflicts, often praising the Cuban military role in Angola and Ethiopia and the Soviet military role in Afghanistan.[53] Nevertheless, Party/civilian writers did not discuss the military aspect of conflict in the Third World in the detail and the volume in which the Soviet military did. Finally, no Party/ civilian writer in the late Brezhnev years called for the separation of military-political considerations from other considerations as V.M. Kulish had done earlier; no military writer did either. This was a rejection of Kulish's implication that ideological factors were not important. Indeed, the increasing stress on socialist development instead of the less ideologically pure non-capitalist development shows that ideological considerations remained of primary importance during the late Brezhnev years.

Pessimism about the ability of nations on the path of socialist development to maintain that path was also increasingly expressed by Party/civilian writers during the late Brezhnev years. This was in part blamed on the intrigues of the Chinese in conjunction with the imperialists.[54] Others, however, saw the source of these setbacks within the Third World itself. V.V. Zagladin, First Deputy Chief of the Central Committee's International Department, noted that resistance to the April 1978 Afghan revolution began only after the Islamic revolution in Iran had taken place.[55] Others noted that a national liberation war gaining independence for a Third World nation and a national democratic revolution against foreign capitalists and local feudalists would not necessarily lead to a socialist revolution.[56] Perhaps the most pessimistic assessment of all, though, was made in a review co-authored by Anatoliy Gromyko (Director of the African Institute of the Academy of Sciences and the son of the Foreign Minister) in which the book under discussion was criticised for classifying all African nations as either (1) capitalist, (2) socialist, or (3) undecided. Instead, the reviewers felt, all African nations should be considered as undecided, including the ones that were now socialist; nothing permanent had been established.[57]

This general pessimism regarding the Third World that both the military and the Party expressed was the result of Soviet experience in the Third World. What at first appeared to be opportunities to easily extend Soviet influence often turned out otherwise. Either Soviet influence was soon lost completely (Egypt, Somalia) or the USSR and its allies had to undertake a protracted military effort to retain their influence (Angola, Ethiopia, Cambodia, Afghanistan). In the latter case, this protracted military effort has not yet resulted in the establishment of secure Third World Marxist regimes; if the USSR or its allies withdrew their forces from any of these countries, the Marxist regimes there would soon collapse. Even the strict conditions set by the Soviet military in the late Brezhnev years for the maintenance of socialism in the Third World (vanguard party ruling internally, reliance on the USSR through a treaty of friendship and co-operation externally) were not guaranteed to work since some of the regimes that met these conditions still face continued local military opposition.

The Soviets could not expect a more permanent alliance from those regimes that did not fulfil both these conditions. A treaty of friendship and co-operation alone was no guarantee of a lasting alliance, as both Egypt and Somalia showed. Other nations, such as India, Iraq and Syria would only comply with Soviet foreign policy in so far as their own foreign policies and their dependence on the Soviets for certain types of assistance (most notably arms) required. Where the treaty with the Soviets no longer served the interests of the Third World nation, their relations would soon deteriorate, as Soviet-Iraqi relations recently have. The Soviets have given Iraq very little assistance in its war with Iran and have signed a treaty of friendship and co-operation with Iraq's rival, Syria; the Iraqis are highly dissatisfied with their Soviet 'friends' as a result. The point here is that these treaties are seen by non-communist Third World nations as serving their interests and not as a desire for them to serve Soviet interests. As for the rest of the non-capitalist but also non-socialist Third World, the Soviets appear to have given up hope of it becoming allied to the USSR.

This experience of growing Third World opposition to the extension of Soviet influence there has been reflected in Soviet military and Party writing about the Third World that has been considerably less optimistic in the late Brezhnev years than during the middle Brezhnev years. So long as many in the Third World saw the USSR as an ally in driving out American and other Western influences, the USSR had been optimistic about its prospects for increasing its own influence in the Third World. This is a situation that still exists in some regions, especially Central

America. However, the desire of the Third World to rid itself of Western influence did not at all mean that it was inviting the USSR to replace it. This, however, is what the Soviets appeared to have thought. As a result, the Soviets are now witnessing former allies which have come to fear the USSR so much that in some instances they have invited the return of Western influence. This situation, though, was not the result of a clever initiative on the part of the West. Instead, it has been the result of many in the Third World itself deciding to turn to the West due to their fear of the USSR. This indigenous Third World opposition to Soviet foreign policy must be bitter to the Soviets who had regarded the Third World as being the natural ally of the USSR.

Notes

1. Colonel G. Malinovskiy, 'Lokal'naya voina', in *Sovetskaya voyennaya entsiklopediya,* vol. 5 (Voyenizdat, Moscow, 1978), p. 22.

2. Lt. Colonel T. Kondratkov, 'Organichennaya voina – orudiye imperialisti-cheskoy agressi', *Kommunist Vooruzhennykh Sil,* no. 8, April 1969, p. 31.

3. Major General S. Tyushkhevich, 'Istochiki voin mnimiye i deistvitel'niye', *Kommunist Vooruzhennykh Sil,* no. 15, August 1979, pp. 80-1.

4. Colonel G. Malinovskiy and Colonel Ye. Rybkin, 'Klassifikatsiya voin', in *Sovetskaya voyennaya entsiklopediya,* vol. 4 (Voyenizdat, Moscow, 1977), p. 200.

5. Ibid. It was evident, though, that the non-class basis of this category of war had been unwelcome to those who wished to maintain ideological purity. In 1977, for example, Colonel T. Kondratkov wrote, 'Certain armed collisions occur between developing states, but obviously they cannot be treated as an independent type of war.' Nevertheless Kondratkov did treat them as an independent type of war and noted that their source often lay in '. . . acute economic, political, religious, ethnic and other problems'; see Colonel T. Kondratkov, 'Tipi i sotsial'niy kharakter voin sovremennoy epokhi', in Major General D. Volkogonov, Major General A. Milovidov and Major General S. Tyushkevich, *Voina i armiya: filosofsko-sotsiologicheskiy ocherk* (Voyenizdat, Moscow, 1977), pp. 84-5.

6. Colonel Ye. Rybkin, 'XXV s''yezd KPSS i osvoboditel'niye voini sov-remennoy epokhi', *Voyenno-Istoricheskiy Zhurnal,* no. 11, November 1978, pp. 11-12.

7. L.I. Brezhnev, *Otchetniy doklad tsentral'nogo komiteta KPSS XXVI s''yezdu Kommunisticheskoy Partii Sovetskogo Soyuza i ocheredniye zadachi partii v oblasti vnutrenney i vneshney politiki* (speech of 23 February 1981) ('Krasnaya Zvezda', Moscow, 1981), p. 5. In acknowledging Soviet assistance to Vietnam in its war with China, the Brezhnev speech mentioned that the USSR had also helped Kampuchea (p. 9).

8. Tyushkhevich, 'Istochiki voin mnimiye i deistvitel'niye', p. 80.

9. See, for example, Colonel Ye. Rybkin, 'Pravda o voine – oruzhiye sil mira', *Kommunist Vooruzhennykh Sil,* no. 10, May 1977, pp. 8-15; Colonel General G. Sredin, 'Velikaya istoricheskaya missiya', *Kommunist Vooruzhennykh Sil,* no. 22, November 1977, pp. 48-57; Captain 1st Rank Yu. Osipov, 'V.I. Lenin, KPSS ob internatsional'nom kharaktere zashchiti zavoyevaniy sotsializma', *Kommunist Vooruzhennykh Sil,* no. 13, July 1978, pp. 74-82; Lt. Colonel A.

Vitkovskiy, 'Natsional'no-osvoboditel'niye voini na sovremennom etape', *Kommunist Vooruzhennykh Sil*, no. 13, July 1978, pp. 88-90; Colonel T. Kondratkov, 'Zloveshchiy kharakter militaristikh dogm', *Kommunist Vooruzhennykh Sil*, no. 19, October 1978, pp. 78-83; and Major General D. Volkogonov, 'Klassovaya bor'ba i sovremennost'', *Kommunist Vooruzhennykh Sil*, no. 4, February 1979, pp. 8-18.

10. See, for example, Major General M. Yasyukov, 'Mirovaya sistema sotsializma – istoricheskoye zavoyevaniye mezhdunarodnogo rabochego klassa', *Kommunist Vooruzhennykh Sil*, no. 24, December 1977, pp. 68-9.

11. Osipov, 'V.I. Lenin', p. 77.

12. Volkogonov, 'Klassovaya bor'ba i sovremennost'', pp. 11-12.

13. B. Vesnin, 'Boyevoy avangard borbi za mir, protiv agressivnoy politiki imperializma', *Kommunist Vooruzhennykh Sil*, no. 11, June 1979, p. 25.

14. See G. Mirskiy, *'Tretiy mir': obshchestvo, vlast', armiya* (Nauka, Moscow, 1976).

15. Colonel Ye. Dolgopolov, 'Molodiye armii i sotsial'niy progress', *Kommunist Vooruzhennykh Sil*, no. 21, November 1976, pp. 90-2.

16. Colonel Ye. Dolgopolov, 'Vazhniy politicheskiy faktor: o roli armiy v razvivayushchikhsya stranakh', *Krasnaya Zvezda*, 21 April 1978.

17. See S.P. Nemanov, 'Partii avangardnogo tipa v afrikanskikh stranakh sotsialisticheskoy orientatsii', *Narodi Afriki i Azii*, no. 2, 1979, pp. 23-5; G. Mirskiy, 'Rol' armii v sotsial'nom razvitii stran Azii i Afriki', *Voprosy Filosofii*, no. 3, March 1979, p. 108; R. Ul'yanovskiy, 'O stranakh sotsialisticheskoy orientatsii', *Kommunist*, no. 11, July 1979, p. 123; A.S. Kaufman, 'Sovremennaya revolyutsionnaya demokratiya i natsional'no-osvoboditel'niye revolyutsii', *Rabochiy Klass i Sovremenniy Mir*, November-December 1979, p. 74; and B. Ponomarev, 'Sovmestnaya bor'ba rabochego i natsional'no-osvoboditel'nogo dvizheniy protiv imperializma, za sotsial'niy progress', *Kommunist*, no. 16, November 1980, pp. 42-3.

18. S. Sergeyev, 'Stanovleniye novoy Efiopi', *Mezhdunarodnaya Zhizn'*, no. 4, 1979, pp. 13-15.

19. G. Mos'ko, 'K voprosu o maoistskoy teoriy "narodov voini"', *Voyenno-Istoricheskiy Zhurnal*, no. 3, March 1979, p. 59.

20. S.A. Mikoyan, 'Ob osobennostyakh revolyutsii v Nikaragua i ee urokakh s tochki zreniya teorii i praktiki osvoboditel'nogo dvizheniya (zaklyuchitel'noye slovo)', *Latinskaya Amerika*, no. 3, March 1980, p. 35.

21. Ibid., pp. 35-7.

22. Brezhnev, Speech of 23 February 1981, p. 15.

23. Colonel Ye. Rybkin, 'Marksizm-Leninizm kak metodologicheskaya osnova prognozirovaniya voyennikh sobitiy', *Voyenno-Istoricheskiy Zhurnal*, no. 7, July 1980, p. 7. By 1980, Colonel Rybkin had been named an Honored Worker of Science of the RSFSR.

24. See A.I. Ionova, 'Sovremennaya ideynaya evolyutsiya islama', *Narodi Azii i Afriki*, no. 6, 1979, pp. 24-35, and I.L. Andreyev, 'Religiya i natsional'no-osvoboditel'naya bor'ba v stranakh vostoka', *Rabochiy Klass i Sovremenniy Mir*, no. 6, November-December 1980, pp. 111-27.

25. For more on the radical Islamic ideology of the Iranian revolution, see William E. Griffith, 'The Revival of Islamic Fundamentalism', *International Security* 4:1 (Summer 1979), pp. 132-8.

26. Seweryn Bialer, *Stalin's Successors: Leadership, Stability and Change in the Soviet Union* (Cambridge University Press, Cambridge, 1980), p. 270.

27. Brezhnev, Speech of 23 February 1981, pp. 13-18.

28. Colonel G. Malinovskiy, 'Natsional'no-osvoboditel'noye dvizheniye na sovremennom etape', *Kommunist Vooruzhennykh Sil*, no. 24, December 1979, pp. 27-8.

29. Ibid.

30. Ibid., p. 33.

31. Colonel Ye. Rybkin, 'Voini sovremennoy epokhi i ikh vliyaniye na sotsial'niye protsessi', *Kommunist Vooruzhennykh Sil,* no. 11, June 1970, p. 16.

32. Lt. Colonel D. Volkogonov, 'The Moral Factor in a Local War', *Voyennaya Mysl'*, no. 12, December 1971, FBIS FPD 0003/74, p. 30.

33. Colonel N. Nikitin, 'Nekotoriye operativno-takticheskiye uroki lokal'nikh voin imperializma', *Voyenno-Istoricheskiy Zhurnal,* no. 12, December 1978, p. 66.

34. Major General V. Matsulenko, 'Po inostrannim armiyam', *Voyenno-Istoricheskiy Zhurnal,* no. 4, April 1979, pp. 54-65.

35. Soviet military writers are fond of assigning credit to the USSR for forcing Israel, Britain and France to withdraw from Egypt in the Suez crisis. Yet while they portray the Soviet Union as foiling these three powers in 1956, they never explain why the USSR was able to force only one, Israel, to withdraw from Arab territory in 1967.

36. Colonel P. Maslennikov, 'Organizatsiya upravleniya voiskami SShA v voine vo V'etname', *Voyenno-Istoricheskiy Zhurnal,* no. 10, October 1975, pp. 42-9.

37. Major General V. Matsulenko, 'O nekotorikh voprosakh upravleniya voiskami v lokal'nikh voinakh', *Voyenno-Istoricheskiy Zhurnal,* no. 3, March 1980, p. 53.

38. Ibid., p. 58.

39. Ibid., p. 63.

40. Major General V. Matsulenko, 'Lokal'niye voini imperializma (1946-1968 gg)', *Voyenno-Istoricheskiy Zhurnal,* no. 9, September 1968, p. 47.

41. See Colonel (ret.) A. Sinitskiy, 'Nekotoriye takticheskiye vivodi iz opita agressivnoy voini SShA protiv V'etnama', *Voyenno-Istoricheskiy Zhurnal,* no. 6, June 1979, pp. 53-7, and Colonel A. Tsvetkov, 'Boyeviye deystviya v tilu protivnika', *Zarubezhnoye Voyennoye Obozreniye,* no. 12, December 1979, pp. 8-14.

42. Sinitskiy, 'Nekotoriye takticheskiye vivodi iz opita agressivnoy voini SShA protiv V'etnama', p. 57. One wonders whether Sinitskiy thought counter-insurgency operations with helicopters would be effective in other mountainous countries, such as Afghanistan.

43. Major General M. Yasyukov, 'Mirovaya sistema sotsializma – istoricheskoye zavoyevaniye mezhdunarodnogo rabochego klassa', *Kommunist Vooruzhennykh Sil,* no. 24, December 1977, p. 68. Soviet and Cuban aid, of course, was given to the MPLA; 'domestic infringements' were the FNLA and UNITA.

44. Malinovskiy, 'Natsional'no-osvoboditel'noye dvizheniye na sovremennom etape', p. 33.

In a book edited by General of the Army I. Shavrov that was published in 1981, several Third World conflicts were discussed in considerable detail, including Angola (1961-1976). In this section, the military actions of Cuban troops were also described: see General of the Army I. Shavrov (ed.) *Lokal'niye voini: istoriya i sovremennost'* (Voyenizdat, Moscow, 1981), pp. 193-200. (See also the plate on military actions in Angola between pages 192 and 193.) More recent conflicts such as Ethiopia, Cambodia and Afghanistan were not treated in this manner.

45. Lt. Colonel N. Khibrikov, 'Krusheniye kolonial'noy sistemi imperializma: osvobodivshiyesya strani Azii, Afriki i Latinskoy Ameriki', *Kommunist Vooruzhennykh Sil,* no. 6, March 1978, p. 74. In the same paragraph, the author castigated Egypt for unilaterally abrogating its Treaty of Friendship and Co-operation with the USSR and for colluding with imperialism. Although it was clear to the author that Egypt was better off before abrogating this treaty, he noted, 'But we do not impose our friendship on anyone.'

46. Osipov, 'V.I. Lenin', p. 76.

47. 'World Communist Solidarity with the Afghan Revolution', *New Times*, no. 3, January 1980, p. 10.

48. Ibid., p. 9. This statement contained a contradiction. If a revolution were victorious, it would not require Soviet military assistance to save it from defeat. Because Soviet military assistance was necessary, it was obvious that the Afghan revolution was far from being victorious.

49. David Binder, 'Brezhnev Doctrine Said to Be Extended', *New York Times*, 10 February 1980.

50. Brezhnev, Speech of 23 February 1981, pp. 14-15.

51. See G. Aliyev (Politburo Candidate Member and First Secretary of the Azerbaidzhani Communist Party Central Committee), 'Oktyabr'skaya revolyutsiya i natsional'no-osvoboditel'noye dvizheniye', *Kommunist*, no. 9, June 1977, pp. 24-38; Anatoliy Gromyko, 'Aktual'niye problemi noveyshey istorii razvivayushchikhsya stran', *Kommunist*, no. 4, March 1979, pp. 117-24; Nemanov, 'Partii avangardnogo tipa v afrikanskikh stranakh sotsialisticheskoy orientatsii', pp. 16-28; and Ul'yanovskiy, 'O stranakh sotsialisticheskoy orientatsii', pp. 114-23.

52. M. Suslov, 'Marksizm-Leninizm i revolyutsionnoye obnovleniye mira', *Kommunist*, no. 14, September 1977, pp. 13-28, and T. Timofeyev, 'Magistral'niye tendentsii revolyutsionnogo protsessa', *Kommunist*, no. 10, July 1978, pp. 75-83.

53. See K.N. Brutents, *Sovremenniye natsional'no-osvoboditel'niye revolyutsii* (Politizdat, Moscow, 1974), p. 293; An. Gromyko, 'Druz'ya i vragi narodov afrikanskogo kontinenta', *Pod Znamenem Leninizma*, no. 8, April 1978, p. 62; Yu. P. Gavrikov, 'Kuba v sovremennom mire: osnovniye napravleniya vneshney politiki', *Latinskaya Amerika*, no. 6, November-December 1978, pp. 102-3; V. Sidenko, 'Leninskiy vneshnepoliticheskiy kurs i natsional'no-osvoboditel'noye dvizheniye', *MEiMO*, no. 2, February 1980, p. 14; V. Teplov, 'Ostoyat' politiku razryadki', *Mezhdunarodnaya Zhizn'*, no. 4, 1980, pp. 109-10; Ye. Tarabrin, 'Afrika: osvoboditel'naya bor'ba i proiski imperializma', *MEiMO*, no. 6, June 1980, pp. 71-4; and 'SSSR i musul'manskiye strani', *Narodi Azii i Afriki*, no. 5, 1980, p. 14.

54. See Yu. Semenov, 'Pekin i natsional'no-osvoboditel'noye dvizheniye', *Mezhdunarodnaya Zhizn'*, no. 12, 1979, pp. 23-33.

55. Intervyu Vadima Zagladina korrespondentam RTL (Radio-Television Luxembourg), 'Neozhidannaya gazeta', *Zhurnalist*, no. 9, September 1980, p. 11.

56. S.L. Agayev and I.M. Tatarovskaya, 'Nekotoriye problemi razvitiya revolyutsionnogo protsessa v osvobodivshikhsya stranakh', *Rabochiy Klass i Sovremenniy Mir*, no. 5, September-October 1978, pp. 45-7.

57. An. Gromyko and G. Starushenko, 'Aktual'niye voprosi razvitiya Afriki', *Kommunist*, no. 2, January 1980, p. 120.

5 CONCLUSION: THE EVOLUTION OF SOVIET MILITARY THINKING ABOUT CONFLICT IN THE THIRD WORLD

Soviet military thinking about conflict in the Third World has evolved during the Khrushchev and Brezhnev eras in both substance and importance. Before Khrushchev, the Soviet military paid almost no doctrinal attention to the problems of Third World conflict. During the Khrushchev era and the early years of the Brezhnev era, the Soviet military began to discuss this question, but not to the same extent that it discussed nuclear war or war in Europe. During the late 1960s and early 1970s, though, the Soviet military discussed conflict in the Third World in much greater depth. This was also a period of relative optimism on the part of the military who believed that foreign policy gains could be made relatively easily without any great effort being expended by the Soviet Union. In the late 1970s and early 1980s, Soviet military concern about this subject has continued, but the relative optimism of before has given way to relative pessimism. It has been seen that gains made easily can also be easily lost. For those gains to be made permanent, it has been recognised that greater and greater involvement by the USSR in the affairs of the Third World is necessary. This greater Soviet involvement in the Third World, though, has tended to provoke indigenous Third World opposition to Soviet foreign policy, making the achievement of Soviet goals even more difficult.

In this study Soviet military thinking about conflict in the Third World has been categorised into six different aspects: the relationship of local war to world war; the nature and types of wars in the Third World; the relationship of peaceful coexistence to wars of national and social liberation; the Soviet view of indigenous forces in the Third World; the Soviet view of American ideas about and actions in local war; and the Soviet role in Third World conflicts. Each of these aspects of Soviet military thought underwent change during the Khrushchev and Brezhnev periods. In conclusion the significance of the changes in Soviet military thinking about each of these aspects will be examined here. In addition, military and Party/civilian thinking will be discussed to see what can be concluded about military-civilian relations in the USSR. Further, the relationship between military thought and Soviet foreign policy will be examined to address the question of what Soviet military thinking about conflict in the Third World tells about the basic intentions of the Soviet Union and whether these intentions are offensive or defensive. Finally, the role of Soviet military thinking will be discussed.

The Relationship of Local War to World War

Soviet military thinking about the relationship between local war and world war underwent a dramatic reversal from the late 1950s and 1960s to the 1970s. At first, they viewed local wars as something only the imperialists waged in order to make strategic gains in an era when world war would be catastrophic to all. Since they did not then view the Soviet Union as being able to wage such wars successfully, Soviet military thinkers emphasised the risk that local war could escalate into world war.[1] In 1956, Khrushchev had stated that world war was no longer inevitable; in 1969, the Party proclaimed that world war could be averted, though it did not say how.[2] In the 1970s, however, the Soviets became increasingly convinced that the growing military strength of the Soviet Union could prevent local war from escalating into world war.[3] What Thomas Wolfe saw in 1964 as glimmerings of disagreement with the dominant view of the 1960s about the relationship between local war and world war became the dominant view of the 1970s and the 1980s.[4] Finally, Soviet military thinkers now regarded local wars as a means by which Soviet interests too could be furthered; the imperialists were no longer seen as the only ones who could use local wars to their own advantage.

The changes in Soviet military pronouncements on the relationship between local war and world war may be seen as a reflection of changes in the correlation of forces between the East and the West. The Soviets did not address the question of the relationship between local war and world war at all before the Soviet Union had developed a relatively substantial nuclear weapons capability in the late 1950s. The immediate effect of this on the West was that the US moved away from the strategy of massive retaliation, in which any military move by the USSR could be met by a nuclear blow against the Soviet Union itself, to a strategy of limited war, in which the US response to Soviet military thrusts into a geographically limited area could also be limited to that area in order to avoid a world nuclear war. This change in Western strategy was seen by the Soviets as a victory for them brought about by their increasing military might. Nevertheless, the Soviets did not want to see the US become involved in local wars either. Yet while the Soviets now had the ability to deter the US from initiating a world war, they could not prevent the US from undertaking local wars in the Third World. Soviet nuclear capability was much less than that of the US, and just as important, Soviet ability to project conventional force into the Third World was extremely limited. Thus, they emphasised the possibility that local war could escalate into world war in order to try to deter the US from undertaking local wars. If the US was not deterred, though, there was little else the Soviets could do since they did not want to risk a world war that could destroy the USSR. At the same time, there was no question of the USSR itself fighting a local war in the Third World. Hence, no provision was made for this in statements on the relationship between local war and world war.

The period of the late 1960s and early 1970s saw another important change in the correlation of forces. This was the period during which Soviet nuclear capability came to equal America's, Soviet conventional forces grew along with Soviet ability to project them into the Third World, and America appeared to have become unable to win a local war (Vietnam) as well as unwilling to become involved in other ones. Through a certain amount of Soviet involvement in local wars, the side the USSR favoured could win, thereby making gains for the USSR as well. Thus, the statement that local wars could lead to world wars was changed to one that the USSR could now keep local wars localised due to its increased strength. In the late 1970s and early 1980s, Soviet involvement in local war increased to the extent that in Afghanistan the USSR has undertaken the major burden of the fighting. When the USSR became this involved in a Third World conflict, it did not want to emphasise the danger that local war might escalate into world war. American involvement in local war, though, is still seen as possessing the risk of wider war; the USSR does not wish to see the US engaged in this kind of activity and does not want to confront the US militarily in a local war.

The changing Soviet military view of the relationship of local war to world war, then, can be seen as a reflection of perceived changes in the correlation of forces in favour of the USSR over time. However, too much should not be made of the notion of the correlation of forces changing in favour of the USSR. The Soviets have claimed this has been happening since 1917 whether it has been true or not. Discussion of the changing correlation of forces not only reflects the growing military strength of the USSR, but also the hope that it will continue to grow. But the 'forces' involved do not include just Soviet military forces, but also the forces of national and social liberation throughout the world.

The Soviets hope that these will grow too. Yet even if they did not grow (say, as a result of increasing Third World opposition to Soviet foreign policy), the Soviets can be expected to continue saying that the correlation of forces has changed in their favour. This would be true if the West increased its military strength *vis-à-vis* that of the USSR also.

The Soviet view of the relationship of local war to world war is important because it has affected other aspects of Soviet military thinking about conflict in the Third World. This is especially true of the Soviet military view of American ideas about local war and the Soviet role in Third World conflicts. Further, the change in the Soviet military view of the relationship of local war to world war provided a change in the assumptions upon which Soviet foreign policy is based. Once it was accepted that the USSR could keep local wars localised through military force, the USSR could then play a larger military role in Third World conflicts, as indeed it has done since the American withdrawal from Vietnam.

The Nature and Types of Conflict in the Third World

The development of Soviet military thinking about the nature and types of wars in the Third World during the Brezhnev era began with a rejection of Khrushchev's formulation of types of wars that mixed ideological and non-ideological factors together.[5] Soviet military thinkers at first asserted the classic four categories of war based solely on sociopolitical bases that had been dominant during the Stalin era: war between opposing social systems; civil war between the proletariat and the bourgeoisie in the developed capitalist countries; national liberation war; and war between imperialist states.[6] Except for national liberation wars, however, none of these types of war was occurring. Other types of war, though, were occurring in the Third World. Beginning with Stepanov and Rybkin, certain Soviet military thinkers expanded the classification of types of wars in order to include these new, and often complex, kinds of Third World conflicts. Thus Stepanov and Rybkin in 1968 introduced civil wars between the people and a regime of extreme reaction and wars between and within developing countries (this latter category underwent several name changes by Rybkin himself), and Rybkin in 1978 introduced wars of nations on the path of socialist development in defence of socialism.[7]

The four classic types of war had relatively distinct sociopolitical bases — all of them involved wars between social classes (either proletariat versus bourgeoisie or bourgeoisie versus bourgeoisie). National liberation wars were somewhat different in that all the classes in a colony fought for national independence, but Soviet military thinking generally expected the national bourgeoisie to come to power. This, however, was considered a progressive development. The two new categories of wars introduced in 1968 could not be as sharply defined in sociopolitical terms. A civil war between the people (both proletariat and bourgeoisie) and a regime of extreme reaction implied that the national bourgeoisie was the enemy of extreme reaction − not the usual Marxist-Leninist assumption. Further, the outcome of such a war was not clear like the older four categories: maybe bourgeois democracy would come to power, maybe socialism. Wars between and within Third World nations, however, had an even more tenuous sociopolitical basis. These wars involved territorial disputes or attempts by regions to secede − class conflict was not involved at all.

The category of wars between and within Third World countries may have had the advantage of accurately describing much of the conflict that actually occurred in the Third World, but it had the disadvantage of not allowing a clear determination of the just nature of each side involved. The other five categories lent themselves easily to the concept of just versus unjust since in each type of war one could easily identify the just and unjust sides from which sociopolitical class they were, except for wars between imperialist states in which both sides were unjust. In other words, justness versus unjustness could be 'objectively' determined in a war from the category or type it belonged to. Such a determination, however, was not possible in wars between and within Third World nations. Soviet military thinkers were unwilling to think of territorial disputes as a type of war between imperialist states because this would make both sides unjust. Since they were unable to ascribe a sociopolitical basis to such conflicts, it was not possible to formulate a general rule about the just nature of each side; class confrontations were not the issue in this type of conflict. As a result, Rybkin stated in 1972 that this type of conflict was so complex that each one had to be judged individually.[8] The following year, Rybkin abandoned this formula, reasserted the idea that the just nature of a war had to be judged from its sociopolitical essence, and then said nothing about how this could be applied to conflict between Third World nations.[9] For whatever reason Rybkin made these two contradictory statements, they pointed out the great difficulty in reconciling the category of conflict between and within Third World nations with the concept of just versus unjust derived from the sociopolitical categorisation of war. In 1974, Colonel

Kondratkov stated that in any war, that side was just whose victory would further the interests of socialism (the USSR).[10] Although this formula had the potential for conflicting with the older view deriving justness 'objectively' from the type of conflict, since what furthered the interests of socialism might not necessarily be in the interests of the just side in a conflict (the result of the civil war in Zimbabwe appears to be an example of this), Soviet military writers did not acknowledge any such potential for conflict of interests.

Of course, Rybkin's innovations were not readily accepted by all Soviet military thinkers. Lt. Colonel Khmara clung to the old four category classification of the types of wars, but sought to explain the complexity of conflict in the Third World by introducing the transformability of national liberation wars into civil wars between the proletariat and the bourgeoisie, and *vice versa*.[11] Interestingly, though, while Khmara did not accept Rybkin's two new categories of war, General of the Army Shavrov, who did accept them, also adopted Khmara's concept of the transformability of conflicts, applying them to Rybkin's as well. Both Khmara and Rybkin believed that sociopolitical factors were of primary importance in discussing war. While Khmara sought to bend the complex phenomenon of conflict in the Third World to fit the orthodox four category classification of types of war, Rybkin sought to revise the orthodox classification to fit the complexity of new types of conflict. In 1975, General Shavrov made a compromise between both these points of view.[12]

Although at the beginning of the Brezhnev era, as was mentioned earlier, Soviet military thinkers rejected Khrushchev's classification of types of war that mixed ideological and non-ideological factors, preferring to rely on ideological ones alone to formulate categories of war, over time they increasingly sought to take into account non-ideological factors such as scale of war and means of combat. The integration of these factors with ideological ones was best achieved by Shavrov. However, while Khrushchev attempted to determine justness from these non-ideological factors in conjunction with ideological ones (world war, unjust; local war, unjust; national liberation war, just), Shavrov kept them separate. Each war could be classified as to sociopolitical factors, scale, and means of combat. Justness was determined from the sociopolitical categorisation alone. Non-ideological factors were by themselves neutral.

Finally, as Rybkin's introduction of a new category of war in 1978 shows, Soviet military thinking about the nature and types of conflict in the Third World is not to be considered definitive and permanent in any of its features, but tentative and temporary. It will undoubtedly change and develop in the future as the complex phenomenon of conflict in the Third World and Soviet involvement in this conflict do so as well.

The three new categories of war developed during the Brezhnev era also deserve study as examples of military thought. In wars between the people and a regime of extreme reaction, a conflict between a right-wing dictatorship on the one hand and all classes of the people, including both bourgeoisie and proletariat, on the other was envisioned. Both communists and non-communists united to fight the dictatorship, with each group hoping later to establish its preferred form of government (dictatorship of the proletariat or republican democracy). The communists in such a civil war may well initially be a relatively small and weak group compared to the non-communists fighting the dictatorship. However, if the United States chooses to support the dictatorship in this conflict, then the communists stand a good chance of eventually coming to power despite their initially weak position. For while the United States is supporting the dictatorship, the Soviet Union will support the communists, making them stronger compared to the non-communist opposition. At the same time, the non-communist opposition continues to fight against the dictatorship, the oppression of which it is familiar with, and not against the communists, whose oppression it has not yet experienced.

Through even minimal support to the dictatorship, the US becomes thoroughly identified with it, as was the case during the civil wars in Iran and Nicaragua. When the dictatorship eventually falls, the communists are often in a position to take power since they have received outside support from the USSR and its allies while the non-communists have received nothing. Further, the non-communists may not be willing to seek American help in preventing the communists from taking over completely due to the hostility remaining toward the US for having supported the dictatorship. Had the US made the effort to identify and support the non-communist, democratic opposition to the dictatorship to begin with, the outcome of the civil war might have been that the non-communists would have come to power, another Third World nation would have achieved democracy, and the US would have gained an ally more stable than an unpopular dictatorship.

However, the United States looks upon civil wars of this type as contests between non-communist and communist forces, and thus supports the dictatorship for fear of the communists coming to power. The Soviet view is much more sophisticated, since it acknowledges that the opposition to the dictatorship consists not just of communists alone, but of non-communists as well. Either one of these could come to power, and so Soviet support of the communists increases the communists' chances of actually doing so. The Americans, of course, also have the opportunity of supporting the non-communist opposition, but because of the rigidity of American thinking, the US does not do this. This is an error that the Soviets can take advantage of. Further, even if the non-communist opposition does come to power despite Soviet aid to the communist forces, as occurred in Iran, the Soviet Union has still gained since the US has lost an ally in the overthrown dictatorship and the non-communist forces in power are hostile to the US for having supported it. Thus, the formulation of the category of civil wars between the people and a regime of extreme reaction is a sophisticated example of Soviet military thought both for making a relatively accurate appraisal of a type of conflict that actually occurs and for seeing an opportunity for the USSR to take advantage of the American error in supporting the unpopular dictatorship instead of the non-communist opposition in these conflicts.

Similarly, the concept of wars between and within Third World nations was a relatively sophisticated one because it saw the source of these conflicts as being local disputes. This was the category that Colonel Rybkin came close to describing as not being governed by traditional Marxist-Leninist concepts of class struggle. Yet even though the Soviets did not go this far, they always emphasised the local aspect of the conflict instead of the larger East-West aspect. This is the opposite of how the US has often regarded these conflicts. However, while wars between and within Third World countries offer opportunities for the USSR to gain influence by supporting one of the contenders, this type of conflict poses problems for the Soviets as well. The Soviet Union wishes to be considered the natural ally of all the Third World. Yet in supporting some Third World countries, it risks alienating others which it does not support. Further, even those countries the USSR does support may decide that Soviet support is inadequate or undesirable, as did Egypt and Somalia.

More important, the growing number of conflicts between and within Third World countries which occur because of local disputes suggests that the Marxist-Leninist prediction that the world is changing from one led by the imperialists to one led by the socialists is not relevant. Many of these conflicts have no relation to the class struggle, but take place over territorial disputes. In addition, the foreign policy of many Third World nations does not accept either the leadership of the West or the East. Some Third World nations even appear to have great power pretensions of their own. It may be that the domination of the world by the East-West conflict is a transitory phenomenon and that in future the major challenge to the *status quo* will come from ideologies indigenous to the Third World that reject Marxism-Leninism, as does radical Islamic fundamentalism. In light of these prospects, the Soviet Union would undoubtedly prefer that conflict between and within Third World countries did not take place at all, but there is little the USSR can do to stop it from occurring. Thus, while this type of conflict might not benefit the United States, it does not necessarily benefit the Soviet Union either.

While the first two new categories of war that were invented in the Brezhnev era appeared in the late 1960s, the third category did not appear until the late 1970s. This was the category of wars of nations on the path of socialist development in defence of socialism. These were wars in which Marxist governments that had come to power in the Third World faced internal and/or external opposition, such as in Angola, Ethiopia, Cambodia and Afghanistan. The Soviets, though, were not as accurate in describing this type of conflict as they were the previous two. Even though it was recognised that the forces fighting against the Third World Marxist governments were indigenous Third World forces, these were not acknowledged to have a legitimate reason for opposing the Marxist governments. They were seen as either 'bandits' or 'reactionaries' backed by the imperialists. The greater the struggle these forces mounted against the Third World Marxist governments, the more the Soviets denounced them as being supported by the imperialists, as in Afghanistan.[13] This, however, is not true. In Angola, the struggle against the Marxist government has the character of an inter-tribal conflict with the ruling MPLA composed primarily of Mbundu people and the opposition UNITA composed primarily of Ovimbundu people. (The now more or less dormant FNLA is composed of Bakongo people.)[14] In the Horn of Africa, Marxist but Christian Ethiopia is opposed by Marxist but Moslem Somali and Eritrean guerrillas.[15] In Afghanistan, Moslem Afghan guerrillas are fighting not only against a non-Moslem Marxist regime, but also a foreign invasion from Russia.[16] Similarly, in Cambodia, Marxist and non-Marxist Cambodian guerrillas are fighting against Marxist Vietnamese invaders.[17] Thus, factors other than Marxist governments fighting a non-Marxist opposition are involved in all these conflicts, though this category does not take account of them.

It is interesting to note that in this one new type of war in which the forces of socialism are on the defensive, Soviet thinking about it is not as accurate as thinking about the other two new types. These wars between a Marxist Third World government and local non-Marxist forces bear a resemblance to another type of war that the Soviets did describe more accurately: wars between the people and a regime of extreme reaction. If the word 'reaction' which implies right-wing were substituted by the word 'oppressive' which can apply to either right- or left-wing dictatorships, then the description would be even more accurate. Indeed, people generally tend to rebel against an oppressive government no matter what its political colouring if they feel they have a chance to successfully overthrow it. This is something that the United States has often failed to recognise concerning conservative Third World dictatorships and that the USSR has also failed to recognise concerning Marxist Third World dictatorships. It would appear, then, that both superpowers are unwilling to regard either their own foreign policies or the internal policies of their Third World allies as a cause for locally based opposition to those allies. Being on the defensive in the Third World does not appear to give rise to clear thinking in either the US or the USSR since both consider opposition to its ally to be caused by the other superpower and not by indigenous Third World forces.

Nevertheless, Soviet military thinking about the nature and types of conflict in the Third World has been noteworthy during the Brezhnev era for its attempt to include local Third World factors in its discussion of the causes of such conflicts. Soviet military thinking made considerable progress in understanding the nature and types of conflict in the Third World to the extent that it accomplished this, but was limited by its insistence on regarding all forms of Third World conflict as a manifestation of Marxist-Leninist notions of class struggle.

Peaceful Coexistence

In the late 1950s and the 1960s, the Party called for peaceful coexistence with the West in order to avoid nuclear war. Concerning the struggle for national and social liberation in the Third World, the Party stated that the provision of peace by the USSR would create an atmosphere in which these struggles could flourish.[18] Little was said about the USSR providing more to them, such as military assistance. The Soviet military indicated its lack of enthusiasm for this position by rarely discussing peaceful coexistence. This, however, changed at the 24th Party Congress held in 1971. The Party now believed that peaceful coexistence with the West was not incompatible with Soviet assistance, including military, to progressive forces in wars of national and social liberation. Since then, the Soviet military has advocated this changed position wholeheartedly.[19]

The basic form of this changed position is that while the Soviet Union and the United States have similar interests in certain areas, such as arms control and East-West trade, on which they can come to terms, the fundamental sociopolitical conflict which exists between the two nations will never allow them to agree on everything, especially where ideological differences are greatest. The US and the USSR are each pursuing their own interests in those areas where they can reach agreement; it is unrealistic for the US to expect the USSR not to pursue its interests in those areas where they do not agree or to demand that the USSR not pursue its interests in those areas as a price for agreeing to what is essentially in the interests of both elsewhere. Among those areas where the US and the USSR disagree is Soviet support of national liberation movements in the Third World.

This is certainly not an unsophisticated view of international relations: the superpowers should be able to reach agreement on eliminating world war between them, which neither wants, thus leaving each of them to pursue in relative safety their basically conflicting interests, even to the extent of military involvement in local conflicts in the Third World. At the same time, this view indicates a degree of activeness in the thinking of Soviet military writers that perceives the Third World as an area where the Soviet Union can make gains for socialism, and also encourages the Soviet Union to attempt to do so.

Still, the Soviet view of peaceful coexistence does not magnanimously call for the United States to act in the same way that the Soviet Union does in the Third World. While peaceful coexistence is seen as allowing Soviet military assistance to its allies in Third World conflicts, it is also seen as a means of dissuading or 'paralysing' America from giving military assistance to its allies in these conflicts. However, even if the US became more actively involved in the Third World than it has been since Vietnam, it is doubtful that the USSR would want to give up pursuing peaceful coexistence bilaterally with the US; the risk of world war is something that the USSR does not wish to see increase.

Indigenous Third World Forces

The Soviet view of indigenous forces in the Third World was at first optimistic about their ability to lead their countries toward socialism, but has gradually become more and more pessimistic in this regard.

During the Khrushchev era, it was thought that radical Third World leaders could successfully lead Third World nations to socialism without any great effort on the part of the USSR.[20] However, after several radical Third World leaders were overthrown by conservative military coups in the mid-1960s, a reassessment was made about how to ensure that Third World nations maintain the path toward socialism once they have embarked upon it. The military concluded that the strongest force in Third World nations was the army. If the army was conservative, then it could overthrow radical leaders. However, if the army was 'progressive', then it could make sure that the nation advanced toward socialism.[21] Thus, the USSR should support radical Third World military regimes. Certain Party/civilian authors (primarily those in the international institutes of the USSR Academy of Sciences), however, thought that radical military regimes were unreliable because there was no force to prevent them from sliding to the right. They felt that only a Marxist-Leninist vanguard party could be trusted to maintain the path toward socialism.[22] The military regarded these civilians as too pessimistic,[23] but during the mid-1970s, certain radical military regimes did exactly what the civilian writers predicted they would do. Egypt, Somalia and Peru all abandoned friendship with the USSR. Since then, the Soviet military has also recognised that a ruling vanguard party is the only force in the Third World that the Soviet Union can rely on.[24]

With regard to guerrilla armies in the Third World, the Soviets have traditionally been sceptical about them even when they were communist.[25] The reason for this was that a guerrilla army that came to power primarily through its own efforts had an independent power base in its own nation and could defy the Soviet Union if it wanted to, as Yugoslavia and China did. After the Vietnam war, guerrilla armies were seen as useful in spreading socialism, but only if they were under the firm control of a Marxist-Leninist vanguard party.[26] A guerrilla army that controlled the party was not acceptable. The Soviets had denounced the Cuban theory of revolution because it called for a guerrilla army to come to power and later create a party. Recently, though, because of the success of the Sandinistas in Nicaragua, the Soviets have spoken more favourably about the Cuban theory. However, they insist that in this kind of revolution, the guerrilla army must surrender authority to the party soon after coming to power.[27] This has not yet happened in Nicaragua.

During the Khrushchev era, the Soviets had assumed that the Third World would naturally become socialist and seek alliance with the Soviet Union. The radical Third World leaders that came to power who proclaimed themselves to be anti-Western seemed to prove this. Many nations in the Third World feared the West and sought the aid of the USSR against it. However, simply because the Third World shared certain anti-Western interests with the USSR did not mean that the interests of the Third World were identical to those of the Soviet Union. These nations that had recently won their freedom from the Europeans did not all look favourably upon the idea of becoming a part of the world socialist system dominated by the USSR.

When this did not happen automatically without any Soviet effort, and when radical Third World leaders were overthrown, the Soviets concluded that a certain amount of Soviet support was needed to help the inevitable course of history. The USSR gave assistance to radical Third World military regimes. However, by the mid-1970s, it was clear that even these would not necessarily maintain the path toward socialism permanently. Now the Soviets feel that only those nations that have (1) a ruling Marxist-Leninist party, and (2) a firm alliance with the USSR (a treaty of friendship and co-operation) will remain socialist. Nations that do not meet both conditions cannot be relied upon.[28]

Aside from the already established socialist states of Cuba, North Korea and Vietnam, these two conditions have been met by only four Third World countries: Afghanistan, Angola, Mozambique and South Yemen. The Marxist military government of Ethiopia has not yet created a vanguard party, but only a centre for the study of forming a party (much to the irritation of the Soviets). In Afghanistan, Angola, Cambodia and Ethiopia, the Marxist governments are facing military opposition from local internal and/or external forces that they have been unable to defeat even with Cuban, Vietnamese, or Soviet armed forces engaging in active combat on their behalf. Thus, it would seem that even if a Third World nation has both a ruling vanguard party and a treaty of friendship and co-operation with the USSR, there is no guarantee that peace and socialism have been established there.

The examples of Afghanistan, Angola, Cambodia and Ethiopia show that socialism encounters many obstacles in the Third World even in countries where socialist nations themselves (including the USSR in Afghanistan) undertake to help establish socialism through military means. Presumably countries which meet the two conditions of having a ruling vanguard party and a treaty of friendship and co-operation with the USSR have the best chance of achieving socialism. What about the countries that meet only one, or neither, of these conditions? The Soviets have become very pessimistic about them achieving socialism.[29]

Nations which do not meet both these conditions, though, form the bulk of the Third World. Far from regarding the Soviet Union as their natural ally, many are wary of its influence; some even regard the USSR as their natural enemy. Why is this? The Soviet search for long-term allies in the Third World has led the Russians to conclude that only those nations over which they have the greatest influence will remain allied to the USSR. However, it is this attempt to gain influence that often alienates Third World nations, sometimes driving them to seek closer relations with the West, obviously the opposite of what the Soviets want to happen.

Increasingly, the Soviets have become reluctant to allow either a reduction or elimination of their influence. This is especially true where a Marxist government is in power. Afghanistan is an example of this. Nearly the entire nation opposed the Marxist government that first came to power in 1978. When the Amin regime was on the point of being overthrown by the people, the Soviets invaded to keep Afghanistan Marxist, setting up in power Babrak Karmal, who was more to their liking than Amin. Yet by preserving Afghanistan for socialism through force, the USSR has alienated much of the rest of the Third World, particularly the Moslem world.

Thus, even if the United States may have become less of an obstacle to the spread of Soviet influence in the Third World, indigenous forces within the Third World have become more of one. This is an ominous development for the Soviet Union since with the US, Western Europe, China and Japan all opposed to the USSR, the Third World was the one area that offered the Soviet Union the greatest opportunity to gain allies. Soviet actions in the Third World, though, have hindered the Soviets from winning over indigenous forces there to its cause. While Soviet military thought does not acknowledge that this has been caused by Soviet actions, the difficulties that the USSR is experiencing in the Third World have been reflected in the pessimism with which the Soviets have lately come to regard this region.

American Ideas and Actions in Local Wars

During the 1950s and 1960s Soviet military thinkers frequently discussed American ideas about local war, but ceased doing this almost completely in the early 1970s. This can best be explained by the fact that the primary criticism Soviet military thinkers made about American limited war theory was that it assumed local conflict could be kept localised and would not escalate into world war. At that time, it was pointed out that such an assumption could well be false. However, when Soviet military thinkers themselves accepted the idea that local wars need not necessarily escalate into world war, the basis for criticising American limited war doctrine was removed. While American military actions could be 'objectively' regarded by a Marxist-Leninist as possessing some correct as well as some incorrect elements, American ideas on limited war were a branch of bourgeois ideology that could not in any way be described as correct.

Up to the mid-1960s, the Soviets had little to say about American actions in local wars. From the time of the Vietnam war to the present, though, they have commented on this at length. During the Vietnam war, the Americans were seen as doomed to failure since even though they were militarily superior to the Vietnamese communists, the US was fighting an unjust war against a morally superior opponent.[30] However, after the Vietnam war, the Soviet evaluation of American actions in local war changed from a sociopolitical basis to a military one. American actions in Vietnam were criticised as poorly executed from a military perspective, unlike those of Israel in the several Arab-Israeli wars which the Soviets saw as well executed.[31] Recently, the Soviets have even begun to evaluate positively certain US military operations in Vietnam, particularly the use of helicopters in mountainous terrain against insurgents (similar to what the Soviets are undertaking in Afghanistan).[32] This meant that the Soviets now saw that local wars could be won or lost through military means alone with sociopolitical factors not necessarily determining the outcome. This was ironic because the change in the basis of evaluation of local wars from a sociopolitical to a military one, along with the notion that local wars could be won or lost by military means, indicated that in the 1970s Soviet military thinkers came to accept these 'bourgeois' ideas on local war, at least as far as conflict in the Third World using conventional armed forces was concerned.

The dropping of American local war theory from their discussions as well as the change of the basis of evaluation of American actions in Third World conflicts from a sociopolitical to a military one might appear to indicate that Soviet military thinkers have during the 1970s eliminated ideological considerations from their view of local war. This, however, is not the case. In any given local war, the Soviet Union would, they hold, only be connected with the side that was ideologically just and would be against the unjust side. The difference now was that local war was no longer seen as a foreign policy instrument that only the West could use. Further, in certain local wars that the USSR might be involved in, the unjust side might use tactics similar to those the Vietnamese communists used against the Americans. Their use of such tactics, though, did not make the unjust side just. In the same manner, tactics adopted by the Soviets from the US to combat such forces did not make the Soviets unjust either. What this development in Soviet military thought did indicate, though, was that as the Soviet Union became more directly involved in Third World conflicts, Soviet military thinkers came to recognise that military factors were vitally important in determining the outcome of these conflicts.

The change in Soviet military thinking about American ideas about and actions in local wars indicates that the Soviet military have come to regard intervention in local war as a military policy that can be successful. Further, it is one that can be successfully undertaken by the Soviet Union. This is a significant change from the 1960s when the Soviets saw local wars as something only the imperialists engaged in and in which the USSR should avoid becoming involved. Yet while the Soviet military is now more willing to intervene in Third World conflicts, their discussion of American actions in local wars reveals something else important. The Soviets now envision themselves as being in a similar position to the Americans in Vietnam – interveners on behalf of an allied government against insurgents. For example, in Afghanistan, the Soviet Union intervened in order to save a Marxist government that was about to be overthrown by non-Marxist forces. What this means is that the Soviet Union has intervened not to fight for change in the *status quo*, but to protect what has already been established, despite the fact that a Marxist government may have only very recently come to power. The Soviets now look at American actions in local wars not to learn how to expand their sphere of influence in the Third World, but to prevent the loss of allies to forces that would be hostile to the USSR if they came to power. This is yet another indication that the Soviets have come to conclude that indigenous forces in the Third World are not always friends, but may sometimes be enemies whom it is necessary to fight against if Soviet interests are to be protected.

The Soviet Role in Third World Conflicts

The first thing to note about Soviet military thinking on the Soviet Union's role in local conflicts in the Third World is that what Raymond Garthoff said in 1966 is still true now: the Soviets have been extremely reticent about making statements on this subject.[33] This reticence is especially noticeable when compared to the relative verbosity of Soviet military writing on all other aspects of Soviet military thought about conflict in the Third World.

In those statements that have been made about the role of the USSR in Third World conflicts, though, a definite trend over time can be seen. At first, in the late 1950s and early 1960s, Soviet military thinkers said nothing specific about the role of the USSR in local conflicts. In the middle and late 1960s, they discussed arms transfers[34] and then in the early 1970s they discussed Soviet training of revolutionary armed forces.[35] In the late 1970s, the role of Cuban armed forces and treaties of friendship and co-operation were discussed.[36] Even some hints of the use of Soviet armed forces were given,[37] though no explicit statements advocating this as a general policy have yet been made. Thus, in these statements there has occurred a progression over time toward increasing Soviet involvement in Third World conflicts. Sending arms to the revolutionary forces allowed them to fight while the USSR remained separate from the conflict. Training the revolutionary forces, either in the USSR or in a Third World nation itself, involved the Soviets in how these forces fought without the USSR being directly involved. With the use of Cuban armed forces, though, the socialist commonwealth, if not the USSR itself, became directly involved in conflict. Treaties of friendship and co-operation created the potential for direct Soviet involvement, as indeed has actually occurred in Afghanistan through the use of Soviet armed forces in combat there.

This progression is also noteworthy, because each of the successive steps of Soviet involvement discussed by Soviet military thinkers was only mentioned *after* they had already occurred in practice. The USSR had been shipping arms to Vietnam, Egypt and other Third World nations long before this was acknowledged in the 1960s by Soviet military writers. Similarly, Soviet military advisers had been in Egypt, Syria, and elsewhere before this policy of training revolutionary armed forces was acknowledged in the early 1970s. Cuban involvement in Angola was only mentioned after it had occurred and met with a certain degree of success. Thus, it is not surprising that no explicit mention has yet been made of the use of Soviet armed forces in Third World conflicts as a policy instrument even though this has already occurred in Afghanistan. Now that Soviet armed forces are being used in Afghanistan, a discussion of this in Soviet military writing may take place.

A question arises as to why Soviet military thinkers have not discussed the policies through which the USSR has become involved in Third World conflicts until after these policies have actually been implemented. Unfortunately, this is not an easy question to answer since the Soviets have never explained why they make certain statements at certain times and not at others. One reason might be the desire to maintain secrecy about new military policies so that they will have the maximum effect when implemented. If the Soviets discussed these new military policies before they were implemented, their opponents might have time to counter them. One difficulty in this explanation, however, is that once a military policy has been announced, the Soviets do not hesitate to proclaim that they will do the same again in the future.

Perhaps a better explanation might be that the Soviets did not really know that they were going to implement new military policies in any given conflict, but improvised new ones as the situation developed. Only when a new policy was seen by the Soviets to be successful did they acknowledge and discuss it. This would appear to be a more plausible explanation since not only did Soviet military thinkers refrain from discussing new military policies before they were implemented, but also while they were first being implemented. It was only when a new military policy was seen to be relatively successful that it was ever discussed.

No matter for what reason Soviet military thinkers did not discuss new Soviet military policies, the conclusion can be drawn that Soviet statements are not useful in predicting in what new ways the USSR might become involved militarily in Third World conflicts. On the other hand, their statements are useful in seeing what are the military policies that Soviet military thinkers regard as being successful, and hence, are likely to be used again in the future.

Finally, it must be noted that during the Brezhnev era, Soviet military thinkers have over time advocated increasingly direct means of Soviet military involvement in Third World conflicts. This trend is frightening not only to Western nations, but also to Third World nations which regard themselves as potential targets of Soviet intervention. However, the reason why the Soviet Union has used increasingly forceful means of military involvement in Third World conflicts is that as time goes by such means are needed for the USSR to be successful in these conflicts. Transfers of arms or training of armed forces alone did not suffice for the USSR to be successful in Angola, Ethiopia, or Afghanistan; increasingly direct commitments have become necessary. Whereas during the Khrushchev era the Soviets thought that socialism would quickly spread throughout the Third World without much assistance from the USSR, by the late Brezhnev era it was recognised that long-term, costly military efforts by the Soviet Union are often required just to protect the gains that socialism has already made. This is not a trend that the Soviets can regard as being beneficial to their interests.

Party-Military Relations

During the Khrushchev and Brezhnev years, there were three occasions on which Party/civilian and military ideas about conflict in the Third World differed from each other: (1) differences over the nature and types of war during the late Khrushchev years; (2) differences on the relationship between peaceful coexistence and wars of national and social liberation during the Brezhnev years before the 24th Party Congress held in 1971; and (3) differences with respect to the reliability of radical military regimes in the Third World from approximately 1966 to 1977.

As was mentioned earlier, the classic Soviet military definition of the nature and types of war inherited from the Stalin years was a fourfold categorisation based solely on ideological factors. In early 1961, though, Khrushchev introduced a threefold categorisation that included both ideological and non-ideological factors (scale of warfare): world war, local war, and wars of national liberation. Khrushchev did this in order to explain why Soviet assistance to Third World conflicts was not as great as the Chinese called for; world war was unjust because it would spell disaster, and local war was unjust too because it could lead to world war. The Soviet military, however, did not accept this new categorisation, and continued to use the traditional one. They criticised the new categorisation because it defined wars as just or unjust based on their scale and not on the class nature of the belligerents. The military, though, never criticised Khrushchev directly. For his part, Khrushchev never said anything at all about the traditional military classification of types of wars. The expression of disagreement by the military with the statements of the Party leader would never have occurred during the Stalin years. It is not surprising that it occurred during the late Khrushchev years when so many groups, including the Party itself, were becoming increasingly dissatisfied with the First Secretary. While Khrushchev was in power, though, the USSR was guided by his notions and not the military's. At the beginning of the Brezhnev era, the military directly criticised Khrushchev for his classification of wars and reasserted the traditional ideologically based classification of types of war. Ironically, the military itself began to introduce non-ideological factors into its discussion of the nature and types of wars beginning in 1968. During the Brezhnev years, this subject was one that the Party left to the military; the Party did not concern itself with this question, but allowed the military to define types of wars within the limits of Marxism-Leninism.

During the years of the Brezhnev era before the 24th Party Congress in 1971, the military was unenthusiastic about the Party's call for peaceful coexistence with the West. The Party desired peaceful coexistence in order to avoid world war. Regarding wars of national and social liberation, it believed that the establishment of peace would allow progressive forces in the Third World to flourish, and was all that the USSR would do to help these forces. The Soviet military expressed its unhappiness with this policy not by criticising it in any way, but simply by not repeating any of the Party's statements in favour of it. At the 24th Party Congress, however, the Party's position on peaceful coexistence changed. Peaceful coexistence was now seen as being compatible with Soviet assistance, including military, to wars of national and social liberation. From this point, the Soviet military enthusiastically repeated the Party's statements on peaceful coexistence. Once again, the military did not criticise the Party directly, and the policy that was actually followed was that of the Party and not the military.

With regard to the dispute over whether or not radical military regimes in the Third World could succeed in maintaining socialism permanently in their countries, the military actually did criticise those who felt such regimes were not reliable. However, the debate on this question took place not between the military and high Party officials, but between the military and the civilian academics of the international institutes of the USSR Academy of Sciences. The Party itself did not comment on this issue; that this debate occurred indicated that it was probably divided over the issue. The Soviet Union, though, did support radical military regimes in the Third World as the military advocated. However, once it was demonstrated that radical military regimes could be unreliable, everyone, including the military, called for Marxist-Leninist parties to be established by military regimes to ensure that the path to socialism was maintained.

What does this indicate about Party-military relations? On certain issues relating to conflict in the Third World, the Soviet military has, in the past, formulated its own independent position. However, where the military position differed from that of the Party leadership, the military made known its views in a highly circumspect manner. Only when the Soviet military was opposed by the civilian academics of the Academy of Science did it directly criticise its opponents — and in this case the military probably had a substantial portion of the Party leadership on its side. It is apparent that the Party is very much in control of the military, and the Party often initiated changes in thinking that were then taken up by the military. This was true of ideas concerning the relationship of local war to world war, peaceful co-existence, and the Soviet role in Third World conflicts.

Nevertheless, while the Party controls the military, the military is the only source of detailed military information that the Party has. There is no civilian Office of the Secretary of Defence or Arms Control and Disarmament Agency offering conflicting advice, as in the United States. Thus, the Party must rely on the military for the information it needs to make decisions on military matters. This, of course, allows the military a large influence in decision making. Some aspects of thinking about conflict in the Third World were left exclusively to the military, without Party comment. In the Brezhnev era, this included the nature and types of war and discussion of American ideas about and actions in local wars. On the whole, though, the ideas of both the Party and the military about conflict in the Third World are similar. The relationship between the two organisations is one based on generally shared interests. The Party is dominant, but the military accepts the role of the Party, and both work toward the same goals.

Military Thought and Foreign Policy

Just what are these goals in terms of Soviet foreign policy? Are the intentions of the Soviet Union basically offensive or defensive? Soviet military thinking about conflict in the Third World sheds some light on these questions.

During the Khrushchev era, the Soviets optimistically thought that socialism would spread throughout the Third World without much effort on the part of the Soviet Union. This would be accomplished by progressive forces within the Third World itself, which, the Soviets felt, would naturally seek to ally with the USSR against the common imperialist enemy. The Soviet Union would give diplomatic, political, ideological, and some economic support to these forces, but very little military support. At most, military support would consist of arms transfers. Thus, while the Soviets saw socialism as being on the offensive politically in the Third World, the Soviet Union played only a minor role there. The USSR was not really on the offensive or the defensive in conflict situations in the Third World; for the most part, it sought to avoid them altogether, emphasising the peaceful road to socialism.

During the early Brezhnev years (1964-68), this view changed. Socialism experienced a number of setbacks in the Third World as radical governments allied to the Soviet Union were overthrown by right-wing military coups. In addition, the United States had steadily increased its military commitment in Indochina to over 500,000 troops during this period. The Soviets realised that there were serious obstacles to the growth of socialism in the Third World. A greater Soviet role in protecting those socialist gains which had already been made was called for. Arms transfers to progressive forces in the Third World were acknowledged as a policy that the USSR did, and would, pursue. The USSR also began to send military advisers to the Third World at this time, most notably to Egypt after the 1967 war, but did not yet discuss this as a policy to be pursued generally. Despite this increased Soviet military involvement in the Third World, the Soviets still expected that indigenous progressive forces would undertake the major part of any fighting to establish or maintain socialism in the Third World. The Soviet role was only an auxiliary one. The increased Soviet military involvement in the Third World that did occur was regarded as defensive against the actions of the main imperialists and indigenous reactionary forces.

The middle Brezhnev years (1969-75) saw the United States withdraw from Indochina and the Portuguese Empire disintegrate. Socialism spread to Indochina, the former Portuguese colonies in Africa, and Ethiopia. Progressive military regimes came to power in Somalia, Peru and elsewhere. Soviet relations with Egypt were troubled, but had not yet reached the point where Egypt abrogated its treaty of friendship and co-operation with Moscow. Though the peaceful road to socialism proved a failure in Chile, Soviet optimism about the spread of socialism in the Third World through revolution was at its highest. However, unlike during the Khrushchev era, the Soviets were now more willing to take steps themselves to ensure that socialism was maintained. Sending Soviet military advisers to the Third World was now advocated as a policy. In 1975, Cuban troops were sent to Angola to help the MPLA defeat its opponents and come to power. The Soviets were opportunistic in taking advantage of Western difficulties in Southeast Asia and Africa to promote socialist forces into power; in this sense, the Soviets saw themselves on the offensive. However, the Soviet Union itself was not directly involved in actual conflict. Its role was to assist the local progressive forces to succeed militarily. It was only at the end of this period that soldiers from an established socialist state intervened in a

Third World conflict; these, however, were not from the USSR, but from Cuba, the leader of which has had more ambitious revolutionary goals than the Soviet Union all along.

During the late Brezhnev years (1976 to the present), Soviet optimism about the spread of socialism in the Third World has given way to growing pessimism in this regard. Both Egypt and Somalia abrogated their treaties of friendship and co-operation with the USSR. Pro-Soviet Marxist governments that had recently come to power faced strong local opposition either from non-Marxist forces, as in Angola and Afghanistan, or from Marxist and non-Marxist forces, as in Ethiopia and Cambodia. In Iran, the revolution that toppled the Shah was originally welcomed by the Soviets as being anti-American, but they now recognise that the radical Islamic fundamentalism it has given birth to is vehemently opposed to Marxism-Leninism.[38] Only in Central America does socialism appear to be on the offensive, with the Sandinistas having come to power in Nicaragua and Marxist guerrillas threatening to topple the government of El Salvador. Elsewhere in the Third World, particularly in nations with pro-Soviet Marxist governments, the forces of socialism are on the defensive. Their opponent, though, is not the United States, but indigenous forces within the Third World itself. This opposition to Soviet foreign policy by indigenous Third World forces is a disappointment to the Soviets who regarded Third World hostility to Western influence as acceptance of, or even an invitation to extend, Soviet influence. The Soviets have not yet realised that indigenous Third World forces, motivated by nationalism and the desire for independence, would not oppose the influence of the West only to replace it by Soviet influence; they want independence from both.

Just to maintain those socialist gains that have already been made the Soviets have come to realise will, in certain instances, require much heavier military commitment than was previously thought necessary. Indigenous socialist forces are no longer seen as being able to provide most of the effort necessary to maintain themselves in power. If socialism is to be maintained in the Third World, long-term military commitments on the part of the existing socialist nations are required. Thus, Cuba has had to keep large numbers of troops in Angola and Ethiopia, as have Vietnam in Cambodia and the USSR itself in Afghanistan, in order to prevent their Marxist governments from falling. More than ever before, the Soviets during the late Brezhnev years feel themselves to be very much on the defensive in the Third World.

Yet how can it be said that the Soviets have become more defensive during the late Brezhnev years when it is this time period in which the USSR and its allies have become more active militarily in the Third World than at any previous time? And how can it be said that the Soviets are merely defending gains already made by socialism in the Third World when these gains were made only very recently, as in Afghanistan? The answer to these questions may be found in what the Soviets define as a 'socialist gain'. This is not treated directly in Soviet military thought, but is implicit in it. The Soviets view history in Marxist-Leninist terms; this is the age when socialism is replacing capitalism throughout the world. This is how history is supposed to develop. Thus, when any group comes to power in the Third World that declares itself Marxist-Leninist or an ally of the Soviet Union, the Soviets regard this as the manifestation of the inevitable progress of history. Further, the Soviets expect that nations which gain socialist governments will continue to remain socialist. They acknowledge that setbacks can occur by socialist governments being overthrown or becoming anti-Soviet, but these are described as temporary. Yet these setbacks have become numerous in the 1960s and 1970s. The Soviets are clearly unhappy when these setbacks occur; however, they have been unwilling to acknowledge that these setbacks for socialism have been inflicted by indigenous Third World forces, instead of through the collusion of the major imperialist powers with local reactionaries.

This is not surprising since the Marxist-Leninist notion of history recognises that the imperialists will fight against the advance of socialism, but not that indigenous popular forces within the Third World will do so. The opposition of the developed capitalist nations to socialism serves to confirm the Marxist-Leninist notion of history, for even if the capitalists are victorious in certain instances, socialism is promised eventual victory over them. Since the end of the Second World War, first the West European capitalists, through the process of decolonisation, and then the United States, through its withdrawal from Vietnam, have experienced defeats in the Third World; their decline should have led to a corresponding gain for socialism. However, the spread of Soviet influence has been resisted within the Third World itself, often in nations where socialism has come to power. The opposition of indigenous Third World forces to socialism is much more threatening to the Soviets than the opposition of the Western capitalists, even though the former may be militarily weaker. The reason for this is that Third World opposition to socialism not only challenges the Soviet desire to increase their influence in the world, but also the entire Marxist-Leninist notion of history which saw the poor regions of the world as seeking to acquire the benefits of both socialism and friendship with the USSR. The fact that this has not happened and that the Third World has developed several different political ideologies of its own that are different from, and some even opposed to, Marxism-Leninism gives rise to questions that the Soviets would prefer not to face. Are the prophecies of Marxism-Leninism irrelevant to the Third World? Will the wave of socialist revolutions give way to a new form of revolution inspired by a completely different ideology, such as Islam, whose success would threaten Soviet interests? Will the Soviet Union, instead of being a revolutionary force spreading a revolutionary ideology throughout the world, become a conservative power trying desperately to maintain an ideology that others see as reactionary?

These are questions that are still in their infancy. The Soviet Union has a definite interest in taking stronger measures to protect Marxist Third World regimes against indigenous Third World forces than against the West in order to prevent these questions from growing large to the point that forces within the Third World and the West opposed to the USSR can unite to pursue joint efforts against the USSR. Socialist forces are having a difficult enough time holding on to their positions in Afghanistan, Angola, Cambodia and Ethiopia against just local Third World forces. This task would be even more difficult if indigenous Third World forces received large-scale military assistance from the West in a co-ordinated effort to defeat Marxist governments. Returning, then, to what the Soviets define as a 'socialist gain' in the Third World, it is seen to occur whenever a Third World government declares itself Marxist-Leninist and/or pro-Soviet. For such a government to be overthrown or to change its mind due to the imperialists is a setback to socialism, but one which can later be rectified, but for such a government to be driven out due to indigenous Third World forces is unacceptable to the Soviets. No matter how recently or by what means these Marxist governments came to power, the fact that indigenous forces currently threaten the existence of several pro-Soviet Marxist governments in the Third World is the reason why the Soviets feel that any actions they take to save them, including military actions, are defensive in nature and not offensive.

This, however, only explains why the Soviets themselves see their actions in the Third World as being defensive. Whether others regard Soviet actions as being either defensive or offensive is a different question altogether. For nations that do not share the Marxist-Leninist notion of history, there is no reason to accept the prediction that the transformation of all nations to socialism is inevitable. All recognise that the Soviet Union is a major power that would like the world to conform to its notion of what the world should be like. Other major powers have shared a similar desire, including the former European colonial powers and, more recently, the United States. However, both the European colonial powers and the United States have been able to accept losses of influence in the Third World in nations or regions which did not accept their view of what the world should be like; the Europeans have withdrawn from nearly all their colonies and the US withdrew from Indochina. The Soviet Union has been forced to withdraw from areas of influence in the past, as when Egypt and Somalia forced the Russians out of their countries. In Afghanistan, though, the Soviet Union has been unwilling to withdraw its influence despite nearly universal opposition to it internally within Afghanistan as well as widespread political opposition in both the Third World and the West. It is this unwillingness to withdraw from a country where its presence is clearly not wanted that is disturbing to others. Hence, while the Soviets might think of their actions in Afghanistan as defensive, it is not difficult to understand why others in both the West and the Third World think of Soviet actions there as offensive.

Afghanistan, though, is a special case since it borders directly upon the Soviet Union. The Soviet Union's unwillingness to withdraw its armed forces from there despite their apparent inability to defeat the Moslem guerrillas points out another serious problem that the USSR faces, but which the United States does not. The Soviet Union is, after all, the last remaining European nation that still possesses a colonial empire in the Third World. This empire includes large regions inhabited primarily by Moslems. With the independence of almost all of the Third World, including the Moslem world, and the rise of radical Islamic ideology in areas that border directly on the USSR, it is doubtful that the desire for independence does not affect Soviet Central Asia as well. The recent assassination of the Soviet premier of Khirgizia reportedly by Moslem rebels shows that there may be the beginning of a movement opposed to Soviet rule in this region.[39] If the Soviets were to withdraw from Afghanistan and acknowledge defeat by the Moslem rebels there, this might well serve to encourage the growth of a large Moslem guerrilla movement in the Soviet Union itself. Although it is doubtful that Moslem guerrillas in Soviet Central Asia could win a military contest with Moscow, they could encourage other opposition movements in the USSR and Eastern Europe. The prospect of having to fight to protect the territorial integrity of the USSR itself cannot be a pleasant one for the Soviet leaders. Thus, for reasons relating to Soviet domestic politics, the USSR may be unable to withdraw from Afghanistan no matter how futile its struggle against the Moslem guerrillas there might be.

Yet while this might be the most basic defensive motive possible for the Soviets to remain in Afghanistan, it is not one that other nations can feel relieved about even though defensive intentions may indicate more limited goals than offensive ones. Historically, the response of great powers to threats toward areas where their hold is tenuous has been to attempt to expand their influence even further. For over half a century following the end of the Napoleonic wars, the British Empire made relatively few colonial acquisitions. It was only when other European nations began to aggressively acquire colonies in the latter part of the 19th century that Britain greatly expanded its colonial empire. For example, in order to protect India, Britain acquired Egypt. But in order to protect Egypt, Britain acquired Sudan and Uganda. Similarly, in order to repress Serbian nationalism in its own province of Bosnia-Herzegovina, Austria-Hungary declared war on independent Serbia. By the same logic, it is possible that the Soviet leaders might become convinced that in order to save their position in Afghanistan, it will be necessary to conquer part or all of Pakistan and Iran. Thus, even with only defensive intentions, it is possible that the USSR will find it necessary to expand its influence further through military means.

Whether this is what the Soviet Union will actually do remains to be seen. What is clear from Soviet military thinking about conflict in the Third World is that while the Soviets do indeed wish to see socialism spread through this region, they have in the late Brezhnev years become relatively pessimistic about this actually occurring. Further, in those Third World nations which have Marxist governments, socialism is often on the defensive against indigenous Third World forces opposing it. In order to remain in power, some of these Marxist governments require relatively large numbers of troops from already established socialist nations to fight the opposition. Even then, this indigenous opposition has not been readily defeated, as Afghanistan, Angola, Cambodia and Ethiopia have shown. Yet while these relatively costly and protracted military commitments directly undertaken by Cuba, Vietnam and the USSR itself have not yet proved successful, so far they have not been overwhelmingly burdensome to the socialist community. But if the opposition to Marxist Third World governments became militarily stronger, or if serious indigenous opposition erupts in other Marxist Third World nations such as Mozambique, South Yemen, or even Cuba or Vietnam, the problem the USSR faces will be greater.

The USSR would then have to decide between two courses of action: (1) making a much greater military effort itself to defend existing regimes, which would ensure greater opposition to its foreign policy from both the West and the Third World and would risk the possibility of domestic opposition within the USSR against the economic and military burden such a policy would entail, without guaranteeing that such a policy would be any more successful than it has been so far in Afghanistan; or (2) allowing Marxist Third World governments to be overthrown (not just letting non-Marxist-Leninist allies such as Egypt and Somalia change their minds) where they are strongly opposed by indigenous forces, and thereby risking the encouragement of opposition to other Marxist Third World governments that would also have to be allowed to fall without the USSR undertaking a major military effort to save them, and perhaps eventually risking the growth of opposition to socialism within the USSR itself. If this is indeed the choice that Soviet foreign policy toward the Third World faces in the future, then Soviet hopes that the Third World would become socialist and that the Third World would willingly accept the USSR as a model for its own economic and political development were woefully optimistic and will never be fulfilled.

The Role of Soviet Military Thought

What can be said about the role military thinking plays in the formulation of Soviet foreign policy? From examining each of the various aspects of Soviet military thought on this subject, as well as its relationship to Soviet domestic politics and foreign policy, it is clear that Soviet military thought is not a rigid, unchanging doctrine that serves as a blueprint from which all Soviet actions can be predicted. Instead, Soviet military thinking has changed over time. Far from being predictive of events, changes in Soviet military thought often reflect events. Yet while Soviet military thought might not actually predict specific Soviet foreign policy actions, changes in Soviet military thought represent changes in the assumptions and attitudes upon which Soviet foreign policy is formulated. Thus, events serve to change Soviet military thinking, which in turn serves to change the formulation of Soviet foreign policy actions. Soviet foreign policy actions, of course, are one factor that shape events in international relations; depending on the success or failure of these actions, Soviet military thinking can either confirm the wisdom of or support modifications to Soviet foreign policy by looking at events in retrospect.

Examples of changes in Soviet military thought changing the assumptions on which Soviet foreign policy is formulated are the changes in Soviet military thinking on the relationship of local war to world war, the relationship of peaceful coexistence to wars of national and social liberation, and American actions in local wars. The change in the Soviet military's views from a belief that local war could escalate into world war to a belief that the USSR could keep a local war localised through its superior military strength in 1974-75 signalled the participation in actual combat in local wars of troops from established socialist countries that began with the Cuban intervention in Angola in 1975. The change in 1971 of the Soviet notion about peaceful coexistence signalled the greater amount of Soviet military assistance to 'progressive forces' in the Third World that has occurred since the early 1970s. Also, the change in the Soviet evaluation of American actions in local wars from a purely ideological perspective during the Vietnam war to a military perspective after it, and the recent favourable evaluation of certain US actions in Vietnam as being effective means of counter-insurgency tactics has shown that the Soviets no longer consider local war to be a policy that can be employed by the imperialists alone, and that the Soviets now see themselves in a position similar to what the American position was in Vietnam — interveners in a local war to protect a friendly government against indigenous opposition.

These three aspects of Soviet military thought can also be seen as reflecting events in international relations. The military did not assert that local wars could be kept localised through Soviet military strength until after the US withdrew from Vietnam and it was clear that American domestic politics would not readily allow US military intervention abroad again. Peaceful coexistence was seen as compatible with Soviet aid to progressive forces in the Third World only in 1971 when it was clear that even though the US would not win in Vietnam it was still willing to pursue strategic arms limitation with the USSR. The Soviet military saw the socialist nations in a position similar to that of the Americans in Vietnam and this was due to military interventions by the established socialist states in Angola, Ethiopia, Cambodia and Afghanistan not being immediately successful in defeating the opposition, as was undoubtedly hoped by the Soviets when these interventions were first launched.

Similarly, the other aspects of Soviet military thought about conflict in the Third World can also be seen as reflective of events. Concerning the nature and types of wars, Soviet military thinking did not attempt to foresee what new types of conflict would occur in the Third World, but rather attempted to understand and classify those types of conflict that were already taking place. Several civil wars between the people and a regime of extreme reaction had already taken place by the time Stepanov and Rybkin had first discussed them in 1968. Similarly, nations on the path of socialist development fighting wars in defence of socialism had already begun to occur before Rybkin first wrote about them in 1978.

Regarding indigenous Third World forces, the Soviet military believed that radical Third World leaders could easily bring their nations to socialism until the mid-1960s when several such leaders were replaced by conservative military regimes. The Soviet military then saw radical military regimes as being able to maintain socialism in their countries until the mid-1970s when some of them abandoned socialism. Now, only a ruling Marxist-Leninist party is seen as capable of performing this task. In each case, change in military thought came only after events showed that the military's expectations were not being met. This was also an example of events affecting thinking which in turn affected Soviet foreign policy, which subsequent events then showed to be unsuccessful, leading to further changes in military thinking and then foreign policy, etc.

Finally, Soviet military thinking about the Soviet role in Third World conflicts always reflected the successful use of new policies (arms transfers, use of military advisers, Cuban troops). Statements about new policies never occurred before a new policy had been introduced in practice and proved successful. Once this occurred, though, a successful policy would be used again later. In this sense, discussion of a policy indicated that it would be used in the future. In contrast to military thought about indigenous forces in the Third World, this was an example of Soviet foreign policy being proved successful by events and Soviet military thinking confirming this success, encouraging the policy to be used again in Soviet foreign policy.

Thus, while changes in military thinking do sometimes signal changes in foreign policy, changing events are more basic to signalling changes both in military thinking and in foreign policy. In attempting to predict changes in future Soviet military thinking and foreign policy, then, it is necessary to predict the future course of events. This is extremely difficult to do. However, there are certain possible developments in international relations that suggest changes that might occur in Soviet military thought.

For example, if the Soviet Union succeeded in defeating the Moslem rebels in Afghanistan, it is likely that the Soviet military would acknowledge and praise the use of Soviet armed forces in Third World conflicts. This would be an ominous development since the Soviets have shown a propensity to repeat actions that have proved successful. However, if the Soviet Union does not succeed in defeating the Afghans, and if the conflict drags on as the Vietnam war did, it is doubtful that they would discuss direct Soviet military intervention in Third World conflicts as a policy to be undertaken elsewhere. Further, the Soviet military might end their praise of certain American actions in Vietnam and might even begin to attack the entire notion of counter-insurgency as being a failure. If a Marxist-Leninist Third World government were ever to fall, or voluntarily renounce either Marxism-Leninism or alliance with the USSR, then a ruling Marxist-Leninist party might also cease to be seen as a guarantee of socialism being permanently established in the Third World; the Soviets might then call for some form of Soviet military presence in socialist Third World nations to better protect socialism. If the United States should ever again become militarily involved in Third World conflicts, and especially if American actions were relatively successful, then the Soviets might re-emphasise the possibility of local wars escalating into world war and state that peaceful coexistence is not compatible with American military involvement in the Third World. Finally, if the trend toward conflicts between socialist nations continues, then the Soviet military might attempt to take more serious account of it in their discussion of the nature and types of wars.

One change in events that could completely change Soviet military thinking about conflict in the Third World would be a change in the leadership of the Soviet Union. Brezhnev's successors might take a more active role in formulating Soviet thinking on military issues; they might be more like Khrushchev and make innovations themselves in one or more aspects of military thinking about conflict in the Third World. On the other hand, they might allow the military to play a more independent role in formulating positions on this subject. Of course, the relationship between the Party and the military may continue under a different leadership much as it has during the Brezhnev era.

These possible changes in Soviet military thinking about conflict in the Third World are, of necessity, speculative. However, if the past is a guide to the future, then thinking about conflict in the Third World will definitely continue to change and evolve over time in response to events. Because of its changing nature, Soviet military thinking about this subject cannot be said to serve as a fixed programme of action that the USSR seeks to implement in the Third World. Soviet military thought is much more reactive to events than it is predictive of them. Nevertheless, the changes in Soviet military thinking about conflict in the Third World are a useful guide to understanding the changing Soviet assumptions and attitudes upon which Soviet foreign policy toward the Third World is based.

Notes

1. See N.S. Khrushchev, 'Za noviye pobedi mirovogo kommunisticheskogo dvizheniya', *Kommunist*, no. 1, January 1961, p. 18; Major General N. Talenskiy, 'Sovremennaya voina: kharakter i sledstviya', *Mezhdunarodnaya Zhizn'*, no. 10, October 1960, p. 36; Marshal of the Soviet Union V.D. Sokolovskiy (ed.), *Voyennaya strategiya*, 1st edn (Voyenizdar, Moscow, 1962), p. 222; Colonel General N. Lomov, 'O sovetskoy voyennoy doktrine', *Kommunist Vooruzhennykh Sil*, no. 10, May 1962, p. 16; Colonel V. Morozov, 'The Third Edition of "Marxism-Leninism on War and the Army"', *Voyennaya Mysl'*, no. 7, July 1963, CIA FDD trans. no. 956, p. 81; Lt. Colonel T. Kondratkov, 'Kharakter i osobennosti sovremennoy voini', *Kommunist Vooruzhennykh Sil*, no. 19, October 1967, p. 81; Major General K. Stepanov and Lt. Colonel Ye. Rybkin, 'The Nature and Types of Wars of the Modern Era', *Voyennaya Mysl'*, no. 2, February 1968, CIA FB FPD 0042/69, p. 73; Colonel V. Iarionov, 'Politicheskaya storona sovetskoy voyennoy doktrini', *Kommunist Vooruzhennykh Sil*, no. 22, November 1968, p. 16; and the note by the RAND Corporation editors of V.D. Sokolovskii, *Military Strategy* (Prentice-Hall, Englewood Cliffs, N.J., 1963), pp. 289-93.

2. *Dokumenti mezhdunarodnogo sobeschaniya kommunisticheskikh i rabochikh partii* (Politizdat, Moscow, 1969), p. 33.

3. Colonel G. Malinovskiy, 'Lokal'niye voini v zone natsional 'no-osvoboditel'nogo dvizheniya', *Voyenno-Istoricheskiy Zhurnal*, no. 5, May 1974, p. 97; General of the Army I. Shavrov, 'Lokal'niye voini i ikh mesto v globalnoy strategii imperializma' (part 1), *Voyenno-Istoricheskiy Zhurnal*, no. 3, March 1975, p. 61; and Colonel G. Malinovskiy, 'Lokal'naya voina', in *Sovetskaya voyennaya entsiklopediya*, vol. 5 (Voyenizdat, Moscow, 1978), p. 22.

4. Thomas W. Wolfe, *Soviet Strategy at the Crossroads* (Harvard University Press, Cambridge, Mass., 1964), pp. 118-24.

5. Khrushchev classified all wars into 'world wars, local wars, and wars of national liberation'; see Khrushchev, 'za noviye pobedi mirovogo kommunisticheskogo dvizheniya', p. 20. For a direct criticism of Khrushchev's classification system, see Colonel I. Sidel'nikov, 'V.I. Lenin o klassovom podkhode k opredeleniyu kharaktera voin', *Krasnaya Zvezda*, 22 September 1965.

6. Major General N. Sushko and Colonel S. Tyushkevich (eds.), *Marksizm-Leninizm o voine i armii*, 4th edn (Voyenizdat, Moscow, 1965), p. 80.

7. Stepanov and Rybkin, 'The Nature and Types of Wars of the Modern Era', pp. 76-9, and Colonel Ye. Rybkin, 'XXV S"yezd KPSS i osvoboditel'niye voini sovremennoy epokhi', *Voyenno-Istoricheskiy Zhurnal*, no. 11, November 1978, pp. 11-12.

8. Colonel Ye. Rybkin, 'Leninskiye printsipi sotsiologicheskogo analiza voin i sovremennost'', in Major General A.S. Milovidov and Colonel V.G. Kozlov (eds.), *Filosofskiye naslediye V.I. Lenina i problemi sovremennoy voini* (Voyenizdat, Moscow, 1972), p. 47.

9. Colonel Ye. Rybkin, 'Leninskaya kontseptsiya voini i sovremennost'', *Kommunist Vooruzhennykh Sil*, no. 20, October 1973, pp. 24-35.

10. Colonel T. Kondratkov, 'Problema klassifikatsii voin i ee otrazheniye

o ideologicheskoy bor'be', *Kommunist Vooruzhennykh Sil,* no. 11, June 1974, p. 20.

11. Lt. Colonel N. Khmara, 'Nekotoriye osobennosti grazhdanskikh voin v sovremennuyu epokhu', *Kommunist Vooruzhennykh Sil,* no. 16, August 1971, pp. 17-18, 23-4.

12. Shavrov, 'Lokal'niye voini i ikh mesto v globalnoy strategii imperializma', pp. 62-3.

13. See, for example, 'World Communist Solidarity with the Afghan Revolution', *New Times,* no. 3, January 1980, pp. 9-10.

14. Colin Legum, 'Angola and the Horn of Africa', in Stephen S. Kaplan *et al., Diplomacy of Power: Soviet Armed Forces as a Political Instrument* (Brookings, Washington, 1981), pp. 573-4.

15. Ibid., pp. 612-27. See also Paul B. Henze, 'To Reagan: Don't Blow It in the Horn of Africa', *Christian Science Monitor,* 3 April 1981. Henze believes that the Ethiopians can contain the military threats against them.

16. See Zalmay Khalilzad, 'Afghanistan and the Crisis in American Foreign Policy', *Survival,* XXII:4 (July/August 1980), pp. 151-60.

17. William S. Turley and Jeffrey Race, 'The Third Indochina War', *Foreign Policy,* no. 38 (Spring 1980), pp. 92-116.

18. See N.S. Khrushchev, *Otchetnii doklad Ts.K. KPSS XX s''yezdu partii* (Politizdat, Moscow, 1956), pp. 36-44; V. Korionov, 'Mezhdunarodnoye znacheniye XXIII s''yezda KPSS', *Kommunist,* no. 6, April 1966, p. 16; and A.A. Gromyko, *The International Situation and Soviet Foreign Policy* (Novosti, Moscow, 1968), pp. 9-15.

19. See, for example, Colonel N. Vetrov, 'Problems of War and Peace and the World Revolutionary Process', *Voyennaya Mysl',* no. 8, August 1971, FBIS FPD 0011/74, p. 18; Colonel V. Serelrayannikov and Colonel M. Yasyukov, 'Mirnoye sosushchestnovaniye i zashchita sotsialisticheskogo otechestva', *Kommunist Vooruzhennykh Sil,* no. 16, August 1972, pp. 10, 15-16; Colonel Ye. Rybkin, 'Pravda o voine – oruzhiye sil mira', *Kommunist Vooruzhennykh Sil,* no. 10, May 1977, pp. 8-15; and Major General D. Volkogonov, 'Klassovaya bor'ba i sovremennost'', *Kommunist Vooruzhennykh Sil,* no. 4, February 1979, pp. 8-18.

20. G. Mirskiy, 'The Proletariat and National Liberation', *New Times,* no. 18, May 1964, pp. 8-9. See also Charles C. Petersen, 'Third World Military Elites in Soviet Perspective', Center for Naval Analyses Professional Paper 262, November 1979, p. 5.

21. Colonel Ye. Dolgopolov, 'Armii osvobodivshikhsya stran', *Krasnaya Zvezda,* 19 May 1968. See also Petersen, 'Third World Military Elites', pp. 11-22.

22. G. Mirskiy, 'O kharaktere sotsial'nikh sil v Azii i Afriki', *Kommunist,* no. 17, November 1968, pp. 89-102; G. Mirskiy, *Armiya i politika v stranakh Azii i Afriki* (Nauka, Moscow, 1970); and G. Mirskiy, *Tretiy mir: obshchestvo, vlast', armiya* (Nauka, Moscow, 1976).

23. Colonel Ye. Dolgoplov, 'Molodiye armii i sotsial'niy progress', *Kommunist Vooruzhennykh Sil,* no. 21, November 1976, pp. 90-2.

24. Colonel Ye. Dolgopolov, 'Vazhniy politicheskiy faktor: o roli armiy v razivayushchiksya stranakh', *Krasnaya Zvezda,* 21 April 1978.

25. This was an issue over which Moscow and Havana disagreed in the 1960s; for a description of each side's position, see Andrés Suarez, *Cuba: Castroism and Communism 1959-1966* (MIT Press, Cambridge, Mass., 1967), pp. 186-91.

26. Colonel V. Andrianov, 'Partizanskaya voina i voyennaya strategiya', *Voyenno-Istoricheskiy Zhurnal,* no. 7, July 1975, pp. 29-32.

27. S.A. Mikoyan, 'Ob osobennostyakh revolyutsii v Nikaragua i ee urokakh s tochki zreniya teorii i praktiki osvoboditel'nogo dvizheniya (zaklyuchitel'noye

slovo)', *Latinskaya Amerika*, no. 3, March 1980, pp. 35-7.

28. Colonel G. Malinovskiy, 'Natsional'no-osvoboditel'noye dvizheniye na sovremennom etape', *Kommunist Vooruzhennykh Sil*, no. 24, December 1979, pp. 27-33.

29. Ibid., p. 28; S.L. Agayev and I.M. Tatarovskaya, 'Nekotoriye problemi razvitiya revolyutsionnogo protsessa v osvobodivshikhsya stranakh', *Rabochiy Klass i Sovremenniy Mir*, no. 5, September-October 1978, pp. 45-7; and An. Gromyko and G. Starushenko, 'Aktaul'niye voprosi razvitiya Afriki', *Kommunist*, no. 2, January 1980, p. 120.

30. Major General V. Matsulenko, 'Lokal'niye voini imperializma (1945-1968 gg), *Voyenno-Istoricheskiy Zhurnal*, no. 9, September 1968, p. 47; Lt. Colonel T. Kondratkov, 'Organichennaya voina – orudiye imperialisticheskoy agressi', *Kommunist Vooruzhennykh Sil*, no. 8, April 1969, p. 28; Major General V. Zemskov, 'Characteristic Features of Modern Wars and Possible Methods of Conducting Them', *Voyennaya Mysl'*, no. 7, July 1969, CIA FP FPD 0022/70, p. 25; V. Perfitov, 'Limited Warfare in U.S. Foreign Policy', *Voyennaya Mysl'*, no. 4, April 1971, FBIS FPD 0019/74, pp. 108-11; and Lt. Colonel D. Volkogonov, 'The Moral Factor in Local War', *Voyennaya Mysl'*, no. 12, December 1971, FBIS FPD 0003/74, pp. 26-7.

31. Colonel P. Maslennikov, 'Organizatsiya upravleniya voiskami SShA v voine vo V'etname', *Voyenno-Istoricheskiy Zhurnal*, no. 10, October 1975, pp. 42-9; Colonel N. Nikitin, 'Nekotoriye operativno-takticheskiye uroki lokal'nikh voin imperializma', *Voyenno-Istoricheskiy Zhurnal*, no. 12, December 1978, p. 66; Major General V. Matsulenko, 'Po inostrannim armiyam', *Voyenno-Istoricheskiy Zhurnal*, no. 4, April 1979, pp. 54-65; and Major General V. Matsulenko, 'O nekotorikh voprosakh upravleniya voiskami v lokal'nikh voinakh', *Voyenno-Istoricheskiy Zhurnal*, no. 3, March 1980, pp. 53-63.

32. Colonel (Ret.) A. Sinitskiy, 'Nekotoriye takticheskiye vivodi iz opita agressivnoy voini SShA protiv V'etnama', *Voyenno-Istoricheskiy Zhurnal*, no. 6, June 1979, p. 57.

33. Raymond L. Garthoff, *Soviet Military Policy: A Historical Analysis* (Praeger, New York, 1966), p. 213.

34. For relatively hesitant statements regarding the transfer of arms, see 'Za edinstvo i splochennost' mezhdunarodnogo kommunisticheskogo dvizheniya', *Pravda*, 6 December 1963; N.S. Khrushchev, *Predotvrashcheniye voini – pervostepennaya zadacha* (Inyazdat, Moscow, 1963), pp. 81-2; and D. Vol'skiy and V. Kudriantsev, 'Real'naya deistvitel'nost' i domisli raskol'nikov', *Krasnaya Zvezda*, 10 October 1963. For a more forthright statement advocating Soviet arms transfers to progressive forces in the Third World, see Matsulenko, 'Lokal'niye voini imperializma (1945-1968 gg)', pp. 40-1.

35. See Khmara, 'Nekotoriye osobennosti grazhdanskikh voin v sovremennuyu epokhu', p. 23; Colonel A. Leont'yev, 'Istoricheskaya pobeda V'etnama', *Kommunist Vooruzhennykh Sil*, no. 6, March 1973, p. 84; Colonel Ye. Dolgopolov, 'Razvivayushchiyesya strani Azii, Afriki i Latinskoy Ameriki', *Kommunist Vooruzhennykh Sil*, no. 16, August 1973, p. 79; Colonel Ye. Dolgopolov, 'Armii razvivayushchiksya stran i politika', *Kommunist Vooruzhennykh Sil*, no. 6, March 1975, pp. 76-81; and Captain 2nd Rank Yu. Morozov, 'Klassoviy kharakter sovetskoy vneshney politiki', *Kommunist Vooruzhennykh Sil*, no. 19, October 1975, p. 14.

36. Major General M. Yasyukov, 'Mirovaya sistema sotsializma – istoricheskoye zavoyevaniye mezhdunarodnogo rabochego klassa', *Kommunist Vooruzhennykh Sil*, no. 24, December 1977, p. 68; Malinovskiy, 'Natsional' no-osvoboditel'noye dvizheniye na sovremennom etape', p. 33; and Lt. Colonel N. Khibrikov, 'Krusheniye kolonial'noy sistemi imperializma: osvobodivshiyesya

strani Azii, Afriki i Latinskoy Ameriki', *Kommunist Vooruzhennykh Sil*, no. 6, March 1978, p. 74.

37. Captain 1st Rank Yu. Osipov, 'V.I. Lenin, KPSS ob internatsional'nom kharaktere zashchiti zavoyevaniy sotsializma', *Kommunist Vooruzhennykh Sil*, no. 13, July 1978, p. 76.

38. L.I. Brezhnev, *Otchetniy doklad tsentral'nogo komiteta KPSS XXVI s"yezdu Kommunisticheskoy Partii Sovetskogo Soyuza i ocheredniye zadachi partii v oblasti vnutrenney i vneshney politiki* (speech of 23 February 1981) ('Krasnaya Zvezda', Moscow, 1981), p. 15; A.I. Ionova, 'Sovremennaya ideynaya evolyutsiya islama', *Narodi Azii i Afriki*, no. 6, 1979, pp. 24-35; Colonel Ye. Rybkin, 'Marksizm-Leninizm kak metodologicheskaya osnova prognozirovaniya voyennikh sobitiy', *Voyenno-Istoricheskiy Zhurnal*, no. 7, July 1980, p. 7; Intervyu V. Zagladina korrespondentam RTL (Radio-Television Luxembourg), 'Neozhidannaya gazeta', *Zhurnalist*, no. 9, September 1980, p. 11; and I.L. Andreyev, 'Religiya i natsional'no-osvoboditel'naya bor'ba v stranakh vostoka', *Rabochiy Klass i Sovremenniy Mir*, no. 6, November-December 1980, pp. 111-27.

39. David Martin, 'Riddle of a Premier's Death', *Far Eastern Economic Review*, 13 February 1981, pp. 32-3.

EPILOGUE: IMPLICATIONS FOR AMERICA AND ITS ALLIES

As this study has shown, Soviet military thinking has changed from an optimistic point of view that envisioned Soviet influence in the Third World easily spreading through only low-cost, short-term Soviet involvement to a pessimistic point of view that recognises the need for a high-cost, long-term effort just to maintain Third World Marxist-Leninist governments in power. This change from optimism to pessimism illustrates how the USSR underestimated the intractability of the Third World and the difficulty in both gaining and retaining influence in it. This is, of course, similar to the American experience in the Third World; the US was initially optimistic about its ability to gain allies in the Third World and to successfully oppose communist insurgency through military means. With America's failure to do this in Vietnam, the US has also become pessimistic about its ability to extend its influence in the Third World. During the early 1970s, many in both the US and the USSR thought that the decline of American influence in the Third World would lead to the rise of Soviet influence there. It is now apparent, though, that the USSR has encountered many of the same obstacles to influence that the US did. These obstacles include the tendency for dictatorial governments allied to either superpower to become unpopular domestically, the inability of the superpowers to defeat guerrilla opposition to these governments, and the extreme difficulty in fostering economic development on either the capitalist or socialist model in many Third World nations.

In this sense, both American and Soviet foreign policies in the Third World experienced similar difficulties. However, the lessons each superpower has drawn from its experience in the Third World have differed in two important respects. First, the Soviet Union has over time reached the conclusion that its most reliable Third World allies are those with Marxist-Leninist governments like itself. The US, on the other hand, has made only half-hearted efforts to support democratic governments like itself. Secondly, since the end of the Vietnam war, American pessimism about the Third World has been reflected in an unwillingness to become militarily involved in Third World conflicts. Soviet pessimism about the Third World, on the other hand, has given rise to greater Soviet military involvement in these conflicts in order to protect what the Soviets see as vital Soviet interests.

Concerning the type of Third World governments that have received superpower backing, both the US and the USSR have frequently supported dictatorships. The Soviet Union has learned that not all dictatorships can be relied upon. Many of them have broken with the Soviet Union after receiving substantial military assistance from it. Hence the Soviets have increasingly sought to encourage radical Third World regimes to form Marxist-Leninist parties and allow them to rule. The Soviets hope that a ruling Marxist-Leninist party would by its very nature seek to co-operate with the Soviet Union and to regard Soviet foreign policy interests as its own. Of course, Marxist-Leninist parties in power can also break away from the Soviet Union, as Yugoslavia, China and Albania have demonstrated. Where ruling Marxist-Leninist parties have a degree of independence from the USSR, it is possible that they too will break away from the USSR. Ruling Marxist-Leninist parties provide no guarantee that their nations will remain allied permanently to the USSR. What the Soviets undoubtedly hope for by having a Marxist-Leninist party in power is a greater opportunity to prevent the Third World nation from breaking away from Soviet influence than is possible in a non-Marxist-Leninist dictatorship: a Marxist-Leninist government may be more receptive to having large numbers of Soviet advisers in the country as well as Soviet assistance in the day-to-day administration of the government than a non-Marxist-Leninist one. By allowing the Soviet Union to have a greater influence in its country, the Marxist-Leninist party would be less able to break free from it later. And yet this very attempt to increase Soviet control may induce the Marxist-Leninist party to resist it. By attempting to increase its control over its allies, the USSR often alienates and loses them − exactly what the USSR wishes to prevent.

The United States, on the other hand, does very little to encourage Third World governments to become democratic. The US would prefer Third World nations to be democracies, but if a Third World dictatorship is anti-Soviet, then the US is usually prepared to work with it. A problem often arises when an anti-communist dictatorship becomes domestically unpopular. Even if the US only gives minimal support to the dictatorship, as the Carter Administration did toward the conservative governments of Iran and Nicaragua, the opposition often regards the US as the force that keeps the dictatorship in power. When these situations arise, the US seldom works to find a political solution in which elections are held so that the competing groups contend for power peacefully. Instead, the US either backs the anti-communist dictatorship against what is perceived as a communist opposition, or does nothing at all. The result is usually that a pro-American dictatorship is replaced by an anti-American one. Thus, while the USSR loses allies by attempting too vigorously to establish its system of government in Third World nations, the US appears to lose allies because it does not work vigorously enough to promote its system of government there.

With regard to the way in which each superpower has responded to failures in the Third World, as was mentioned earlier, the US has become less militarily involved in the Third World while the USSR has become more so. Perhaps the explanation for this lies in the fact that the US government must obey the desire of the American public not to become involved in protracted military conflicts while the Soviet government is subject to no such constraint. Yet even if the Soviet Union intervenes militarily for what it regards as defensive purposes, this trend is one that is disturbing to the rest of the world, as both Western and Third World reaction to the Soviet invasion of Afghanistan has demonstrated.

What often takes place in international relations is a sort of paradox. Soviet actions in the Third World are intended to gain allies for the USSR there, but often they have the opposite effect of losing Soviet allies to the US. Similarly, American policy is intended to prevent the spread of Soviet influence, but often results in the opposite. Through relying on unpopular dictatorships as allies, the actions of each superpower frequently serve to benefit the other when local opposition to the dictatorship occurs. What is most significant about this process is how each superpower now responds to it. While the US would intervene militarily in previous times, since Vietnam it no longer does so. If the pro-American dictatorship falls, the US loses an ally. The USSR, on the other hand, has in the past seen allies fall when it does not intervene militarily. Recently, though, the socialist community has intervened militarily to save Marxist-Leninist governments in the Third World. Through doing this, the Soviet Union does not need to depend on local forces to retain its allies; the armed forces of Cuba, Vietnam, or the USSR itself can guarantee that a nation's government remains allied to the socialist community. Thus, even in a country such as Afghanistan where most of the populace actively opposes the Marxist-Leninist government in Kabul, the presence of Soviet armed forces ensures that the government remains in power. The Soviets have thus found a way in which they can overcome the faithlessness or unpopularity of Third World dictatorships that can result in the loss of an ally. Soldiers from the socialist community may not succeed in defeating local opposition to Marxist-Leninist governments in the Third World, but so far their inability to do this has not prevented them from continuing to try to do so.

What does all this mean for American foreign policy? Can America do anything to help remove Soviet influence from countries that do not want it? How can the US avoid becoming involved in military conflicts in the Third World that risk being protracted, and hence, domestically unpopular, or that risk a wider conflict with the Soviet Union? At the same time, in those instances where Soviet influence in a Third World nation is maintained through military intervention by the USSR or other Soviet-bloc country, can Soviet influence be removed through anything less than American military intervention? In short, is it at all realistic for the US to attempt to counter Soviet influence in the Third World with any hope of success?

The answer to these questions probably depends to a large extent on what the ultimate goal of American foreign policy toward the Third World is. If it is the goal of the United States to keep pro-American governments in power even if these governments are unpopular dictatorships, then it will be difficult for the US to succeed. Unpopular pro-American dictatorships present the most promising opportunity for the spread of Soviet influence in the Third World. If opposition to the dictatorship is widespread, so usually is opposition to the nation seen as responsible for maintaining it in power. Popular attention is focused on the unjustness of the present regime, and not on the unjustness of the regime to follow if it is a pro-Soviet Marxist one. As the American experience in Vietnam showed, it is extremely difficult to defeat widespread guerrilla opposition even with large-scale US military intervention. Nor is it likely that the American public would support direct military intervention in the Third World very readily after Vietnam. Yet without such support, the pro-American dictatorship is usually less able to maintain itself in power, even if it receives US arms transfers. Thus, keeping pro-American dictatorships in power where they are domestically unpopular is a policy that is not likely to succeed.

If, however, the goal of American foreign policy were not to maintain unpopular pro-American dictatorships in power at all costs, but instead to help Third World nations be rid of unwanted Soviet influence and to develop independently as they see fit, then the US would have a much greater opportunity to successfully achieve this goal. As has been noted here, Soviet foreign policy encounters two main difficulties in the Third World: (1) Soviet efforts to control Third World allies often lead these allies to break with the Soviet Union, and (2) leftist dictatorships supported by the USSR are often domestically unpopular. In order to weaken or diminish Soviet influence in the Third World, American foreign policy can work to exacerbate these two difficulties that the Soviets are encountering.

The tendency of the Soviet Union to alienate its Third World allies is one that the US has taken advantage of in the past, but which it could take even greater advantage of. In the past, the US has waited until relations between the USSR and its ally have deteriorated to the point of open mutual hostility before doing anything. In some cases, such as Egypt and Somalia, the initiative in establishing better relations with the US has come from the former Soviet ally. The US, however, could probably induce more Soviet allies to either become American allies, or at the least, to become neutral, if American foreign policy took the initiative to do this. One of the reasons that Third World governments cling to the USSR despite Soviet efforts to control them is that these governments perceive the United States as being unremittingly hostile to them. If the United States would end its stance of refusing to deal with these regimes, but instead make quiet diplomatic efforts to assure them that the US would not undertake hostile actions against them, then the Third World government might well be induced to seek American friendship, or even protection, when the almost inevitable differences arise between it and the Soviet Union. This is not a policy that would cost the United States very much to implement. What it would require is that the US should not assume that radical Third World governments are firmly under the control of the Soviet Union even if they declare eternal friendship toward the USSR and hostility toward the US. It should be clear by now that in those countries where Marxism-Leninism does not come to power mainly through the efforts of Soviet or other socialist bloc armed forces, the government actually does have a degree of independence from the USSR which it desires to maintain, and that Soviet attempts to reduce this independence give the US an opportunity to pry an ally away from the Soviet Union.

The tendency for dictatorships allied to the Soviet Union to become domestically unpopular is also one that the US can take advantage of. Where local opposition to the dictatorship is widespread, the US can give it political and diplomatic support. In those instances where the Soviet-backed dictatorship faces armed opposition, the US could help the latter through arms transfers and other means of assistance. Direct US military intervention might not be advisable due to the risk of wider conflict with the USSR or of unpopularity within America such a policy might have. However, direct US military intervention might not be necessary if American arms transfers enable the domestic opposition in the Third World nation to defeat, or at the minimum, deny victory to the Soviet-backed dictatorship. If the Soviet Union or another socialist-bloc nation intervenes militarily to protect the regime, American aid to the domestic opposition should continue so that victory is denied to the Marxist-Leninist forces. As both the American experience in Vietnam and the Soviet experience in Afghanistan have shown, counter-insurgency warfare cannot easily succeed even if the intervening forces are vastly superior in military terms to the guerrillas. In addition, there is no reason why the US should acquiesce to Soviet persistence at attempting to conquer a nation that does not wish to be conquered. Even if the US is unwilling or unable to participate in the fighting, it should at least give to those nations that do wish to fight against Soviet attempts to conquer them the means with which they can effectively do so.

The US, then, can either assist radical or Marxist Third World regimes in loosening or ending their dependence on the Soviet Union and Soviet attempts to control them, or it can assist opposition groups in these Third World nations to avoid domination by, or even to topple, Soviet-backed dictatorships. Either of these policies can serve to decrease Soviet influence in specific Third World countries. However, it must be noted that it is not possible for the United States to successfully pursue both policies at the same time in any one country. If the United States gave political or military assistance to a domestic opposition movement in a Third World nation ruled by a Soviet-backed dictatorship, it is doubtful that the US could convince the dictatorship to break away from Soviet influence; indeed, the dictatorship would most likely cling to the USSR more strongly than ever in the face of an American supported internal threat to its rule. What the US should do is determine which policy is more likely to be successful in any given country. If the regime is strong and the opposition is weak, then the US should attempt to pry the regime away from Soviet influence. If the regime is weak and the opposition is strong, then US support to the opposition might be most fruitful. In those cases such as Afghanistan where the regime owes its very existence to the presence of Soviet armed forces and thus the regime cannot possibly be pried away from Soviet influence, the only policy that has a chance of succeeding (i.e. of preventing the USSR from conquering Afghanistan) is for the US to aid the opposition.

Yet while it can be relatively easy for the US to weaken an unpopular Soviet-backed dictatorship through giving aid to the opposition the US must remember that it is also easy for the Soviet Union to weaken an unpopular American-backed dictatorship in a similar fashion. Indeed, even without Soviet involvement, American-backed Third World dictatorships can be overthrown by internal forces alone, as occurred in Iran. When these situations arise, the US should not attempt the extremely difficult task of keeping the dictatorship in power through military means, but instead should attempt to achieve a political solution involving all parties. Finding a peaceful solution to a civil conflict can be difficult to accomplish; hence, the US should encourage dictatorships allied to it to transform themselves into democracies before armed domestic opposition to them arises. It is, however, possible to find peaceful solutions to bitter and prolonged civil wars, as the example of Zimbabwe demonstrated. Not only can the attempt to find a peaceful solution to a civil war succeed, but it also provides the opportunity to foster democracy. In Zimbabwe, Robert Mugabe was considered to be the most radical and Marxist-oriented leader, yet after winning the election he has surprised the West by committing himself to the maintenance of democracy. Finally, by working toward a peaceful solution to civil conflicts and respecting the outcome of free elections that occur even if the group that comes to power might not be the one most favoured by the US, the US denies the Soviet Union the opportunity to dominate the opposition to the unpopular dictatorship and to make the struggle an anti-American one. Surely the US is better off if a neutral but relatively stable democratic government that does not want to be dominated by either the US or the USSR is in power than if a pro-American but relatively unstable dictatorship is in power which is likely to be replaced by a pro-Soviet dictatorship.

Of course, internal opposition to either Soviet or American supported dictatorships is not the only type of conflict that occurs in the Third World. Other types of conflict frequently occur between nations, as when one nation wishes to conquer all or part of the territory of another one; and within nations, as when a portion of a nation (religious, tribal, ethnic, or other group) wishes either to secede from or rule all of the rest of the country. Many of these conflicts occur regardless of the ideological coloration or the alliances with either superpower that the Third World forces involved may have. For example, Somalia has wished to obtain the Ogaden from Ethiopia in the past when Somalia was allied to the USSR and Ethiopia to the US as well as more recently when the two nations reversed their alliances. It is probable that the three ethnic groups in Angola would struggle for power and that the Vietnamese would attempt to dominate the rest of Indochina no matter what ideology each group espoused. There are a great number of such conflicts between and within Third World nations; a partial list would include the Arab-Israeli conflict, the Lebanese civil war, the Iran-Iraq war, the Moroccan attempt to dominate the Western Sahara, separatist movements in India and the Philippines, the black-white struggle in southern Africa, and many others.

Perhaps the best policy that the US could adopt toward such conflicts is to offer to help those involved achieve a peaceful solution by means of plebiscites or other elections. The US may not be successful in implementing such a policy in every case (indeed, it may only succeed in relatively few cases), but there really is no better alternative. These conflicts have their roots in the Third World itself, and not in the Soviet-American competition. Should the US favour one side in this type of conflict, it would invite the Soviet Union to aid the opposing side. In this way, the US will have lost the opportunity to remain friends with both sides as well as the ability to act as a neutral party seeking a peaceful political solution. Should the Soviet Union take sides in such a dispute first and support one side militarily, then the US might have to support the other side. The US should only do so, though, to the extent that the side facing a Soviet-backed opponent is able to defeat aggression from it; the US should not help its own ally to launch aggression against the other side, perhaps even with direct US military intervention. Again, although peaceful political solutions are difficult to achieve in conflicts that stem from contending nationalisms or other indigenous Third World causes, the US would be much better able to make friends with those forces desiring peace and stability if it makes a genuine attempt to find a peaceful solution to Third World conflicts. The Soviet Union often seeks to prevent resolution to conflicts since its Third World allies are dependent on the USSR so long as the conflict continues. Once a conflict ends, Soviet allies no longer need to depend on the USSR and thus tend to drift away from it. By offering the genuine prospect of resolving conflicts peacefully, the US can encourage this process to take place.

The resolution of Third World conflicts through peaceful means is an area where America's allies can play an important role. This was proved by the successful British effort to resolve the civil war in Zimbabwe. Zimbabwe, of course, was unique in that it was a colony that had not been granted formal independence and in which all sides to the dispute accepted the return of British authority while free elections took place. It is doubtful that the participants in other Third World conflicts would all accept the return of the former colonial powers in order to resolve their disputes. Nevertheless, Western Europe, Japan and other nations can often use their political, diplomatic and economic influence to help resolve conflict in areas or nations that are of particular importance to them.

One important asset that America's allies often possess is a greater knowledge of Third World conflict situations that is derived from more extensive experience in certain areas of the Third World than the US has had. In those instances when conflict erupts in an area where the US has had little experience, this knowledge can be of great value in finding a peaceful political solution.

At times, America's allies have also become militarily involved in Third World conflicts. In some cases, they have been relatively successful, as Britain was in ending insurgencies in Malaya, North Borneo and Oman, and as France and Belgium were in turning back insurgent forces attempting to enter Zaire's Shaba province. In other cases, though, they have been notably unsuccessful; for example, France's military efforts failed in Indochina, Algeria and Chad, while Britain's failed in Aden. The US can learn from both the successes and the failures of its allies. In addition, as dictatorships supported by the US can become domestically unpopular and provide an opportunity for the spread of Soviet influence, pro-Western dictatorships supported by America's allies are also subject to the same weaknesses.

Another important role that America's allies can play is to inform the United States when they feel American efforts to halt the spread of Soviet influence are becoming counter-productive. This is especially necessary when American efforts to prop up a pro-American dictatorship through military means do not seem likely to succeed. America's allies might then take the lead in attempting to find a political solution to the conflict. This may appear to be a formula for creating a rift between the US and its allies. However, if America's allies do not make their views known, there is a risk that domestic opposition to American foreign policy will grow in Western Europe and elsewhere which will make co-operation between the US and its allies more difficult over a broad range of issues. In other words, issues relating solely to the US and its allies may be affected by US foreign policy in the Third World. If America's allies had made a vigorous effort to achieve a political solution in South Vietnam that involved a negotiated settlement and free elections, it is possible that the spread of Soviet influence in Indochina might have been halted, America might have been saved from a humiliating defeat, and tensions between the US and its allies might have been avoided. The Hanoi government may still have both attempted and succeeded in establishing its influence throughout the rest of Indochina by military means. However, even if this did occur, Vietnam may not have become such a firm Soviet ally than if the US had sought a political solution — not just a military one — to this conflict. It is possible that the proposals made by France and Mexico concerning the peaceful resolution of the conflict in El Salvador could serve as the basis for avoiding a repetition of the problems that arose from US involvement in Vietnam.

Since the interests of America's allies are affected by American involvement in the Third World, America's allies do not serve either their own or America's long-run interests by not expressing their reservations about US foreign policy actions they think will be counterproductive. If America's allies wish to prevent the spread of Soviet influence in the Third World, the deterioration of their alliance with the US, and the weakening of America's position in the world, they must make their views known. The US should accept the views of its allies with these broader issues in mind. At the same time, America's allies should also be receptive to American views about their involvement in the Third World.

The Third World has proved to be a region that not only was difficult for the US to extend its influence over, but is also proving difficult for the USSR to do the same. There are forces in the Third World that work to make it intractable to attempts to control it by either superpower. At present, the Soviet Union has resorted to increasingly forceful methods to spread and maintain its influence in the Third World against those forces of intractability. If it is the goal of the US and its allies to prevent the further spread of Soviet influence in the Third World, and to weaken Soviet influence where it already exists, then the US should work with these forces of intractability in order to frustrate Soviet attempts to dominate Third World nations that do not want to be dominated by it; they should not fight against these forces and thereby assist Soviet aims in the Third World. Through pursuing these policy recommendations, the nations of the Third World will not necessarily become firm allies that the US can easily control, but at least they will not be nations that the Soviet Union can easily control either. This alone would surely be of great value to the United States and its allies.

BIBLIOGRAPHY

Agayev, S.L. 'Razryadka mezhdunarodnoy napryazhennosti i kommunisticheskoye dvizheniye', *Rabochiy Klass i Sovremenniy Mir*, no. 4 (July-August 1974), 14-27

Agayev, S.L. and Tatarovskaya, I.M. 'Nekotoriye problemi razvitiya revolyutsionnogo protsessa v osvobodivshikhsya stranakh', *Rabochiy Klass i Sovremenniy Mir*, no. 5 (September-October 1978), 44-56

Alimov, Yu. 'Retsidivi kolonializma', *Kommunist*, no. 9 (June 1978), 109-15

Aliyev, G. 'Oktyabr'skaya revolyutsiya i natsional'no-osvoboditel'noye dvizheniye', *Kommunist*, no. 9 (June 1977), 24-38

Andreyev, I.L. 'Religiya i natsional'no-osvoboditel'naya bor'ba v stranakh vostoka', *Rabochiy Klass i Sovremenniy Mir*, no. 6 (November-December 1980), 111-27

Andrianov, Colonel V. 'Partizanskaya voina i voyennaya strategiya', *Voyenno-Istoricheskiy Zhurnal*, no. 7 (July 1975), 29-38

Andronova, V.P. 'Revolyutsiya monsen'orov?' *Latinskaya Amerika*, no. 2 (March-April 1971), 76-91

Avakov, M. and Chernichenko, S. 'Zhiznennaya sila leninskikh printsipov mirnogo sosushchestvovaniya', *Kommunist Vooruzhennykh Sil*, no. 23 (December 1973), 19-26

Babich, Colonel V. 'Strategicheskaya aviatsiya i takticheskiye zadachi', *Aviatsiya i Kosmonavtika*, no. 2 (February 1974), 46-7

―――― 'Taktika ognevogo vozdeystviya', *Aviatsiya i Kosmonavtika*, no. 9 (September 1975), 46-7

Bagdasarov, S. 'Krusheniye kolonial'noy sistemi imperializma', *Kommunist Vooruzhennykh Sil*, no. 15 (August 1975), 63-72

Baskakov, V. 'Ob osobennostyakh nachal'nogo perioda voini', *Voyenno-Istoricheskiy Zhurnal*, no. 2 (February 1966), 29-34

Belousov, Colonel L. 'Konferentsiya o sovetskoy voyennoy doktrine', *Voyenno-Istoricheskiy Zhurnal*, no. 10 (October 1963), 121-6

Bel'skiy, A. 'Natsional'no-osvoboditel'naya revolyutsiya: zakonomernosti i perspektivi', *Aziya i Afrika Segodnya*, no. 3 (March 1975), 28-32

Benke, Valeria 'Sovetskiy Soyuz s chest'yu vipolyaet internatsional'niy dolg', *Kommunist*, no. 17 (November 1972), 42-8

Bennigsen, Alexandre 'Les musulmans de l'URSS et la crise afghane', *Politique Étrangère*, 45, no. 1 (March 1980), 13-25

Bialer, Seweryn *Stalin's Successors: Leadership, Stability, and Change in the Soviet Union* (Cambridge University Press, Cambridge, 1980)

Binder, David 'Brezhnev Doctrine Said to Be Extended', *New York Times*, 10 February 1980

Bobkov, Captain 2nd Rank I. 'Russkiye i sovetskiye korabli v Srediyemnom more', *Voyenno-Istoricheskiy Zhurnal*, no. 9 (September 1970), 37-47

Bochkarev, Major General K., Prusanov, Colonel I., and Babakov, Colonel A. *Programma KPSS o zashchite sotsialisticheskogo otechestva*, 1st edn (Voyenizdat, Moscow, 1963)

—— *Programma KPSS o zashchite sotsialisticheskogo otechestva*, 2nd edn (Voyenizdat, Moscow, 1965)

Bogdanov, K. and Rumyantsev, V. 'Nasushchniye voprosi revolyutsionnogo dvizheniya v Afrike', *Kommunist*, no. 3 (February 1967), 80-92

Borisov, D. 'SSSR – Somali: otnosheniya razvivayutsya', *Mezhdunarodnaya Zhizn'*, no. 10 (October 1975), 113-14

Borisov, O.B. and Koloskov, B.T. *Sovetsko-kitayskiye otnosheniya 1945-1970* (Mysl', Moscow, 1971)

'Boyevoy avangard bor'bi protiv imperializma', *Kommunist*, no. 10 (July 1969), 8-19

Brezhnev, L.I. 'Kommunisticheskoye dvizheniye vstupilo v polosu novogo pod"-ema', *Problemi Mira i Sotsializma*, no. 8 (August 1969), 1-9

—— *Leninskim kursom: rechi i stat'i*, 7 vols. (Politizdat, Moscow, 1970-79)

—— *Otchetniy doklad tsentral'nogo komiteta KPSS XXVI s"yezdu Kommunisticheskoy Partii Sovetskogo Soyuza i ocheredniye zadachi partii v oblasti vnutrenney i vneshney politiki* ('Krasnaya Zvezda', Moscow, 1981)

—— *O vneshney politike KPSS i Sovetskogo gosudarstva: rechi i stat'i*, 3 vols, (Politizdat, Moscow, 1973-78)

Brutents, K.N. *Sovremenniye natsional'no-osvoboditel'niye revolyutsii* (Politizdat, Moscow, 1974)

—— 'Voprosi ideologii v natsional'no-osvoboditel'nom dvizhenni', *Kommunist*, no. 18 (December 1966), 37-50

Bulatov, Colonel A., and Glazov, Colonel V. 'Imperialist Aggression in the Near East', *Voyennaya Mysl'*, no. 9 (September 1967), CIA FB FPD 0132/68, 75-85

Chernyak, Colonel N. 'V.I. Lenin on Proletarian Internationalism and Its Role in Defense of the Achievements of Socialism', *Voyennaya Mysl'*, no. 2 (February 1969), CIA FB FPD 0060/69, 10-22

Chernyshev, Rear Admiral F., and Konyukhovskiy, Colonel V. 'The Army of Friendship of Peoples and of Proletarian Internationalism', *Voyennaya Mysl'*, no. 11 (November 1967), CIA FB FPD 0157/68, 79-90

Chuvrikov, Colonel P. *Kratkiy ocherk marksistsko-leninskoy teoril o voine i armii* (Voyenizdat, Moscow, 1949)

—— *Marksizm-Leninizm o voine i armii (kratkiy populayarniy ocherk)*, 2nd edn (Voyenizdat, Moscow, 1956)

Colton, Timothy J. *Commissars, Commanders, and Civilian Authority: The Structure of Soviet Military Politics* (Harvard University Press, Cambridge, Mass., 1979)

'Congo-Soviet Friendship Treaty', *The Washington Post*, 14 May 1981

Dashichev, Vyacheslav 'Theory and Practice of "Little Wars"', *New Times*, no. 37 (September 1957), 7-10

Debray, Régis, *Révolution dans la révolution?* (François Maspero, Paris, 1967)

'Development of Military Theory – An Important Factor in Increasing Fighting Power of the Armed Forces', *Voyennaya Mysl'*, no. 2 (February 1973), FBIS FPD 0045/73, 1-15

Deych, T. '"Noviy kurs" Pekina i Afrika', *MEiMO*, no. 2 (February 1974), 39-49

Dinerstein, Herbert S. *The Making of a Missile Crisis: October 1962* (Johns Hopkins Press, Baltimore, 1976)

—— *Soviet Doctrine on Developing Countries: Some Divergent Views*, P-2725

(RAND Corp., Santa Monica, March 1963)

—— *War and the Soviet Union* (Praeger, New York, 1959)

Dokumenti mezhdunarodnogo sobeschaniya kommunisticheskikh i rabochikh partii (Politizdat, Moscow, 1969)

Dolgin, V.G. 'Mirnoye sosushchestvovaniye i faktori ego uglubleniya i razvitya', *Voprosy Filosofii,* no. 1 (1974), 57-68

Dolgopolov, Colonel Ye. 'Armii osvobodivshikhsya stran', *Krasnaya Zvezda,* 19 May 1968

—— 'Armii razvivayushchiksya stran i politika', *Kommunist Vooruzhennykh Sil,* no. 6 (March 1975), 76-81

—— 'Molodiye armii i sotsial'niy progress', *Kommunist Vooruzhennykh Sil,* no. 21 (November 1976), 90-92

—— 'Natsional'no-osvoboditel'naya voina', *Sovetskaya voyennaya entsiklopediya* (Voyenizdat, Moscow, 1978) V, 536-9

—— *Natsional'no-osvoboditel'niye voini na sovremennom etape* (Voyenizdat, Moscow, 1977)

—— *Natsional'no-osvoboditel'niye voini v sovremennuyu epokhu* (Voyenizdat, Moscow, 1960)

—— 'Razoblacheniye burzhuaznikh i maoistskikh fal'sifikatorov istorii lokal' nikh voin', *Voyenno-Istoricheskiy Zhurnal,* no. 6 (June 1980), 56-63

—— 'Razvivayushchiyesya strani Azii, Afriki i Latinskoy Ameriki', *Kommunist Vooruzhennykh Sil,* no. 16 (August 1973), 72-9

—— 'Vazhniy politicheskiy faktor: o roli armiy v razvivayushchikhsya stranakh', *Krasnaya Zvezda,* 21 April 1978

Dominguez, Jorge I. 'Cuban Foreign Policy', *Foreign Affairs,* 57, no. 1 (Fall 1978), 83-108

Donaldson, Robert H. (ed.) *The Soviet Union in the Third World: Successes and Failures* (Westview Press, Boulder, Colo., 1981)

Drambyants, G. 'Aktual'niye problemi natsional'no-osvoboditel'nogo dvizheniya', *Kommunist,* no. 18 (December 1968), 109-12

—— 'Politika internatsional'noy solidarnost'', *Kommunist,* no. 5 (March 1972), 84-95

Dudinskiy, I.V. 'Internatsional'niye i natsional'niye interesi sotsialisticheskikh gosudarstv', *Voprosy Filosofii,* no. 10 (1973), 64-76

Duncan, Raymond W. (ed.) *Soviet Policy in the Third World* (Pergamon Press, New York, 1980)

Ebinger, Charles, K. 'External Intervention in Internal War: The Politics and Diplomacy of the Angolan Civil War', *Orbis,* 20, no. 3 (Fall 1976), 669-99

Ermarth, Fritz. *The Soviet Union and the Third World: Purpose in Search of Power,* P-4072 (RAND Corp., Santa Monica, April 1969)

Fedorov, Colonel G.A., Sushko, Colonel N. Ya. and Beliy, Colonel B.A. *Marksizm-Leninizm o voine i armii,* 2nd edn (Voyenizdat, Moscow, 1961)

—— *Marksizm-Leninizm o voine i armii,* 3rd edn (Voyenizdat, Moscow, 1962)

Fromkin, David 'The Great Game in Asia', *Foreign Affairs,* 58, no. 4 (Spring 1980), 936-51

Galin, Yu. and Kashirin, V. 'Latinskaya Amerika v planakh Pentagona', *Kommunist Vooruzhennykh Sil,* no. 9 (May 1961), 85-8

Garthoff, Raymond L. *Soviet Military Policy: A Historical Analysis* (Praeger, New York, 1966)

—— *Soviet Strategy in the Nuclear Age* (Praeger, New York, 1958)

—— 'Soviet Views on the Interrelation of Diplomacy and Military Strategy', *Political Science Quarterly*, 94, no. 3 (Fall 1979), 391-405

—— 'Unconventional Warfare in Communist Strategy', *Foreign Affairs*, 40, no. 4 (July 1962), 566-75

Gavrikov, Yu. P. 'Kuba v sovremennom mire: osnovniye napravleniya vneshney politiki', *Latinskaya Amerika*, no. 6 (November-December 1978), 96-109

—— 'SSSR – Kuba: sotrudnichestvo i solidarnost'', *Latinskaya Amerika*, no. 1 (January-February 1973), 6-16

Genri, Ernst 'Porazheniye pravoy sotsial-demokratii v 'tret'em mire'', *Kommunist*, no. 3 (February 1969), 107-20

Geronimus, A. *Marksizm-Leninizm o voine i armii* (Partizdat, Moscow, 1932)

Glassman, Jon D. *Arms for the Arabs: The Soviet Union and War in the Middle East* (Johns Hopkins University Press, Baltimore, 1975)

Glazov, Colonel V. 'Chto takaye lokal'naya voina?', *Krasnaya Zvezda*, 16 May 1961

—— 'O reaktsionnoy sushchnosti teorii lokal'nikh voin', *Kommunist Vooruzhennykh Sil*, no. 10 (May 1961), 59-66

Golan, Galia 'Soviet Power and Policies in the Third World: The Middle East', *Prospects of Soviet Power in the 1980s: Part II*, Adelphi Papers, no. 152 (International Institute for Strategic Studies, London, Summer 1979)

Golub, P. 'Revolyutsia i demokratizatsiya armii', *Voyenno-Istoricheskiy Zhurnal*, no. 3 (March 1974), 3-13

Gorshkov, Sergei G. *Red Star Rising at Sea* (US Naval Institute, Annapolis, Md., 1974)

Grechko, Marshal of the Soviet Union A. *The Armed Forces of the Union of Soviet Socialist Republics* (Novosti, Moscow, 1972)

—— *Vooruzhenniye sili sovetskogo gosudarstva* (Voyenizdat, Moscow, 1975)

Griffith, William E. 'Communist Esoteric Communications', in Ithiel de Sola Pool (ed.), *Handbook of Communication* (Rand McNally, Chicago, 1973), 512-20

—— 'The Revival of Islamic Fundamentalism: The Case of Iran', *International Security*, 4, no. 1 (Summer 1979), 132-8

—— 'Soviet Power and Policies in the Third World: The Case of Africa', *Prospects of Soviet Power in the 1980s: Part II*. Adelphi Papers, no. 152 (International Institute for Strategic Studies, London, Summer 1979)

Griffiths, Franklyn J.C. 'De la justification des transferts d'armes par l'Union Soviétique', *Etudes Internationales*, 8, no. 4 (December 1977), 600-17

Gromyko, Anatoliy, 'Aktual'niye problemi noveyshey istorii razvivayushchikhsya stran', *Kommunist*, no. 4 (March 1979), 117-24

—— 'Druz'ya i vragi narodov afrikanskogo kontinenta', *Pod Znamenem Leninizma*, no. 8 (April 1978), 59-62

Gromyko, An., and Starushenko, G. 'Aktual'niye voprosi razvitiya Afriki', *Kommunist*, no. 2 (January 1980), 118-20

Gromyko, Andrei A. *The International Situation and Soviet Foreign Policy (Speech of June 27, 1968)* (Novosti, Moscow, 1968)

—— 'Predisloviye', in I.D. Ovsyaniy (ed.) *Vneshnyaya politika Sovetskogo Soyuza* (Politizdat, Moscow, 1975), 3-24

—— *Vo imya torzhestva leninskoy vneshney politiki: izbranniye rechi i stat'i* (Politizdat, Moscow, 1978)

Heikal, Mohamed *The Cairo Documents* (Doubleday, Garden City, 1973)
—— *The Road to Ramadan* (Ballantine, New York, 1975)
—— *The Sphinx and the Commissar: The Rise and Fall of Soviet Influence in the Middle East* (Harper & Row, New York, 1978)
Henze, Paul B. 'To Reagan: Don't Blow It in the Horn of Africa', *Christian Science Monitor*, 3 April 1981
'Increasing Focus on Central America', *Soviet World Outlook*, 5, no. 4 (15 April 1980), 2-3
Inozemtsev, N. 'Leninizm – nauchnaya osnova sovetskoy vneshney politiki', *Kommunist*, no. 7 (May 1966), 12-25
Intervyu Vadima Zagladina korrespondentam RTL (Radio-Television Luxembourg), 'Neozhidannaya gazeta', *Zhurnalist*, no. 9 (September 1980), 9-13
Ionova, A.I. 'Sovremennaya ideynaya evolyutsiya islama', *Narodi Azii i Afriki*, no. 6 (1979), 24-35
Ivanashchenko, Captain 1st Rank (ret.) L.A. 'Rezhim morskoy blokadi po sovremennomu mezhdunarodnomu pravu', *Morskoy Sbornik*, no. 11 (November 1967), 85-90
Ivanov, Colonel O. 'Leninskaya strategiya mira', *Kommunist Vooruzhennykh Sil*, no. 17 (September 1979), 8-16
Ivanov, General S. 'Soviet Military Doctrine and Strategy', *Voyennaya Mysl'*, no. 5 (May 1969), CIA FB FPD 0116/69, 40-51
Ivan'shin, S. and Osotov, I. 'V'etnam – pobeda istoricheskogo znacheniya', *Kommunist*, no. 2 (January 1973), 15-23
Izmaylov, Colonel V. 'Kharakter i osobennosti sovremennikh voin', *Kommunist Vooruzhennykh Sil*, no. 6 (March 1975), 67-75
Jacobsen, C.G. *Soviet Strategic Initiatives: Challenge and Response* (Praeger, New York, 1979)
Jones, Christopher D. 'Just Wars and Limited Wars: Restraints on the Use of the Soviet Armed Forces', *World Politics*, 28, no. 1 (October 1975), 44-68
Jones, David R. (ed.) *Soviet Armed Forces Review Annual*, 3 vols. (Academic International Press, Gulf Breeze, Fla., 1977-79)
Joshua, Wynfred and Gilbert, Stephen P. *Arms for the Third World: Soviet Military Aid Diplomacy* (Johns Hopkins University Press, Baltimore, 1969)
Kanet, Roger E. (ed.) *The Soviet Union and the Developing Nations* (Johns Hopkins University Press, Baltimore, 1974)
Kang, Young-Hoon 'The Kinds of War in Communist Military Doctrine and Their Relationship to Deterrence', *The Korean Journal of International Studies*, 9, no. 3 (Summer 1978), 35-56
Kapitsa, M.S. *Leveye zdravogo smysla (O vneshney politike gruppi Mao)* (Politizdat, Moscow, 1968)
Kaplan, Stephen S. *et al. Diplomacy of Power: Soviet Armed Forces as a Political Instrument* (Brookings Institution, Washington, 1981)
Kartsa, Gabor 'O razvitii revolyutsionnogo protsessa v Latinskoy Amerike', *Latinskaya Amerika*, no. 1 (January-February 1972), 6-24
Katz, Mark N. 'The Origins of the Vietnam War 1945-1948', *Review of Politics*, 42, no. 2 (April 1980), 131-51
Kaufman, A.S. 'Sovremennaya revolyutsionnaya demokratiya i natsional'no-osvoboditel'niye revolyutsii', *Rabochiy Klass i Sovremenniy Mir*, no. 6 (November-December 1979), 68-79

Kazakov, Major D. 'Teoreticheskaya i metodologicheskaya osnova sovetskoy voyennoy nauki', *Kommunist Vooruzhennykh Sil*, no. 10 (May 1963), 7-15

Khalilzad, Zalmay 'Afghanistan and the Crisis in American Foreign Policy', *Survival*, 22, no. 4 (July/August 1980), 151-60

Khalipov, Colonel V. 'Mir sotsializma v istoricheskom nastuplenii', *Kommunist Vooruzhennykh Sil*, no. 12 (June 1973), 18-25

Khibrikov, Lt. Colonel N. 'Krusheniye kolonial'noy sistemi imperializma: osvobodivshiyesya strani Azii, Afriki i Latinskoy Ameriki', *Kommunist Vooruzhennykh Sil*, no. 6 (March 1978), 68-75

Khmara, Lt. Colonel N. 'Nekotoriye osobennosti grazhdanskikh voin v sovremennuyu epokhu', *Kommunist Vooruzhennykh Sil*, no. 16 (August 1971), 17-24

Kholodov, Rear Admiral M. 'Defense of Sea Lines of Communication', *Voyennaya Mysl'*, no. 4 (April 1967), CIA FB FPD 1135/67, 63-9

Khrushchev, N.S. *O natsional'no-osvoboditel'nom dvizhenii* (Inyazdat, Moscow, 1963)

—— *Otchetnii doklad Ts.K. KPSS XX sy"ezdu partii* (Politizdat, Moscow, 1956)

—— *Predotvrashcheniye voini – pervostepennaya zadacha* (Inyazdat, Moscow, 1963)

—— 'Za noviye pobedi mirovogo kommunisticheskogo dvizheniya', *Kommunist*, no. 1 (January 1961), 3-37

—— *Za prochniy mir i mirnoye sosushchestvovaniye* (Politizdat, Moscow, 1958)

Khvostov, V. 'V. I. Lenin o printsipakh vneshney politiki sovetskogo gosudarstva', *Kommunist*, no. 9 (June 1969), 79-89

Kim, G. 'Mirovoy sotsializm i sovremenniye natsional'no-osvoboditel'niye revolyutsii', *Mezhdunarodnaya Zhizn'*, no. 7 (July 1977), 70-80

Kiva, A. 'Aziya i Afrika: glubokiye peremeni', *Aziya i Afrika Segodnya*, no. 11 (November 1975), 18-22

Kolkowicz, Roman *The Soviet Military and the Communist Party* (Princeton University Press, Princeton, 1967)

Kondratkov, Lt. Colonel T. 'Kharakter i osobennosti sovremennoy voini', *Kommunist Vooruzhennykh Sil*, no. 19 (October 1967), 79-84

—— 'Organichennaya voina – orudiye imperialisticheskoy agressi', *Kommunist Vooruzhennykh Sil*, no. 8 (April 1969), 24-31

—— (Colonel) 'Problema klassifikatsii voin i ee otrazheniye v ideologicheskoy bor'be', *Kommunist Vooruzhennykh Sil*, no. 11 (June 1974), 20-4

—— 'Sotsial'niy kharakter sovremennoy voini', *Kommunist Vooruzhennykh Sil*, no. 21 (November 1972), 9-16

—— 'Sotsial'no-filosofskiye aspekti problemi voini i mira', *Voprosy Filosofii*, no. 4 (1975), 14-24

—— 'Zloveshchiy kharakter militaristikh dogm', *Kommunist Vooruzhennykh Sil*, no. 19 (October 1978), 78-83

Korionov, V. 'Mezhdunarodnoye znacheniye XXIII sy"ezda KPSS', *Kommunist*, no. 6 (April 1966), 16-36

Korkeshkin, Colonel (res.) A. 'Fighting for Independence', *Soviet Military Review*, no. 4 (April 1978), 57-8

Korotkin, I.M., Slepenkov, Z.F., and Kolyzayev, B.A. *Avianostsy i vertoletonostsy* (Voyenizdat, Moscow, 1972)

Kortunov, V. 'Leninskaya politika mirnogo sosushchestvovaniya i klassovaya bor'ba', *Mezhdunarodnaya Zhizn'*, no. 4 (April 1979), 91-101
—— 'Mirnoye sosushchestvovaniye i ideologicheskaya bor'ba', *Voprosy Istorii KPSS*, no. 7 (1972), 66-79
Kosygin, A.N. *Zayavleniye pravitel'stva SSSR ob osnovnikh voprosakh vnutrenney i vneshney politiki* (Politizdat, Moscow, 1966)
Kozlov, Major General S. 'Voyennaya doktrina i voyennaya nauka', *Kommunist Vooruzhennykh Sil*, no. 5 (March 1964), 9-16
Krasil'nikov, A. 'Politika Pekina i razvivayushchiyesya strani', *Aziya i Afrika Segodnya*, no. 1 (January 1975), 44-7
Krasnov, Colonel A. and Koryuk, Lt. Colonel A. 'Primeneniye aviatsiy v lokal' nikh voinakh', *Voyenno-Istoricheskiy Zhurnal*, no. 8 (August 1972), 87-92
Kruglov, L.L. (ed.) *Vooruzhennaya bor'ba narodov Afriki za svobodu i nezavisimost'* (Nauka, Moscow, 1974)
Kulakov, Captain 1st Rank V. 'Proiskhozhdeniye i sushchnost' strategii "gibkogo reagirovaniya"', *Voyenno-Istoricheskiy Zhurnal*, no. 3 (March 1968), 40-9
Kulikov, General V. 'The Indestructible Unity of Peoples – The Builders and Defenders of Communism', *Voyennaya Mysl'*, no. 12 (December 1972), FBIS FPD 0047/73, 1-22
Kulish, V.M. (ed.) *Voyennaya sila i mezhdunarodniye otnosheniya* (Izdatel'stvo 'Mezhdunarodniye Otnosheniya', Moscow, 1972)
Kunayev, D. 'V.I. Lenin i natsional'no-osvoboditel'noye dvizheniye', *Kommunist*, no. 17 (November 1969), 50-60
Laqueur, Walter *The Struggle for the Middle East: The Soviet Union and the Middle East, 1958-70* (Penguin, Harmondsworth, 1972)
Larionov, Colonel V. 'Politicheskaya storona sovetskoy voyennoy doktrini', *Kommunist Vooruzhennykh Sil*, no. 22 (November 1968), 11-18
Lebanov, Colonel I.N., Beliy, Colonel B.A. and Novoselov, Colonel A.P. *Marksizm-Leninizm o voine i armii*, 1st edn (Voyenizdat, Moscow, 1957)
Legum, Colin 'The Soviet Union, China and the West in Southern Africa', *Foreign Affairs*, 54, no. 4 (July 1976), 745-62
Legvold, Robert *Soviet Policy in West Africa* (Harvard University Press, Cambridge, Mass., 1970)
'Leninism – The Banner of the Modern Era', *Voyennaya Mysl'*, no. 1 (January 1969), CIA FB FPD 0087/69, 1-12
'Leninskaya vneshnyaya politika Sovetskogo Soyuza', *Kommunist*, no. 14 (September 1970), 3-14
LeoGrande, William M. 'The Revolution in Nicaragua: Another Cuba?' *Foreign Affairs*, 58, no. 1 (Fall 1979), 28-50
Leont'yev, Colonel A. 'Istoricheskaya pobeda V'etnama', *Kommunist Vooruzhennykh Sil*, no. 6 (March 1973), 83-8
Lider, Julian *On the Nature of War* (Saxon House, Westmead, Farnborough, 1977)
—— *The Political and Military Laws of War* (Saxon House, Westmead, Farnborough, 1979)
Lomov, Colonel General N. 'O sovetskoy voyennoy doktrine', *Kommunist Vooruzhennykh Sil*, no. 10 (May 1962), 11-21
—— (ed.) *Scientific-Technical Progress and the Revolution in Military Affairs*,

transl. US Air force (US Government Printing Office, Washington, D.C., 1973)

Lowenthal, Richard *Model or Ally? The Communist Powers and the Developing Countries* (Oxford University Press, New York, 1977)

Malinovskiy, Colonel G. 'Lokal'naya voina', *Sovetskaya voyennaya entsiklopediya* (Voyenizdat, Moscow, 1978), V, 21-2

—— 'Lokal'niye voini v zone natsional'no-osvoboditel'nogo dvizheniya', *Voyenno-Istoricheskiy Zhurnal*, no. 5 (May 1974), 91-8

—— 'Natsional'no-osvoboditel'noye dvizheniye na sovremennom etape', *Voyenno-Istoricheskiy Zhurnal*, no. 24 (December 1979), 25-36

Malinovskiy, Colonel G. and Rybkin, Colonel Ye. 'Klassifikatsiya voin', *Sovetskaya voyennaya entsiklopediya* (Voyenizdat, Moscow, 1977), IV, 199-200

Malinovskiy, Marshal R. Ya. *Bditel'no stoyat'na strazhe mira* (Voyenizdat, Moscow, 1962)

Malyanchikov, Colonel S. 'On the Nature of Armed Struggle in Local Wars', *Voyennaya Mysl'*, no. 11 (November 1965), CIA FDD Trans. No. 953, 12-24

Mamayev, Captain 1st Rank Ye. 'The Disruption of Sea and Ocean Transport', *Voyennaya Mysl'*, no. 12 (December 1968), CIA FB FPD 0102/69, 50-5

Manchkha, Petr I. *Avangardniye otryadi revolyutsionnoy bor'bi v Afrike* (Politizdat, Moscow, 1971)

—— 'Narodnoye dvizheniye za osvobozhdeniye Angoli', *Agitator,* no. 8 (April 1972), 60-1

Marcum, John A. *The Angolan Revolution. Volume I: Anatomy of an Explosion (1950-1962)* (MIT Press, Cambridge, Mass., 1969)

—— *The Angolan Revolution. Volume II: Exile Politics and Guerrilla Warfare (1962-1976)* (MIT Press, Cambridge, Mass., 1978)

—— 'Lessons of Angola', *Foreign Affairs,* 54, no. 3 (April 1976), 407-25

Martin, David 'Riddle of a Premier's Death', *Far Eastern Economic Review* (13 February 1981), 32-3

Maslennikov, Colonel P. 'Organizatsiya upravleniya voiskami SShA v voine vo V'etname', *Voyenno-Istoricheskiy Zhurnal,* no. 10 (October 1975), 42-9

Matsulenko, Major General V. 'Lokal'niye voini imperializma (1945-1968 gg)', *Voyenno-Istoricheskiy Zhurnal,* no. 9 (September 1968), 36-51

—— 'O nekotorikh voprosakh upravleniya voiskami v lokal'nikh voinakh', *Voyenno-Istoricheskiy Zhurnal,* no. 3 (March 1980), 52-63

—— 'Po inostrannim armiyam', *Voyenno-Istoricheskiy Zhurnal,* no. 4 (April 1979), 54-65

Maydanik, K.L. and Polyakov, M.I. 'Pobeda kubinskogo naroda i mirovoy revolyutsionniy protsess', *Latinskaya Amerika,* no. 4 (July-August 1973), 36-49

Mayzel, Matitiahu 'Soviet Military Theory in Local Wars' (Tel Aviv University Institute of Strategic Studies, Tel Aviv), 8 December 1976

Mazurkevich, V. and Petrov, M. 'Voyennaya "pomoshch" SShA – orudiye ekspansii amerikanskogo imperializma', *Kommunist Vooruzhennykh Sil,* no. 18 (September 1972), 76-80

McConnell, James M. and Dismukes, Bradford 'Soviet Diplomacy of Force in the Third World', *Problems of Communism,* 28, no. 1 (January-February 1979), 14-27

McGwire, Michael 'The Rationale for the Development of Soviet Seapower', *U.S. Naval Institute Proceedings,* 106, no. 5 (May 1980), 154-83

Mikoyan, S.A. 'Ob osobennostyakh revolyutsii v Nikaragua i ee urokakh s tochki zreniya teorii i praktiki osvoboditel'nogo dvizheniya (zaklyuchitel' noye slovo)', *Latinskaya Amerika*, no. 3 (March 1980), 34-44

———— 'Peru posle 5 fevralya', *Latinskaya Amerika*, no. 3 (May-June 1975), 221-4

Milovidov, Major General A. 'War and the Socialist Revolution', *Voyennaya Mysl'*, no. 11 (November 1971), FBIS FPD 0004/74, 1-16

Milovidov, Major General A. and Kozlov, Colonel V. (eds.) *Filosofskoye naslediye V.I. Lenina i problemi sovremennoy voini* (Voyenizdat, Moscow, 1972)

'Mirnoye sosushchestvovaniye gosudarstv i klassovaya bor'ba', *Problemi Mira i Sotsializma*, no. 3 (March 1974), 39-43

Mirskiy, Georgiy *Armiya i politika v stranakh Azii i Afriki* (Nauka, Moscow, 1970)

———— 'O kharaktere sotsial'nikh sil v Azii i Afriki', *Kommunist*, no. 17 (November 1968), 89-102

———— *Problems of the National-Liberation Movement* (Novosti, Moscow, 1971)

———— 'Rol' armii v sotsial'nom razvitii stran Azii i Afriki', *Voprosy Filosofii*, no. 3 (1979), 97-108

———— 'The Proletariat and National Liberation', *New Times*, no. 18 (May 1964), 6-9

———— *Tretiy mir': obshchestvo, vlast', armiya* (Nauka, Moscow, 1976)

———— 'Vazhniye problemi natsional'no-osvoboditel'nogo dvizheniya', *Kommunist*, no. 9 (June 1974), 124-8

Molodtsigin, Colonel (ret.) M. 'Leninskiy printsip internatsionalizma v organizatsii voyennoy zashchiti sotsialisticheskikh stran', *Voyenno-Istoricheskiy Zhurnal*, no. 9 (September 1974), 3-10

Morozov, Colonel V. 'The Third Edition of "Marxism-Leninism on War and the Army"', *Voyennaya Mysl'*, no. 7 (July 1963), CIA FDD Trans. No. 956, 76-87

Morozov, Captain 2nd Rank Yu. 'Klassoviy kharakter sovetskoy vneshney politiki', *Kommunist Vooruzhennykh Sil*, no. 19 (October 1975), 9-17

Mos'ko, G. 'K voprosu o maoistskoy teoriy "narodov voini"', *Voyenno-Istoricheskiy Zhurnal*, no. 3 (March 1979), 58-63

Moskrin, Colonel I. 'The Aggressive Plans of the U.S. in Southeast Asia', *Voyennaya Mysl'*, no. 8 (August 1965), CIA FDD Trans. No. 958, 84-94

———— 'The War in South Vietnam', *Voyennaya Mysl'*, no. 3 (March 1966), CIA FDD Trans. No. 967, 73-85

'Narod V'etnama pobedit', *Kommunist*, no. 9 (September 1966), 92-8

Nassar, Fuad 'Lenin i osvoboditel'naya bor'ba arabskikh narodov', *Kommunist*, no. 5 (March 1970), 113-19

Nemanov, S.P. 'Partii avangardnogo tipa v afrikanskikh stranakh sotsialisticheskoy orientatsii', *Narodi Afriki i Azii*, no. 2 (1979), 16-28

Nikitin, Colonel N. 'Nekotoriye operativno-takticheskiye uroki lokal'nikh voin imperializma', *Voyenno-Istoricheskiy Zhurnal*, no. 12 (December 1978), 60-6

Nikolayev, Rear Admiral K. 'The Navy in Local Wars', *Voyennaya Mysl'*, no. 3 (March 1969), CIA FB FPD 0101/69, 74-82

Osborne, Milton 'Kampuchea and Viet Nam', *Survival*, 20, no. 4 (July/August 1978), 63-9

Osipov, Captain 1st Rank Yu. 'V.I. Lenin, KPSS ob internatsional'nom kharaktere zashchiti zavoyevaniy sotsializma', *Kommunist Vooruzhennykh Sil*, no. 13 (July 1978), 74-82

Perfilov, V. 'Limited Warfare in U.S. Foreign Policy', *Voyennaya Mysl'*, no. 4 (April 1971), FBIS FPD 0019/74, 105-20

Petersen, Charles C. 'Third World Military Elites in Soviet Perspective', Professional Paper 262 (Center for Naval Analyses, Alexandria, Va.), November 1979

Petrovskiy, V. 'Kontseptsii sili i ikh evolyutsiya', *MEiMO*, no. 4 (April 1979), 36-44

Ponamarev, Boris 'Istoricheskiye uroki VII kongressa kominterna i sovremennost'', *Problemi Mira i Sotsializma*, no. 12 (December 1965), 3-11

―――― 'Mezhdunarodnoye znacheniye obrazovaniya i razvitiya SSSR', *Problemi Mira i Sotsializma*, no. 10 (October 1972), 4-11

―――― 'Nekotoriye voprosi revolutsionnogo dvizheniya', *Problemi Mira i Sotsializma*, no. 12 (December 1962), 7-16

―――― 'Neodolimost' osvoboditel'nogo dvizheniya', *Kommunist*, no. 1 (January 1980), 11-27

―――― 'Rol' sotsializma v sovremennom mirovom razvitii', *Problemi Mira i Sotsializma*, no. 2 (February 1969), 4-12

―――― 'Slavnaya godovshchina v istorii kommunisticheskogo dvizheniya', *Problemi Mira i Sotsializma*, no. 2 (February 1969), 1-17

―――― 'Sovmestnaya bor'ba rabochego i natsional'no-osvoboditel'nogo dvizheniy protiv imperializma, za sotsial'niy progress', *Kommunist*, no. 16 (November 1980), 30-44

Ponomarev, Colonel N. 'Avanturizm voyenno-politicheskikh kontseptsiy imperializma', *Kommunist Vooruzhennykh Sil*, no. 1 (January 1966), 42-8

―――― 'Izmeneniye sootnosheniya sil v mire i krizis voyennikh doktrin imperiaizma', *Kommunist Vooruzhennykh Sil*, no. 14 (July 1971), 13-20

Porter, Bruce D. *Soviet Military Intervention: Russian Arms and Diplomacy in Third World Conflicts, 1958-78.* PhD dissertation, Harvard University, September 1979

Potapov, Captain 1st Rank I. 'Evolutsiya strategicheskikh kontseptsiy imperializma v poslevoyenniy period', *Voyenno-Istoricheskiy Zhurnal*, no. 5 (May 1971), 42-50

―――― 'Morskiye desantnyiye sili SShA v poslevoyenniy period', *Voyenno-Istoricheskiy Zhurnal*, no. 1 (January 1973), 39-46

Pyazdishev, B. 'Podnogotnaya "gryaznoy voini"', *Kommunist*, no. 10 (July 1971), 103-14

Quandt, William B. 'Soviet Policy in the October Middle East War – I', *International Affairs*, 53, no. 3 (July 1977), 377-89

―――― 'Soviet Policy in the October Middle East War – II', *International Affairs*, 53, no. 4 (October 1977), 587-603

Ra'anan, Uri *The USSR Arms the Third World: Case Studies in Soviet Foreign Policy* (MIT Press, Cambridge, Mass., 1969)

Radványi, János *Delusion and Reality: Gambits, Hoaxes, and Diplomatic One-Upmanship in Vietnam* (Gateway Editions, South Bend, Ind., 1978)

Reed, Stanley F., III 'Dateline Syria: Fin de Régime?', *Foreign Policy*, no. 39 (Summer 1980), 176-90

Rubinstein, Alvin Z. *Red Star on the Nile: The Soviet-Egyptian Influence Relationship since the June War* (Princeton University Press, Princeton, 1977)

Rumyantsev, V. 'Arabskiy vostok na novom puti', *Kommunist*, no. 16 (November 1969), 90-101

'Russia in Afghanistan', *The Economist*, 23 May 1981, pp. 33-7

Rybalkin, I. 'Chiliyskiy opit: obschchiye zakonemernosti i svoeobraziye revolyutsionnogo protsessa', *Kommunist*, no. 8 (May 1972), 120-7

Rybkin, Colonel Ye. 'Leninskaya kontseptsiya voini i sovremennost'', *Kommunist Vooruzhennykh Sil*, no. 20 (October 1973), 21-8

——— 'Marksizm-Leninizm kak metodologicheskaya osnova prognozirovaniya voyennikh sobitiy', *Voyenno-Istoricheskiy Zhurnal*, no. 7 (July 1980), 3-10

——— 'Pravda o voine—oruzhiye sil mira', *Kommunist Vooruzhennykh Sil*, no. 10 (May 1977), 8-15

——— 'Voini sovremennoy epokhi i ikh vliyaniye na sotsial'niye protsessi', *Kommunist Vooruzhennykh Sil*, no. 11 (June 1970), 9-16

——— 'V poiskakh vikhoda iz tupika', *Kommunist Vooruzhennykh Sil*, no. 1 (January 1973), 20-6

——— 'XXV s''yezd KPSS i osvoboditel'niye voini sovremennoy epokhi', *Voyenno-Istoricheskiy Zhurnal*, no. 11 (November 1978), 10-17

Rybkin, Colonel Ye. *et al. Filosofiya i voyennaya istoriya* (Nauka, Moscow, 1979)

Rybkin, Colonel Ye. and Tyushkevich, Colonel S. 'Marksizm-Leninizm o vzaimosvyazi voyennoy istorii i sotsiologii', *Voyenno-Istoricheskiy Zhurnal*, no. 11 (November 1975), 3-11

Schwartz, Morton *Soviet Perceptions of the United States* (University of California Press, Berkeley, 1978)

Scott, Harriet Fast, and Scott, William F. *The Armed Forces of the USSR* (Westview Press, Boulder, Colo., 1979)

Scott, William F. *Soviet Sources of Military Doctrine and Strategy* (Crane Russak, New York, 1975)

Second Congress of the Communist International (New Park, London, 1977)

Semenov, Yu. 'Pekin i natsional'no-osvoboditel'noye dvizheniye', *Mezhdunarodnaya Zhizn'*, no. 12 (December 1979), 23-33

Serelrayannikov, Colonel V. and Yasyukov, Colonel M. 'Mirnoye sosushchestvovaniye i zashchita sotsialisticheskogo otechestva', *Kommunist Vooruzhennykh Sil*, no. 16 (August 1972), 9-16

Sergeyev, K. 'O kriteriyakh v otsenke kharaktera voin i vneshney politiki', *Voyenno-Istoricheskiy Zhurnal*, no. 9 (September 1966), 104-13

Sergeyev, S. 'Stanovleniye novoy Efiopi', *Mezhdunarodnaya Zhizn'*, no. 4 (April 1979), 13-22

Shavrov, General of the Army I. 'Lokal'niye voini i ikh mesto v global'noy strategii imperializma' (part 1), *Voyenno-Istoricheskiy Zhurnal*, no. 3 (March 1975), 57-66

——— 'Lokal'niye voini i ikh mesto v global'noy strategii imperializma' (part 2), *Voyenno-Istoricheskiy Zhurnal*, no. 4 (April 1975), 90-7

——— (ed.) *Lokal'niye voini: istoriya i sovremennost'* (Voyenizdat, Moscow, 1981)

Sherr, Ye. S. (ed.) *Somali v bor'be za sotsialisticheskuyo orientatsiyu* (Nauka, Moscow, 1974)

Shesterin, Colonel F. 'Protivovozdushnaya oborona v lokal'nikh voinakh', *Voyenno-Istoricheskiy Zhurnal*, no. 10 (October 1977), 75-81

Shul'govskiy, A.F. 'Ideologicheskiye i teoreticheskiye aspekti revolyutsionnogo protsess v Peru', *Latinskaya Amerika*, no. 4 (July-August 1975), 8-28

Shurin, L. 'Solidarnost' po-pekinski', *Aziya i Afrika Segodnya*, no. 2 (February 1975), 38-40

Sidel'nikov, Colonel I. 'V. I. Lenin o klassovom podkhode k opredeleniyu kharaktera voin', *Krasnaya Zvezda*, 22 September 1965

Sidenko, V. 'Leninskiy vneshnepoliticheskiy kurs i natsional'no-osvoboditel'noye dvizheniye', *MEiMO*, no. 2 (February 1980), 3-18

Sikoyev, Ruslan *Firm Friends for 60 Years: Sixty Years of Diplomatic Relations Between the USSR and Afghanistan* (Novosti, Moscow, 1979)

'Sili progressa v istoricheskom nastuplenii', *Kommunist Vooruzhennykh Sil*, no. 7 (April 1971), 63-8

Simes, Dmitri K. 'Deterrence and Coercion in Soviet Policy', *International Security*, 5, no. 3 (Winter 1980-81), 80-103

Sinitskiy, Colonel (ret.) A. 'Nekotoriye takticheskiye vivodi iz opita agressivnoy voini SShA protiv V'etnama', *Voyenno-Istoricheskiy Zhurnal*, no. 6 (June 1979), 53-7

Skril'nik, Captain 1st Rank A. 'Mirnoye sosushchestvovaniye i bor'ba idey', *Kommunist Vooruzhennykh Sil*, no. 21 (November 1973), 10-24

Slobodenko, Major General A. 'Strategiya yadernogo avantyurizma', *Mezhdunarodnaya Zhizn'*, no. 12 (December 1980), 28-36

Smolansky, Oles H. *The Soviet Union and the Arab East Under Khrushchev* (Bucknell University Press, Lewisburg, Pa., 1974)

Sokolovskii, V.D. *Military Strategy*. Eds. Herbert S. Dinerstein, Leon Gouré, and Thomas W. Wolfe (Prentice-Hall, Englewood Cliffs, N.J., 1963)

Sokolovskiy, Marshal of the Soviet Union V.D. *Soviet Military Strategy: Third Edition*. Ed. Harriet Fast Scott (Crane, Russak, New York, 1975)

Sokolovskiy, Marshal of the Soviet Union V.D. (ed.) *Voyennaya strategiya*, 1st edn (Voyenizdat, Moscow, 1962)

—— *Voyennaya strategiya*, 2nd edn (Voyenizdat, Moscow, 1963)

—— *Voyennaya strategiya*, 3rd edn (Voyenizdat, Moscow, 1968)

Sokolovsky, Marshal V.D. *Military Strategy: Soviet Doctrine and Concepts*. Intro. by Raymond L. Garthoff (Praeger, New York, 1963)

Solodovnikov, V. 'Leninizm i osvobozhdayushchayasya Afrika', *MEiMO*, no. 4 (April 1970), 67-78

Sredin, Colonel General G. 'Velikaya istoricheskaya missiya', *Kommunist Vooruzhennykh Sil*, no. 22 (November 1977), 48-57

'SSSR i musul'manskiye strani', *Narodi Azii i Afriki*, no. 5 (1980), 3-14

Stalbo, Rear Admiral K. 'The Significance of the Seas and Oceans in Combat Actions', *Voyennaya Mysl'*, no. 3 (March 1971), FBIS FPD 0028/74, 53-63

Starushenko, G. 'Bor'ba s neokolonializmom—delo vsekh narodov', *Kommunist*, no. 3 (February 1966), 109-17

Stepanov, Major General K. and Rybkin, Lt. Colonel Ye. 'The Nature and Types of Wars of the Modern Era', *Voyennaya Mysl'*, no. 2 (February 1968), CIA FB FPD 0042/69, 68-80

Stepanov, V. 'Mirovaya sistema sotsializma—vedushchaya revolyutsionnaya sila sovremennosti', *Kommunist*, no. 10 (July 1969), 20-31

Stern, Ellen P. (ed.) *The Limits of Military Intervention* (Sage Publications, Beverly Hills, 1977)

Suarez, Andrés *Cuba: Castroism and Communism 1959-1966* (MIT Press, Cambridge, Mass., 1967)

Sushko, Major General N. and Kozlov, Lt. Colonel V. 'The Development of Marxist-Leninist Teaching on War and the Army', *Voyennaya Mysl'*, no. 4 (April 1968), CIA FB FPD 0052/69, 86-99

Sushko, Major General N., and Tyushkevich, Colonel S. (eds.) *Marksizm-Leninizm o voine i armii,* 4th edn (Voyenizdat, Moscow, 1965)

Suslov, Mikhail 'Leninizm i sovremennaya epokha', *Problemi Mira i Sotsializma*, no. 5 (May 1969), 1-15

—— 'Marksizm-Leninizm i revolyutsionnoye obnovleniye mira', *Kommunist*, no. 14 (September 1977), 13-28

Suturin, M. 'On the Peking "Theory" of People's War', *Voyennaya Mysl'*, no. 1 (January 1968), CIA FB FPD 0093/68, 62-74

Talenskiy, Major General N. 'Sovremennaya voina: kharakter i sledstviya', *Mezhdunarodnaya Zhizn'*, no. 10 (October 1960), 31-7

Tarabayev, P. and Shishkin, N. 'Prodazhi i postavki vooruzhenniy v strategii imperializma', *MEiMO*, no. 3 (March 1979), 37-47

Tarabrin, Ye. 'Afrika: osvoboditel'naya bor'ba i proiski imperializma', *MEiMO*, no. 6 (June 1980), 64-74

Tarasenko, N. 'Leninskiy printsip edinstva sotsialisticheskogo internatsionalizma i patriotizma', *Kommunist Vooruzhennykh Sil*, no. 16 (August 1973), 9-17

Teplov, V. 'Ostoyat' politiku razryadki', *Mezhdunarodnaya Zhizn'*, no. 4 (April 1980), 108-12

Tikhmenev, V. 'Leninizm i revolyutsionniy protsess v Latinskoy Amerike', *Kommunist*, no. 3 (February 1971), 114-19

Tikhvinskiy, S. 'Klyucheviye problemi sovremennogo natsional'no-osvoboditel'-nogo dvizheniya', *Kommunist*, no. 16 (November 1972), 110-12

Timofeyev, T. 'Magistral'niye tendentsii revolyutsionnogo protsessa', *Kommunist*, no. 10 (July 1978), 75-83

Titov, Captain 1st Rank K. 'Indiyskiy okean na kartakh Pentagona', *Morskoy Sbornik*, no. 7 (July 1973), 92-8

Tomashevskiy, D. 'Leninskiy printsip mirnogo sosushchestvovaniya i klassovaya bor'ba', *Kommunist*, no. 12 (August 1970), 101-13

Trepetov, A. 'Latinskaya Amerika: revolyutsionniy protsess i vooruzhenniye sili', *Kommunist*, no. 2 (January 1974), 124-7

Trifonenkov, Colonel P. 'Ob"yektivniye zakoni voini i printsipi voyennogo iskusstva', *Kommunist Vooruzhennykh Sil*, no. 1 (January 1966), 8-16

Troitskiy, Ye. S. and Agafonov, V.D. 'Ideologiya sovremennoy revolyutsionnoy demokratii', *Nauchniy Kommunizm*, no. 4 (1973), 55-64

Tsvetkov, Colonel A. 'Boyeviye deystviya v tilu protivnika', *Zarubezhnoye Voyennoye Obozreniye*, no. 12 (December 1979), 8-14

Tunkin, Professor G. 'Leninskiy printsip mirnogo sosushchestvovaniya i ego protivniki', *Pravda,* 9 October 1970

Turley, William S. and Race, Jeffrey 'The Third Indochina War', *Foreign Policy,* no. 38 (Spring 1980), 92-116

Tyagunenko, V. 'Mirovoy sotsializm i natsional'no-osvoboditel'niye revolyutsii', *Kommunist*, no. 8 (May 1973), 42-54

Tyushkevich, Colonel S. 'Development of the CPSU Marxist-Leninist Doctrine of War', *Voyennaya Mysl'*, no. 8 (August 1967), CIA FB FPD 0125/68, 1-11

—— (Major General) 'Istochiki voin mnimiye i deistvitel'niye', *Kommunist Vooruzhennykh Sil*, no. 15 (August 1979), 78-83

—— (Colonel) 'Politicheskiye tseli i kharakter voini', *Kommunist Vooruzhennykh Sil*, no. 7 (April 1969), 31-8

Tyushkevich, Colonel S., Sushko, Major General N. and Dzyuba, Colonel Ya. *Marksizm-Leninizm o voine i armii*, 5th edn (Voyenizdat, Moscow, 1968)

Ulam, Adam B. *Expansion and Coexistence: Soviet Foreign Policy 1917-73*, 2nd edn (Praeger, New York, 1974)

Ul'yanovskiy, R. 'Nauchniy sotsializm i osvobodivshiyesya strani', *Kommunist*, no. 4 (March 1968), 92-106

—— 'Nekotoriye voprosi nekapitalisticheskogo razvitiya', *Kommunist*, no. 4 (March 1971), 103-12

—— 'Nekotoriye voprosi nekapitalisticheskogo razvitiya osvobodivshikhsya stran', *Kommunist*, no. 1 (January 1966), 109-19

—— 'O stranakh sotsialisticheskoy orientatsii', *Kommunist*, no. 11 (July 1979), 114-23

—— 'Osvoboditel'naya bor'ba narodov Afriki', *Kommunist*, no. 11 (July 1969), 36-47

Ustinov, D.F. *Izbranniye rechi i stat'i* (Politizdat, Moscow, 1979)

Valenta, Jiri 'From Prague to Kabul: The Soviet Style of Invasion', *International Security*, 5, no. 2 (Fall 1980), 114-41

Van Ness, Peter *Revolution and Chinese Foreign Policy* (University of California Press, Berkeley, 1970)

Vesnin, B. 'Boyevoy avangard bor'bi za mir, protiv agressivnoy politiki imperializma', *Kommunist Vooruzhennykh Sil*, no. 11 (June 1979), 22-30

Vetrov, Colonel N. 'Problems of War and Peace and the World Revolutionary Process', *Voyennaya Mysl'*, no. 8 (August 1971), FBIS FPD 0011/74, 10-22

Vieira, Hilberto 'O taktike revolyutsionnoy bor'bi kommunistov Kolumbii', *Kommunist*, no. 4 (March 1968), 84-91

Vigor, P.H. *The Soviet View of War, Peace, and Neutrality* (Routledge & Kegan Paul, London, 1975)

Viktorov, Major B. 'Reaktsionniye proiski Pekina v Afrike', *Kommunist Vooruzhennykh Sil*, no. 2 (January 1980), 81-5

Vitkovskiy, Lt. Colonel A. 'Natsional'no-osvoboditel'niye voini na sovremennom etape', *Kommunist Vooruzhennykh Sil*, no. 13 (July 1978), 88-90

Volkogonov, Colonel D. 'The Ideological Struggle at the Present Stage', *Voyennaya Mysl'*, no. 12 (December 1973), FBIS FPD 0048, 15-30

—— (Major General) 'Klassovaya bor'ba i sovremennost'', *Kommunist Vooruzhennykh Sil*, no. 4 (February 1979), 8-18

—— (Lt. Colonel) 'The Moral Factor in a Local War', *Voyennaya Mysl'*, no. 12 (December 1971), FBIS FPD 0003/74, 20-31

Volkogonov, Major General D., Milovidov, Major General A. and Tyushkevich, Major General S. *Voina i armiya: filosofsko-sotsiologicheskiy ocherk* (Voyenizdat, Moscow, 1977)

Vol'skiy, D. and Kudriantsev, V. 'Real'naya deistvitel'nost' i domisli raskol'nikov', *Krasnaya Zvezda*, 10 October 1963

Vorob'yev, Major K. 'V. I. Lenin o klassovoy sushchnosti sovetskikh vooruzhennikh sil', *Kommunist Vooruzhennykh Sil*, no. 17 (September 1969), 9-16

V'yunenko, Captain 1st Rank N. 'Naval Support of Ground Forces', *Voyennaya Mysl'*, no. 7 (July 1963), CIA FDD Trans. no. 956, 62-75

Warner, Edward L., III *The Military in Contemporary Soviet Politics: An Institutional Analysis* (Praeger, New York, 1977)

Whetten, Lawrence L. *The Canal War: Four-Power Conflict in the Middle East* (MIT Press, Cambridge, Mass., 1974)

Wolfe, Thomas W. *Soviet Power and Europe, 1945-1970* (Johns Hopkins Press, Baltimore, 1970)

—— *Soviet Strategy at the Crossroads* (Harvard University Press, Cambridge, Mass., 1964)

'World Communist Solidarity with the Afghan Revolution', *New Times*, no. 3 (January 1980), 8-10

Yablochkov, L.D. *Printsipy vneshney politiki afrikanskikh gosudarvst* (Nauka, Moscow, 1974)

Yakovlev, Vice Admiral V. 'Joint Operations of the Navy and Ground Troops in Modern Warfare', *Voyennaya Mysl'*, no. 9 (September 1965), CIA FDD Trans. No. 952, 1-13

Yasyukov, Major General M. 'Mirovaya sistema sotsializma–istoricheskoye zavoyevaniye mezhdunarodnogo rabochego klassa', *Kommunist Vooruzhennykh Sil*, no. 24 (December 1977), 61-9

Yefremov, A.Y. *Za shirmoy 'organichennykh' voin* (Voyenizdat, Moscow, 1960)

Yermakov, Lt. Colonel S. '"Counterinsurgency Measures" in the System of Military Plans of American Imperialism', *Voyennaya Mysl'*, no. 5 (May 1968), CIA FB FPD 0012/69, 60-8

Yezhov, Colonel P. 'Experience of the War in Vietnam and Its Use in the U.S. Armed Forces', *Voyennaya Mysl'*, no. 8 (August 1973), FBIS FPD 0038, 98-110

'Za edinstvo i splochennost' mezhdunarodnogo kommunisticheskogo dvizheniya', *Pravda*, 6 December 1963

Zagladin, V.V. (ed.) *Mezhdunarodnoye kommunisticheskoye dvizheniye* (Politizdat, Moscow, 1970)

—— 'Rabochiy klass, sotsializm i mir', *MEiMO*, no. 11 (November 1979), 3-24

—— 'Strategiya edinstva vsekh revolyutsionnikh sil', *Voprosy Istorii KPSS*, no. 4 (1969), 5-21

Zagoria, Donald 'Into the Breach: New Soviet Alliances in the Third World', *Foreign Affairs*, 57, no. 4 (Spring 1979), 733-54

Zaytsev, Major General of Aviation A. and Kondrashov, Colonel (ret.) V. 'Krusheniye kolonial'noy sistemi imperializma', *Kommunist Vooruzhennykh Sil*, no. 5 (March 1980), 75-83

Zelentsov, V. 'Pravoye delo v'etnamskogo naroda vostorzhestvuet', *Kommunist*, no. 10 (July 1966), 112-18

Zemskov, Major General V. 'Characteristic Features of Modern Wars and Possible Methods of Conducting Them', *Voyennaya Mysl'*, no. 7 (July 1969), CIA FB FPD 0022/70, 19-27

—— 'Wars of the Modern Era', *Voyennaya Mysl'*, no. 5 (May 1969), CIA FB FPD 0116/69, 52-63

Zhilin, Lt. General P. 'Voyenniye aspekti razryadki napryazhennosti', *Mezhdunarodnaya Zhizn'*, no. 11 (November 1973), 31-4

Zhukov, Ye. 'Natsional'no-osvoboditel'noye dvizheniye narodov Azii i Afriki', *Kommunist*, no. 4 (March 1969), 31-42

INDEX